Eye Witness Accounts Of The Kiowa In Transition

Tahan: Out of Savagery into Civilization
and
Andele, or The Mexican-Kiowa Captive

Introduction
by
Peter N. Jones

Bauu Institute and Press
2013

Copyright © 2013

Library of Congress Cataloging-in-Publication Data

Griffis, Joseph K.
Tahan: Out of Savagery into Civilization
Methvin, J.J.
Andele, or The Mexican-Kiowa Captive

p.cm

1. Native Americans - Ethnography. 2. Kiowa.

ISBN 13: 978-1-936955-13-8

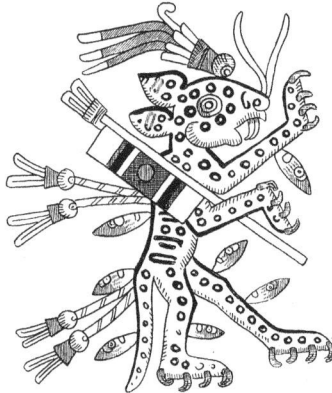

Bauu Press
Golden Colorado
http://www.bauuinstitute.com

Eye Witness Accounts Of The Kiowa In Transition

Tahan: Out of Savagery into Civilization
and
Andele, or The Mexican-Kiowa Captive

Introduction
by
Peter N. Jones

Bauu Institute and Press
2013

INTRODUCTION

The Kiowa are a nation of Native Americans from the Great Plains region of the United States. Originally migrating from western Montana southward into the high plains of present-day Colorado in the 17th and 18th centuries, they finally moved into the southern plains of present-day Oklahoma, Colorado, and Texas by the early 19th century. Historically the Kiowa were a society traditionally based upon the buffalo, which they followed in a seasonal pattern throughout the southern plains. As Euroamerican settlers began to arrive within the traditional lands of the Kiowa, conflicts arose over land, resources, and the buffalo. The result was that the United States negotiated several treaties with the Kiowa that ceded traditional lands and eventually forced them onto reservations. However, not all Kiowa agreed to the terms of the treaties, and many wanted to maintain their traditional lifeways. The result was the so-called Red River War, which was a military campaign launched by the U.S. Army in 1874 to remove the Kiowa, as well as the Comanche, Southern Cheyenne, and Arapaho tribes from the southern plains, and forcibly relocate them to reservations in Oklahoma.

Lasting only a few months, the war saw several army columns crisscross the Texas Panhandle in an effort to locate, harass and capture the highly skilled Kiowa bands. Most of the engagements were small skirmishes in which neither side suffered many casualties. The war wound down over the last few months of 1874 as fewer and fewer bands had the strength and supplies to remain in the field. Though the last significantly sized group did not surrender until mid-1875, the war marked the end of free roaming Kiowa bands on the southern plains.

Tahan (also spelled Tehan) was a Euroamerican captive of the Kiowa who played a small role in the Red River War of 1874, and which briefly propelled him into the limelight during the colonization of traditional Kiowa lands in western Oklahoma and the Texas Panhandle. Known later in life as Rev.

Joseph K. Griffis, Tahan was born in Pike County, Illinois on February 28, 1862. Shortly after his family moved to the Texas frontier he was captured by the Kiowa in infancy, where he was adopted and grew up in the family of a chief without knowledge of his Euroamerican ancestry. The Kiowas called him Tahan, a corruption of Texan. Except for his red hair, fair skin, and non-Native features, Tahan grew up to be pure Kiowa, and he reportedly committed several depredations on Euroamericans as an apprentice brave during the early 1870s. When the Red River War broke out in the summer of 1874, Tahan was a young brave. In the fall of that year after the battle of Adobe Walls in the Texas Panhandle, Tahan and a group of Kiowas from the Wichita Agency in Oklahoma camped near the upper Washita River in what is now Hemphill County, Texas while traveling west toward Palo Duro Canyon, a traditional trade, hunting, and camping ground. On September 8 Tahan rode back toward a previous campsite to look for stray horses, but was captured by Lt. Francis D. Baldwin and three army scouts who were carrying dispatches from Col. Nelson A. Miles, who was in the Texas Panhandle, to Camp Supply in Oklahoma. Although Tahan pretended to be grateful for his "deliverance," Lt. Baldwin took no chances and kept a rope tied about his neck to prevent any escape attempt. After meeting with Capt. Wyllys Lyman's supply wagons near the Texas and Oklahoma border, Lt. Baldwin left Tahan and scout William Schmalsle with Capt. Lyman in the belief that Col. Miles would want to question the "white Indian." In the meantime, Kiowa scouts sent out to look for Tahan discovered Capt. Lyman's wagontrain and reported the location to the main Kiowa camp. As a result, the Kiowas besieged the supply train from September 9 to 14, during which time Tahan escaped from his guards and rejoined his adopted tribe, disappearing into the rugged country around Palo Duro Canyon.

After this event, the historic accounts of Tahan diverge down two opposite paths of history and oral tradition. One version indicates that Tahan died shortly after his escape somewhere in western Texas. The other paints a picture of Tahan rediscovering his Euroamerican heritage and reintegrating into Euroamerican society.

The first version comes from Rev. J. J. Methvin, a missionary at the Wichita Agency, who stated that shortly after the battle of Adobe Walls, Tahan had gone on a raid into Texas with Kiowa leader Za-ko-yea (Big Bow), who was said to have murdered and plundered more than any other Kiowa leader. Indeed, he was among the last of the Kiowa chiefs to surrender to the federal authorities in the spring of 1875. According to this oral history, before surrendering Za-ko-yea, in a desperate bid to cover up his crimes, shot and killed Tahan with his bow and arrow. Since Tahan knew of Za-ko-yea's exploits, the chief, in a moment of madness, feared that his companion's "white blood" would eventually prompt him to reveal all he knew to the military authorities, thus leading to Za-ko-yea's possible execution. After Za-ko-yea's surrender, he and his family told everyone that Tahan had died of thirst while retreating from soldiers out on the parched Llano Estacado of Texas.

The other oral history, much more detailed in specifics, comes from Tahan's Kiowa foster sister Hoodle-tau-goodle (Red Dress). According to a Comanche with whom Hoddle-tau-goodle spoke, Tahan had come to his camp and subsequently joined the Comanches on several raids. However, when Tahan learned that his Kiowa foster father had died in a prison in Florida, he decided to go to Fort Sill in Oklahoma to take care of his Kiowa foster mother. Shortly after Tahan's Kiowa foster mother died, and after having slowly become accustomed to the Euroamerican culture around Fort Sill, he enlisted in the U.S. Army in 1878 and served two and a half years as interpreter, scout, and guide. The military proved to not be well suited to Tahan's disposition, and he and two others deserted, but were soon captured, tried and sentenced to be shot. The captain, however, ordered them sent to Fort Reno, and there with one companion he escaped by cutting through the roof of the guard house. He went to Texas, Mexico, New Orleans, up the Mississippi and to London, Canada, where he was converted to Christianity. Later, as this version of the oral history tells, he was arrested and imprisoned for ten days for preaching in the streets. Afterward he became an officer in the Salvation Army where he engaged in evangelical work and in September 1893 was ordained as a Presbyterian minister in Buffalo, New York. According to the oral history, he regularly told of this earlier, thrilling life among the Kiowa when preaching, but he never returned to the southern plains and remained in New York and Ohio for the remainder of his life.

The first book reproduced here, *Tahan: Out of Savagery into Civilization* is the autobiography of Tahan (Joseph K. Griffis). Originally published in

1915, the autobiography tells the story of Tahan from his birth to his capture and life among the Kiowa, to his years within the military and finally as a preacher and missionary. Along with the second book reproduced here, *Andele, or The Mexican-Kiowa Captive* by J.J. Methvin, Tahan provides one of the only known sources of direct ethnographic accounts of traditional Kiowa life prior to the reservation period. Although both books have shortcomings and biases in their presentations, they provide invaluable information on traditional Kiowa life that cannot be found in any other sources. Like Tahan, Andele concerns a non-Kiowa who came to live and spend many years among the Kiowa during the last few decades when they were still able to practice their traditional lifeway prior to being forced onto the reservation. Recorded by Methodist missionary John Jasper Methvin in 1899, Andele is also a biography of life among the Kiowa, providing a unique look into the culture, traditions, and lifeway of the Kiowa prior to the reservation period.

Methodist missionary John Jasper Methvin, son of John and Mourning Glover Methvin, was born December 17, 1846, near Jeffersonville, Georgia. After attending school, he left to serve in the Confederate army in the Civil War. Afterward, he studied law and was admitted to the bar but quickly changed his profession to religion. The church called him to become superintendent of New Hope Seminary for girls, co-sponsored by the Choctaw Nation, and in 1885 Methvin relocated to Indian Territory in present-day Oklahoma. Almost immediately after his arrival, a disagreement between the church and the Choctaw resulted in the closing of the school, and Methvin was left on his own to make a living. He became a circuit rider for the Indian Mission Conference of the Methodist Episcopal Church, South. In 1887 the Methodist conference named Methvin "missionary to the Western Tribes" and sent him to Anadarko in western Indian Territory where he ministered primarily to the Kiowa, but also to the Comanche and Apache. Methvin established a church and also a school called the Methvin Institute, built on federal land and opened in 1890. The facility remained open until 1907.

As did most missionaries, Methvin focused on changing Native American cultures, and he tried very hard to end the practice of polygamous marriage and the use of peyote and the Native American Church. However, Methvin also worked closely with many Kiowa and recorded one of only three existing New Mexico captivity narratives, told to him by José Andrés Martínez, or

Andele, a boy abducted by Apaches (presumably) in 1866. The boy became an adopted Kiowa and later one of Methvin's converts and aides and in 1899 Methvin published Martínez's biography as Andele, A Story of the Kiowa-Mexican Captive. J. J. Methvin died in Anadarko, Oklahoma on January 17, 1941.

As with our information on Tahan, the story of Andele is somewhat clouded by conflicting oral histories and historical accounts. Jose Andres Martínez (Andele) was born November 13, 1855 in a place then called "Monton de Los Alamos" near present day Las Vegas, New Mexico. His parents were Juan Martin and Pabla Padilla. In the fall of 1866 when he was just eleven years old, Martínez was captured by some Mescalero Apache in a raid. Early in the following spring of 1867, Kiowa chief Many Bears (Set-daya-ite) paid a Mescalero Apache one mule, two buffalo robes and a red blanket to purchase Jose Andres Martinez, eventually adopting him as his grandson. Martínez quickly adapted to his new life and grew to manhood amongst the Kiowas, taking part in Kiowa raiding parties and marrying three times to Kiowa women.

Confined to a reservation in Oklahoma after 1875, Andele in the 1880s sought to reclaim his former life and returned to his family in Las Vegas, New Mexico. But in 1889, feeling "his interests were all identified with the Kiowa, and that he had learned to love them," he returned to the reservation and taught industrial arts at the agency school. He also aided the Kiowas in defense of their lands. In 1894 he served as interpreter and spokesman for a Kiowa, Comanche, and Apache delegation to Washington D.C that argued against allotment of the reservation under the Dawes Act of 1887.

In the 1890s Andele began serving as an informant to a generation of anthropologists studying the Kiowa and Apache societies, as well as an aide to J.J. Methvin, and his captive narrative published in 1899 is an invaluable eyewitness description of a transitional period for the Kiowa.

Together, *Tahan: Out of Savagery into Civilization* and *Andele, or The Mexican-Kiowa Captive* provide unique, important information on a pivotal period in Kiowa history. Within a short period of time, the Kiowa were forced onto reservations and prevented from practicing much of their traditional lifeway, including their seasonal movements with the buffalo herds. Both Tahan and Andele lived among the Kiowa during this period, and the two books published here provide essential information on this transition.

Peter N. Jones, Ph.D.

August 2013

Golden, Colorado

TAHAN IN THE COSTUME OF AN INDIAN CHIEF
AS HE APPEARS ON THE LECTURE PLATFORM TODAY

TAHAN

Out of Savagery into Civilization

AN AUTOBIOGRAPHY
BY
JOSEPH K. GRIFFIS

NEW YORK
GEORGE H. DORAN COMPANY

DEDICATION

To the Red Heroes and Patriots of America who fought to the last gasp for their rights and suffered defeat without self-pity, and to those who with resolution are struggling to adjust themselves to the trend of modern progress, I dedicate this book.

JOSEPH K. GRIFFIS (TAHAN)

INTRODUCTION

TO have a life story so remarkable that it is difficult to tell it in all its romantic details, does not often fall to the lot of a writer of autobiography.

In order to insure interest and a glamour of excitement, most men who write of strange adventures are compelled to use the arts of rhetoric coupled with a subtle touch of imagination.

Here is an author, however, whose life-story is so thrillingly strange that he actually omits many a stirring adventure and tones down his experiences lest they pass the limit of human credence when related.

Tahan is a man who has passed through a series of transitions that have led him up from savagery, through the experiences of an Indian warrior, a medicine man, an outlaw, a scout, a deserter under sentence of death, a tramp, a Salvation Army captain, a successful evangelist and a clergyman, to the state of broad culture that fits him for his association and friendship with scientists, statesmen and leaders of world-thought.

An adept in the languages of the classic world as well as in many tongues of the Indians of the Great Plains, Tahan is an accomplished student of

7

Introduction

science, art, music and literature. Yet he never studied for a single day in any school.

Tahan's adventures on the plains will be found interesting and instructive. Some chapters may sound impossible, but he has not exaggerated a single incident in his tale. I happen to know this, for all unknown to him, I took the pains to follow his old trail through the west, and I learned from the lips of the Indians with whom he lived, and from captives with whom he bunked in tepee and barracks, the story just as he tells it, and in many cases with more wonderful detail. I covered the trail in old Indian Territory and in Oklahoma, and followed it through its windings into Canada and on to the City of Buffalo. Besides, I have quizzed Tahan himself by the camp fire and at his table, and in this way I have corroborated the tale he tells so well.

The student of anthropology or of social science will find much of pertinent interest in what Tahan relates. The ethnologist will learn things he maybe merely suspected before. The psychologist will recognise an especial appeal. And the lover of plain truth will find his pulses quickened by the dramatic features he finds revealed in this unvarnished tale.

It is difficult to believe that the cultured gentleman whom one knows as Joseph K. Griffis, the friend of the scientist and literary critic, was once a be-feathered warrior who was the most reckless bareback rider that ever rode a bronco or trotted off with a herd of cattle that didn't belong to him; who was the most prized

Introduction

captive, the most honoured too, among the Kiowas, Comanches and Apaches, for his ability to plan successful raids. Indeed, he nearly precipitated intertribal wars because the tribes all wanted him as an "expert specialist" in devising means to get horses and cattle without buying them.

To-day magazines and lecture bureaus do the warring over Tahan, for as of old, "he delivers the goods."

There is not a man who reads this book, unless it be the old plainsman, but will remark, "I did not believe that such a man lived."

The theorist who holds that man is made by his environment, may pause as he reads and reflect how in the life of Tahan it was the overcoming of environment that made the man. And yet, each reader will have the puzzle to solve for himself, for each one will be compelled to inquire just why the vagabond of the plains, the hunted deserter, and the tramp of the cotton belt, did not stay in the lower levels,—a man of the underworld. Was it luck, was it Providence, was it heredity, or was it a ceaseless desire to achieve something better, that civilised and educated Tahan?

This book is a book of facts, of concrete examples of theories over which learned men have puzzled for decades. It at once awakens interest, then curiosity, then the question, is it fact or only fiction? Discovering it fact the reader will find himself wondering how

Introduction

likewise to find success, fame, culture, and broad use-
fulness in the world.

I hope every sociologist, every ethnologist, every
friend of man, every lover of the strangeness of real
life, will read this life story of Tahan, for beyond the
value of his tale, there is a potency in his message
that is good for every man.

ARTHUR C. PARKER,

*State Archæologist of New York, Curator of Ethnology, N. Y.
State Museum, Secretary Society of American Indians,
Editor of the Quarterly Journal, S. A. I., Fellow Ameri-
can Ethnological Society, etc., etc.*

ALBANY, N. Y.

CONTENTS

Contents

ILLUSTRATIONS

TAHAN

T A H A N

CHAPTER I

PARENTAGE—MOTHER'S DEATH

SOMEWHERE west of the Mississippi River, somewhere between the borders of Canada and Mexico I was born. Just where and just when, I do not know.

My father—hunter, trapper, goldseeker and scout, in turn—and companion of such men as Jim Bridger, Kit Carson, "Wild Bill" and "Buffalo Bill"—was well known for many years on the frontier as "California Joe."

By this title and this only do I know him. Through many, many moons I have hunted diligently, patiently, for the trail that would lead me to his real name and to his people. Not even his most intimate friends could help me strike it.

My mother, Al-Zada—known among the Indians as Hazel Eye—was of the Osage tribe. This fact was brought to light but recently, in the long search for my ancestry.* From as far back as 1868, when, with

---

* For this information I am indebted principally to Mr. Horace P. Jones of Fort Sill, Oklahoma.

the Indians, I was captured by Gen. Geo. A. Custer, during the Battle of the Washita, I had supposed myself to be a full-blood white man.

My mother's father was a hunter and trapper, familiarly and widely known in the early days as "Pap" Reynolds. When but a girl, Mother was captured by the Northern Cheyennes. "California Joe," my father, rescued and married her.*

Mother's brother, known as Kinch West, who was with the James boys and the Youngers during the Civil War, and who refused to surrender to United States authorities at its close, was killed near Fort Gibson, I. T., by a posse of marshals in eighteen hundred and eighty-eight.

It must have been in the year eighteen hundred and fifty-five or six, when father and several other men of nomadic habits, located with their families, temporarily, in the State of Texas, by a small stream near where the city of Gainesville now stands. And on this spot occurred the tragic episode which was the first of a train of events that have wrought me into the only man of the kind in the world—and one of the kind is quite enough—to the credit or discredit of which I lay no claim.

It appears that during the absence of the men, a small Kiowa war party raided along the stream and killed or captured the women and children, not one escaping. I was too young to remember, but the story

* This incident is the theme of a poem by Capt. Jack Crawford.

"MY FATHER—HUNTER, TRAPPER, GOLDSEEKER AND SCOUT, WAS FOR MANY YEARS WELL KNOWN ON THE FRONTIER AS 'CALIFORNIA JOE'"

Parentage—Mother's Death

of the raid was told in my hearing long years afterwards, by warriors of the tribe.

Mother was alone with me in the cabin, so the story runs, when the wild riders of the plains swooped down upon us. She met them with one of father's rifles, and her cool, well-directed aim tumbled one of the marauders, dead, from his horse, and brought down another, mortally wounded. Her expert marksmanship and her valiant defence, led the attacking party to believe that a man was back of both, and this unexpected reception sent the horsemen scurrying to cover. They found it in a nearby ravine. Then, afoot, they returned, by way of the sheltering bank of the creek, and crept up to renew the attack. Convenient for their use lay the ax by the woodpile, and with it they rushed against the door, breaking it in.

It seems that I had toddled around in front of Mother, and was clinging to her dress when the Indians burst through the doorway. The leader raised the ax to strike me. As Mother stooped over to snatch me away from it, the blow intended for me fell on her head.

I was brushed aside until the raiders ransacked the house. When they turned to go, they discovered me sitting on the floor, dabbling my hand in a little pool of blood, and patting Mother's cheek. A young warrior snatched me up to dash my brains out against the wall, but I grabbed his long hair and held on so tenaciously that he decided it would be bad medicine to kill me. So I saved my own life by pulling the hair of my captor. He was no less than Zepkhoeete or Big Bow, the young Kiowa chief.

He returned to his camp with me half dead upon the pommel of his saddle. He dropped me into the arms of his wife, Tsilta, with the words,

"Here is a present for you, wife."

"Where did you get him?" she asked.

"In Texas," was his reply.

"Then," said she, "his name shall be Tahan." That is, Texas Man, or Fighting Man.

For years after I came into civilised life, I went under this translation of my Indian name, which became corrupted into "Texas Joe."

The young chief and his wife took me not only into their tepee but into their hearts as well. They cared for me as well as they cared for their own children, and my affections twined about them as does the love of any normal child in response to kindness.

CHAPTER II

MY first recollection is one of hunger.

The prairie grass had taken fire and the flame, driven by a strong wind, across a wide area, chased the game before it. As the tornado of flame whirled toward our village, buffalo, deer, antelope and wolf intermingled and fled in terror. The men set the grass afire to the leeward of the camp and moved our belongings into the black, burnt stretch. We were saved, but many of our horses stampeded and were lost.

The supply of food in the camp being small, the only hope of escaping starvation was to reach speedily a part of the country untouched by the fire, where game could be found.

I was too young to remember much about the "Big Burning" and the forced journey across the desert. The lasting vividness of the episode is due to its repeated rehearsals, for, through long years afterwards, the people discussed it in all its horrible details.

What I do recall personally is my hunger. I need no tradition to keep keen this memory.

Under the blazing sun, without water and without food, we made our way across that black land of death, and the suffering was intense.

Tahan

One day some of the young men found a buffalo. With hair singed and eyes blinded by the fire, he was staggering about with lolling tongue. He furnished easy prey and a welcome supply of meat.

Another day one of our few horses became too weak to carry his load, so he made food for us. We children attempted to take one of the bones of that horse away from a half-famished dog. He sprang savagely at us and was killed in consequence. His flesh came good to the hungry people.

The days of suffering entirely exhausted several of the older men and women, and they found place upon the travois drawn by horses. One old warrior, no longer able to walk, refused to ride and begged to be left so that he would not be an encumbrance. He had lived long enough, he said, and at such a time was content to die. So he was left behind.

There was no murmuring. The Indian's philosophy of life teaches him to suffer without complaint, to go unflinchingly into the future, to fight to the last breath for his own, and to die without a whimper.

Many, many dead dotted that fire-blackened trail. There were no poles to make burial scaffolds, so the bodies were left on the ground where they fell.

There was no plaint from the dying, none from the living. When the men became weak of body and of heart, the women, although as weak and pinched as they, cheered them on to further endurance, until at last the fainting feet touched a land of grass-grown hills and sparkling streams, where game abounded.

22

First Recollections

Then the camp knew once more the feasting and the singing.

Close on the trail of the memory of the "Big Burning," follows the acute recollection of the "Big Long Cold" when the horses froze, when the buffalo and deer perished in numbers for want of water because the Spirit of the Cold overcame the Spirit of the Heat.

Many, many of our people went on the Long Trail that winter.

CHAPTER III

MY FOSTER-PARENTS

MY foster father and mother were real comrades and in the higher sense, I believe, loved each other.

They two went to visit the Navajos one summer, leaving us children in the care of a friend. They were gone so long we thought never to see them again. But at last, when the leaves—the messages from Those Above—began to flutter down to us, they came back with a wonderful story to tell:

A company of soldiers chased them into the mountains. They had a great fight. Father killed a number of the pursuers before he got away—with four shotwounds in his body. He and Mother took refuge among the rocks.

Again and again the enemy surrounded them. From hiding-place to hiding-place they crept till Father fell from loss of blood. Then Mother hid him and left him. The soldiers brushed against his covert. But like the doe leading the hounds from the hiding-place of her young, she lured them away. First here, then there—always the mountain-gorge between, she showed herself to the enemy till darkness fell. Then

24

back to her helpless mate she made her way. Night did not hide from her the trail she meant to follow.

She carried Father on her back down into a deep canyon to living water. She dressed his wounds with healing herbs, and cared for him untiring all through the summer. For food she picked berries and snared rabbits, and once she killed a deer.

As we children sat in the fireshine of the crackling sticks in the long winter evenings, Mother often repeated the story. She would tell how Father had sent his bullets straight and the soldiers had fallen; how after his first wound he had stoutly declared that in spite of it, he would still defeat the enemy; how she had begged to help him away and how he had fought on, until he had counted another and yet another bullet in his breast; how, when he had fallen back exhausted from loss of blood, and she had thought him dead, he had opened his eyes and smiled the message he could not speak—encouragement.

Then Father's voice would carry on the story. We would hear of Mother's ingenuity and heroic exertions in saving him, until with Father we knew that Mother was the greatest woman in the world.

CHAPTER IV

THE INDIAN WOMAN AS A MOTHER

THE Indian woman is a good mother.

She is alone when her child is born, and rarely does she let it out of her sight until it is able to care for itself. As she toils at her duties, her babe, in its pocket-cradle, swings from the friendly arm of a tree. She sings to it a heart-song, or hushes its fretfulness by calling its attention to the twittering birds, or the breath of the Spirit in the quivering leaves.

To the older little ones she chants her legends.

Often has my foster-mother led me into the Sleep-Land in the footsteps of some great hero of the past, the telling of whose wonderful deeds expressed the hopes of her mother-heart for me. And she had the mother-heart for me as well as for her own two boys and girl.

My foster-sister, Giawamahye (Kiowa-Girl), was an agreeable, diligent child. She responded well to her mother's teaching.

The Indian woman is careful to guard her little girl from evil and to train her in virtue and modesty and industry.

My foster-brothers—Tsaeepahgo (One Horse) and Seeseh (Arrow-Head)—and I were not always as

26

The Indian Woman as a Mother

agreeable as Giawamahye. We children loved each other as well as do those of any well-regulated, civilised family, but we boys were as rough in our playing as little brother-bears. So there were frequent bites and scratches to call Mother's attention to us. Her reproof was all that was needed to shame us into agreement.

Our parents were always kind to us. Indeed all Indian parents greatly loved their children, and they taught them to obey.

Obedience is the first law of the savage Indian. He believes it as vital to his existence as to that of animal creation. As the buffalo, the deer, the beaver and the turkey trained their young to obey, so did our parents train us.

For us to disobey meant a day shut up in the tepee alone, or sitting apart with no food when all the others were eating. Rarely, if ever, did a father or mother punish a child by whipping.

The nearest I ever came to getting a thrashing—which was, by no means, the nearest I ever came to needing one—was one day when Mother was pounding up some dried meat. She was sitting by the tepee door, not far from where I was playing. I decided it would be fun to throw a handful of sand into the meat. I threw it. Mother had the fun. She grabbed me by the hair and gave it a vigorous jerk. I squalled.

Father looked reproachfully through the doorway. Mother, meeting his look, hung her head as though she had been caught in a crime. She softened at

Tahan

once, threw her arms around me, gave me a kiss, and sent me back to my play with a light heart.

Father—the big, strong warrior, known by his enemies as the relentless Zepkhoeete—was as loving and tender towards us as is any white civilised man towards his children. For hours at a time he would dandle little Giawamahye upon his knee, singing her a Sleepsong the while. And at times he would romp with us as though we were all young bears together.

We always had the greatest respect for our parents. To me my father was the greatest man that lived; my mother the best and wisest of women.

When we boys were able to take care of ourselves around the camp, we enjoyed a wide range of liberty. We went and came when we pleased, slept when we felt like it, ate when we were hungry. But night always found us at Mother's tepee.

THE BIG, STRONG WARRIOR, KNOWN BY HIS ENEMIES AS THE
RELENTLESS ZEPKHOEETE, FROM A LATER PHOTOGRAPH.

CHAPTER V

FIRST LESSONS

AS soon as I was able to walk, an old man taught me the rabbit dance, for, like every other boy, I was called a Pho-ly-yoh-yeh—"rabbit," though not born a Kiowa. The girls as well as the boys took part in the dance. They formed a circle, imitated the peculiar motions of the rabbit, and with the first two fingers of each hand kept time to the beat of the tom-tom.

I was hardly able to walk when they put me on horseback alone—a common sport with the child. The men picked out some sleepy, trusty old nag for the mount, and the onlookers thought it great fun to see the small rider clutch frantically at the mane as the horse was whipped up. If the child fell off, the hurt never amounted to much. But he rarely fell off. His tiny hands clutched the mane so tightly, they helped him keep his seat.

When I had learned to manage a horse, Father took me with him. It was always a great delight to me to be awakened by Father's calling me to hurry. That meant that I was to go with him. Out from under the robes I would scramble, mount my horse and follow along after him, my heart proud of the privilege.

Shortly after we had made camp in a new country,

we were out together. Father asked me suddenly in what direction camp lay. I did not know. He told me where, explaining how he knew. He told me how to find my way when the sun is hidden.

"When you leave camp, know from what direction blows the wind. Know by the grass, by the leaves, by the clouds, if it changes. If they do not tell you, still the wind breathes. Wet your finger. Hold it up. Where it begins to dry, the breath of the wind has dried it."

Then he pinched my ear. I thought his nails would go clear through the lobe. I did not cry out. I did not make a sound. I did not dare. I was learning to be a man. I set my teeth and listened to Father saying:

"This is not to punish you. It is to make you remember. Always make your eyes big. Not only look at things, but see them. Make your ears wide. Not only hear things, but listen to them."

In the sand near a stream he noticed a moccasin track. He told me to dismount and examine it carefully—to note its shape, to look for its every peculiarity.

That night, when we were resting in the tepee, besides the blazing sticks, I was called upon to relate everything that I could remember having seen and heard; I had to tell the different directions in which we had travelled and the quarter the wind was in; to describe the prairie, the hills, the streams and their banks, just where wooded, just where bare; and, after

First Lessons

many other details, I finally had to attempt to draw the shape of the moccasin-track that we had seen in the sand. On the floor of the tepee I drew it with my finger. When I got it wrong Father corrected me, explaining that it was a Comanche track and that no two prairie tribes had the same shaped moccasin.

Sometimes in our wanderings, we would dismount at the edge of a stream where animals had been to drink. Singling out a deer's track, Father would ask me to tell him the length of time which had elapsed since it had been made. Or, pointing to the pebbles, would ask me why their upper surface was of a lighter colour than their under sides.

Indeed, from everything beneath, around and above, were drawn the lessons that were taught me.

Early I learned how to cure myself of nervousness—"buck ague." Came my first chance to shoot a deer. A fine buck appeared in an opening in the forest. In the act of firing under Father's gaze, I trembled like an aspen leaf.

"Bite your finger on the nail—hard," he whispered. Quickly I obeyed. The immediate pain centred my mind, and the buck went down under my steady aim. To this day, if I find myself nervous in hunting, I use this means to bring steadiness.

Once on a hunting trip in the mountains, we heard a voice which greatly puzzled us. It was a low murmuring sound something like um-um-um-m-m-m!

We would travel in the direction from which it

31

seemed to come, when presently it would seem to be in another direction. It apparently changed locality so often, I began to think it must be an evil spirit seeking to do us harm. It would stop for a little while and then begin again, um-um-um-m-m-m!

Frightened, I kept close to Father, glad to remember that he was a great hunter and warrior.

Finally, Father sat down under a tree and thought for a long time. Then he said,

"Boy, this is a strange sound to me. At first I thought it the voice of the wind speaking through the splinters of a storm-torn treetop. It is not. Never have I heard anything like it."

I asked him if he thought it was an evil spirit.

"It must be," he replied. "We have walked into weariness."

And weariness lies in the trail not of kindly but of evil spirits. Surely the sound was one of them, for with good eyes and good ears we had not been able to locate its body.

Presently we heard it again. Father put his ear close to the ground, where he could hear it more distinctly. Then he rose and together we began to walk in a circle among the trees. At last Father stopped close to a big tree, and with his ear against the trunk, declared that the sound was somewhere in its top. It was a tree of immense girth and height and with dense foliage. From every side I looked up into it to discover eventually what made my heart jump almost out of my mouth.

First Lessons

Close to the top and but partially hidden among the leaves, was a great black something. I pointed it out to Father. When he had taken one glance at it, he sat down at the root of the tree and shook with silent laughter.

The thing that had uttered the strange, weird sound was a big black bear. He was busy robbing a bees' nest, and the bees, resenting the intrusion into their storehouse, were busy assailing him. Whenever they attacked his nose, the robber dashed his paw against it, and the strange, nasal murmur was the result.

Father shouted up. We looked for the bear to come crashing down—the usual habit when shouted at—but he was too busy with his sweetmeat. So he only tipped his head a bit to peer down at us.

"You thief!" cried Father. "You thief! Worse even than an Apache! The poor little bees work so hard for their honey. You coward! to steal their sweetmeat! You enemy! Come down! Not a blood-drop shall stay in your sneaking body. Come down! I want your skin to sleep on; I want your tongue to feast on!"

The robber seemed to listen to all Father had to say, but apparently he had no notion of accepting the invitation. Then Father raised his rifle and fired. The thief came tumbling down through the branches, and the thud with which he landed gave ground for believing that the fall had broken every bone in his body.

Father rushed forward with his knife. The bear

33

struck him in the breast and sent him sprawling. Instantly he was on his feet and running for his gun. He had leaned it, unloaded, against a tree.

The bear was on his feet, too, and not many paces behind Father, who kept the tree between them as he tried vainly to pour a charge of powder into the gun.

Round and round the tree they went, and I dug out through the woods. Then Father took after me, calling,

"Come back! Bring your gun!"

He was getting out of breath and the bear was closing up on him.

"Quick!" he shouted, "your gun, breech first!"

I obeyed as rapidly as my frightened feet could carry me.

When he snatched my gun and fired, the bear was so close the powder burned his neck. The creature dropped dead in his tracks. We found the first shot had grazed his skull. It had stunned him just enough to bring him down. We also found we had as trophy one of the biggest beasts of his kind.

I shouted with joy. But father did not speak a joy like that I spoke.

"Boy," said he, "they call me mighty hunter. With my bow I drive an arrow into a buffalo till the point sticks out on the other side. Yet I let our brother-bear outwit me. I let him knock me down. Me—Zepkhoeete! I felt myself too sure I hit the spot I aimed at. I let myself forget to load my gun.

34

First Lessons

Even Zepkhoeete—tried and mighty hunter—can be taught!"

"And you, boy, you ran," he went on sternly. "Never do that again. Never feel fear."

Then he spoke more kindly.

"Unarmed I have met the wild things of the forest. With unflinching eye upon them, I have walked around and away. They do not follow him who feels no fear. The instant you feel that, the wild thing knows it. That instant you are his.

"Remember my mistakes. Remember, too, my care to study out the brother-bear's queer voice. Make your ears true in the forest. There are creatures that cry in the voices of those they seek to kill and devour. The panther cries like a child, like a woman in distress, like a man who halloos."

Of such sort was the training and education my father gave me.

Like any child I gleaned many lessons unconsciously. I cannot remember when I first knew that the paints we used had a colour meaning. Yellow was the sacred colour. For certain religious ceremonies it was put not only on the face but over the whole body. Red and other bright tints told that the wearer's heart was glad and that he was in trim to attend a feast or friendly dance. Streaks of black in addition meant readiness for the war trail. Black alone was the sign of mourning.

To this day I dislike to recall some of the memories associated with that all-black paint. Like any other

35

Tahan

child I was interested in the burial ceremonies—particularly those of a warrior. I liked to watch the men put up the scaffolding poles out on the prairie; I liked to watch them wrap the dead warrior in his robes, and lay beside him his trappings of war and the food he would need on the Long Dark Trail. I liked to see the men relatives appear with their hair cut. On one side of the head it was always cut even with the lower part of the ear. This was a mark of mourning.

I did *not* like to see the burning of the dead man's things or the killing of his horses, especially his war pony which was always shot beside the scaffolding, to be ready for the first call of his master.

I did *not* like the chanting of the funeral dirge, and to-day I fight off the vision of the women seated on the ground and gashing themselves across the breast and arms; of a mother cutting off a finger-joint in token of the loss of a son or brother, and coaxing the spirit to stay near and comfort her. And to-day I fight off the sound of the wailing.

Never in all my varied experiences among white men have I ever seen or heard anything to exceed the expressions of our Indian women's grief. Their heart-rending wails would smite the heart of any listener and lay upon it a weight never to be forgotten. I have known a bereft mother to break out into wails of grief many years after the death of a child and to cry and mourn for hours together.

From the stories told in the fireshine of the long

36

First Lessons

winter evenings I learned what the warriors had learned on the hunt and the warpath. Their return meant the narration of every incident that took place from the time they left home. But principally I learned how friend or foe was painted, how he was dressed, how his hair was arranged; what was the shape of his moccasin tracks; whether he camped in the timber or on the prairie—all of which set forth the tribe to which he belonged, as well as the purpose of his mission. So, every boy had a pretty good idea of the game he was to hunt and the foes he would face, long before the years fitted him for hunter and warrior.

CHAPTER VI

THE INDIAN GIRL'S TRAINING

THE girl, too, learned the duties that were to be hers, long before she was old enough to help. The Indian mother was careful to teach her little daughter to observe particularly the method of preparing the skins for robes, clothing and tepees.

The deerskin was used for clothing. In the process of tanning, it was spread on the ground, and every particle of flesh scraped off with a knife. Then came the sprinkling with ashes to remove the grease. After the lapse of a day or two, the hide was spread over a log and the hair scraped off with the rib of a buffalo. The ashes removed, the skin was washed in the stream until clean. Then the brains of the animal were worked into the leather, which was rubbed and pulled and stretched until it was dry and soft. To give it a yellowish-brown colour, it was smoked.

In making it into clothing, the women used a small bone for a needle or awl, and for thread the sinew of an animal's leg. Being natural artists, they ornamented the wearing apparel in most beautiful patterns, using besides beads the eye-teeth of the elk.

By the time the girl was old enough for courtship, she was an expert at this work, and not infrequently

38

The Indian Girl's Training

showed her artistic ability by making a shirt for the young man who was to become her husband.

But she never made his war-bonnet. Only the warrior himself could do this, and he couldn't do it without getting the consent of the other warriors of his band or order. Then the event became one of ceremony and of song. Before a feather was put into its place, a war honour was recounted and bestowed upon it by the brother warriors. Thus a war-bonnet was the history of its maker's deeds.

The women and girls never made any head ornaments for themselves. In the long-ago time they never wore anything of any kind on the head, and now any such occasional adornment is simply a concession to the white man's fancy.

The girls were also taught how to prepare buffalo meat for winter use. It was cut into thin strips and placed upon a scaffolding of poles in the sun, where it would dry quickly. When it was pounded fine enough, it was put into skin bags in alternate layers with melted tallow and dried berries. It was then packed solid in these bags and hung up in the tepee for future use either on a journey or during the time when game was scarce.

All parts of edible animals were used for food, except the lungs, gall bladder, and one or two other organs. Parts, such as the liver, kidneys, stomach and small intestines, were frequently eaten raw. Some of the small intestines were often stuffed with long thin strips of tender meat, the entrail having first been turned inside out and washed. This was considered a great delicacy. The greatest was the roasted unborn calf of the buffalo. Prairie dog, roasted by simply covering it up in the ashes and heaping coals of fire on it, was good, and roasted polecat much better than jack-rabbit and finer than squirrel.

Fresh meat was usually roasted or broiled. Sometimes it was boiled, and the women used kettles of green hide, if there were no cooking utensils of other material.

In the country where the mesquite bush grew in abundance, the beans of it were used by the women to make a kind of meal, which they mixed with water and baked on the coals.

Once in a while a little cornmeal, sugar and coffee varied our fare. These highly prized articles were among the booty taken while raiding white men and Mexicans.

The women also prepared a kind of wild potato, which was dug in the autumn and half-roasted. It would keep then until needed.

We were a prairie people and the small band in which I grew up was nearly always at war, either with some other tribe or with the white man. So we were on the move much of the time, never staying long enough in one place to raise a crop of any kind, had we wished to raise any.

CHAPTER VII

THE INDIAN BOY'S SPORTS

THE Indian boy's sports are suggested by the narratives of the men and by the things he expects to do when he comes to the age and strength of a hunter and warrior. He plays at what he will do in earnest when he becomes a man. So the first thing he plays at, is how to make a living—*the last thing the white boy undertakes.*

Among our earliest sports was the hunt for prairie dogs, which we played were bear or deer, and the game of "Hunt the Buffalo." In the latter, a number of the boys would go away out upon the prairie in the morning, taking along provisions of some kind, usually a piece of dried or boiled meat. These boys were the buffaloes. Another company were the hunters. The game was to catch the buffaloes and capture the provisions, when the successful hunters would have a feast together.

We were engaged in this sport one day when I was one of the hunters. We had gone a distance of perhaps four or five miles when I had an adventure which came near costing me my life.

Creeping through the weeds and grass I came upon

a buffalo-wallow. In it was an old shaggy bull which had been hooked out of the herd.

A heroic idea took possession of me. I would kill the old fellow and make a name to be sounded loudly through the camp. So, selecting a sharp-barbed arrow, I crept up within a few feet of my quarry.

In my conceit and eagerness to distinguish myself, I did not stop to consider that, with my puny strength, it would be impossible to drive an arrow far enough into a buffalo's side to kill him. I discovered it, however, a few moments later.

I knew where to aim—just behind the left shoulder. Rising to one knee, I fitted the arrow to the string and drawing it back to the head, I let it go.

With a grunt the buffalo jumped up. So did I.

He was stung enough to make him curious to find out what the thing was that had disturbed his repose. When he caught sight of me, he evidently made up his mind I was the thing. For a moment we gazed at each other. Then I stood not upon the order of my going, but went at once. If ever a boy wished for wings I was that boy.

The creek was a little distance away, and there lay safety. I glanced over my shoulder at my pursuer. He was as high as a mountain. His eyes were coals of fire, each as big as the moon. In my flight my little rag of a blanket slipped off my shoulders. He stopped to fight it. This gave me time. I gained the bank of the creek and flung myself down into the top of a tree.

The Indian Boy's Sports

The buffalo, who, doubtless, had enjoyed the chase far more than I had, galloped on down the trail, in evident disgust.

After a while, some of our young men who were riding back to the camp, passed near me. I signalled to them, hurriedly told of the adventure, and pointed out down the valley the course the old straggler had taken. He had not long to enjoy the memory of the chase, for he soon fell victim to the arrows of the grown-ups I had set upon his tracks.

The hunters took me into camp, and told the story—*not* of how I had hunted the buffalo, but of how the buffalo had hunted me—at which there was a great laugh, and with common consent they called me Gwah-tahe-lam-khe-ah, or Boy-Chased-by-a-Buffalo.

Unquestionably I had made a name to be sounded loudly through the camp!

One of the chief delights of us boys was the war game.

We painted our faces red and yellow streaked with black, and tied on our heads tufts of buffalo hair for imitation scalp-locks. This was to keep safe the real scalp-locks and yet give the victors their tokens of conquest. Dividing into two parties, each with its chief, and armed with our bows and blunt-headed arrows, we then disappeared into the bushes and woods for the battle. It was not always bloodless.

Once, while engaged in this always exciting sport, I saw a boy of the other side in a clump of bushes.

"Hah!" I exulted, "his scalp shall dangle at my

belt before this battle is over. To-night I will dance around it in the fireshine, and tell of my victory."

Creeping up behind a log, so as to get a quick shot at him, I poked my head above it, arrow-notch to bowstring.

No sooner did my head appear than another boy who had been watching me, let fly his arrow. It struck me near my right eye. The blood blinded me. But according to the rules of the game, I could not so much as lift my hand to wipe it away. I must act as though dead. My enemy with an exultant whoop dashed up and took my "scalp."

And that night I had another humiliation—seeing my "scalp" tied to a pole, the victor holding it aloft as he danced around in the firelight and boastfully told of his victory, while the other members of his "tribe" shouted in chorus at every pause in the recital of the story.

Another one of our favourite sports was to lasso and ride the wildest horses of the herd.

On horseback we cut out and roped an unbroken mustang. To mount him was a much harder thing to do. Once in a while one of us was thrown, but the rider was always ready for another trial.

At the age of eight or nine we began to herd the horses.

At night we brought the best and fleetest close to camp to picket them in readiness for emergency.

Often while engaged in the duty of herding, a contest with the ropes took place. A boy was caught and

44

The Indian Boy's Sports

jerked from his horse, or the animal thrown. Then his rider struck out afoot for the bushes, were we could not use the lasso.

We learned to ride on the side of the horse, clinging to his mane or to a rope around his neck, with nothing but one foot showing above his back; to leap to the ground, still clinging to the mane, and to remount the horse on the run.

One of our sports was to take a supposedly wounded comrade from the field. As he lay flat upon the ground, a horseman rode up on either side of him, grasped legs or arms and dragged or carried him to a considerable distance. Or two riders dropped a robe to him. He would clutch it, roll on top of it and be hauled away.

In this manner many a warrior fallen in battle, has been saved by his comrades from capture or death.

We had "boxing" matches. In these any number of us could take part at the same time.

We chose sides, and each side formed a line, facing the other ten or fifteen feet apart. At the word, each line rushed forward until within three or four feet of the other. Then every boy jumped into the air and whirled and kicked backwards at his antagonist in the opposing line. This was repeated until one side or the other was knocked down. Sometimes a foot landed against the stomach of an opponent who did not whirl quick enough. But this taught the victim to be quicker next time.

And we had wrestling matches.

45

Tahan

One of our best wrestlers was a white captive who had blue eyes and hair white as thistledown. From exposure to sun and wind his skin was as dark as that of any Indian, and this in contrast with the long white hair floating down over his shoulders, gave him a most unique appearance. We called him White Hair. He was fond of wrestling, and with his fine physical mould was well fitted for it.

One day there came a young wrestler—Kheabone—with several of his companions, to visit our camp. Our young men made a match between him and our champion. So great was their confidence in White Hair's ability that they staked on him nearly everything they possessed. On Kheabone the visitors did likewise.

The whole village gathered to witness the match. It was to consist of two falls out of three, of the style which might be called "catch-as-catch-can."

The two youths faced each other, stripped to the breech-clout. The Indian was the taller; the white boy the more muscular. On the whole they were pretty evenly matched.

Began the contest. They rushed together, each seeking an advantageous hold. Their supple bodies twisted, bent and writhed. Kheabone was the quicker; White Hair the stronger. Strength, however, did not avail against the marvelous dexterity with which the Redskin wriggled out of his antagonist's grasp and by a grapevine twist of the leg, laid the white champion on his back for the first fall.

The Indian Boy's Sports

The next was White Hair's victory, after much manœuvring and display of agility.

For the third time they grappled.

Every trick known to either was tried without effect. Finally, to our intense surprise, White Hair tore himself from the embrace of the Indian and darted away across the prairie with the speed of an antelope, the Redskin hard after him.

Our hearts sank. White Hair had the heart of a coyote.

Suddenly, as Kheabone gained on him, White Hair stopped, and with a whirling duck, caught his pursuer round the legs, tossed him clear over his head, pounced upon him like a panther and pinned him to the ground.

Kheabone and his friends were not satisfied. They had little left to wager, but they would bet everything, even to their moccasins, upon the Redskin's ability to beat the White-haired one in a fight.

The challenge was accepted. Our young men covered their bets. Kheabone laid a knife, a gun, a bow and arrows on the ground in a row at the feet of White Hair. He could have his choice of weapons. Our champion held up his fists.

"I fight with these," he said.

Kheabone, after some hesitation, held up his fists and declared that babies and girls fought with their hands, but that he would accommodate the White Head.

Nearby was the bank of the stream, at the bottom of which, some fifteen feet sheer down, was thin black

47

mud of an unguessed depth. On the edge of this bank White Hair took his stand in readiness.

"Knock him over the bank into the mud," whispered Kheabone's advisers.

The Indian approached White Hair on the run, with fist high in the air. When near enough, he lunged, throwing his body with the blow.

White Hair side-stepped, and Kheabone plunged headfirst over the bank into the mud. He sank to his middle, his legs waving like mullein-stalks in a whirl-wind, in his endeavour to extricate himself.

His friends hauled him out and washed the oozy slime out of his eyes and ears.

The drollness of the thing struck us with such force that we screamed in laughter, rolled on the ground, pulled up grass and threw it into the air and shouted. Anyone with the belief that Indians never laugh should have witnessed that scene.

Kheabone was wild with anger. It was not fair, he declared. He had been tricked and he wanted satisfaction. He seized a gun and went hunting for White Hair, who had vanished.

The victors arrayed themselves in the trophies they had won on the match, mounted their horses, and shouting lustily the name of White Hair, circled round the crest-fallen visitors, who sat together almost naked.

Tiring of their sport, they gave back nearly all of the stuff they had won, and when Kheabone returned from his unsuccessful hunt, they mollified him, found White Hair and made peace between the two.

The Indian Boy's Sports

We always enjoyed our sports whole-heartedly, even though our life was full of hardships and uncertainties. When we left our tepees in the morning, there were many chances for our scalps to be drying before the lodge of an enemy ere the sun walked down over the edge of the world. But this thought never troubled us.

One of the most interesting captives among the Kiowas was a Mexican boy. The Apaches captured him in New Mexico. The Kiowas took a fancy to him and traded a blind mule and two buffalo robes for him. His name was Andrez Martinez. But as the Kiowas were unable to pronounce the name Andrez, they called him Andele. As the boy grew up he became completely Indianized. He forgot his name, his identity, and the fact that he was a captive, and he became one of the fiercest warriors of the tribe, making many raids into Texas. He was discovered by a missionary and sent back to his people. But he returned to the Kiowas, married a white woman, and became a useful man among the Indians.

CHAPTER VIII

THE INDIAN GIRLS' GAMES

THE girls as well as the boys, played at things which they expected to do in earnest when they grew up. So they imitated their mothers. They played at housekeeping. They set up tiny tepees made of pieces of robes or blankets. They built little fires, broiled bits of meat and feasted together as the grown-ups feasted.

One of their most popular games was "Hunt the Baby." A girl took a doll out to the edge of the camp and dropped it in the grass, when her companions were not looking. At a signal the hunt began. The finder of the baby was called the mother, and was honoured with a little feast by her playmates.

One day when the sky was smiling, and the breezes were shaking the perfume from the prairie flowers, a company of little girls were busy with their doll-game.

We boys were looking about for some new diversion, and we made up our minds those girls should furnish it.

We crept up around the tepees, keeping out of sight lest they take alarm, find refuge with their mothers and spoil our sport. With wild whoops and in a body we dashed upon our prey. Uttering their girl-cries,

50

The Indian Girls' Games

they ran like young partridges towards the tepees. But we were too quick for them. We surrounded them and danced among them, brandishing our arms, our yells adding to their confusion.

One of the larger boys singled out the "mother" of the game, and snatching the doll-baby from her, began to tear it to pieces, greatly to the grief of the little "mother."

Now I had a particular fondness for that little maid, and an intense dislike for the boy, who, a short while before, had held my head under water until I was nearly drowned. Although he was larger than I, I rushed upon him, seized his scalp-lock and gave it a jerk—an insult no boy would stand. For that lock of hair was to be his badge of manhood when he arrived at this longed-for estate. He, therefore, turned his attention at once to me.

We met in furious combat, to the delight of our companions who suddenly lost all interest in the girls. They thronged around us and with voice and gesture encouraged each of us to do his best.

My husky foe dealt me a severe pummelling, besides sundry scratches which blood-smeared my face. But I fought on until I succeeded in turning him onto his back. Then, astride of him, I chugged his head against the ground until he, at least, was satisfied.

As I rose triumphantly, my eyes fell upon the little "mother." She was sitting huddled down on the ground with one of her playmates—a most interested and delighted witness of my victory.

Tahan

I called to her in the most manly voice I could command.

"Come, Nacoomee! I go to the lodge now."

Proudly I walked on, she following close behind.

At the lodge waited the mother, who had been a witness of the bloody struggle. As I turned my charge over to her, the little maid, looking coyly into my blood-stained face, exclaimed,

"How brave and strong you are, Tahan!"

"And," added the mother, smiling at the marks of the scrimmage, "he will be a great warrior some day."

I went on my way proud that I had played such a part for the little maiden, and naturally unconscious that she was destined to play an important part for me in later years.

CHAPTER IX

HOW WE TOOK CARE OF OUR BODIES

LIVING as we did under the great blue of heaven, where nothing interfered with the caress of the sun nor kept the pure breath of the Four Ways from our bare skins, there was little sickness among us.

Dyspepsia, for example, was unknown. For our articles of food were limited in number and prepared in the simplest way. At times we, as individuals, fasted from choice, or we all went hungry from compulsion. Occasionally, we ate to repletion, but always at what might be termed our regular meals we were sparing eaters. The less the variety, the smaller the appetite.

We did not suffer from colds. In winter time we thought it fun to run barefooted through the snow, to tumble naked into the soft drifts, and to plunge into icy water. On the approach of cold weather we rubbed a little bear oil on our bodies to keep the dampness out, and in winter time we mixed paint with the oil in the belief that it not only gave added protection against the cold, but that the colours enhanced our appearance as well.

Our men were proud of their strong, well-proportioned bodies and they used to believe that white men

53

wore clothes because they were ashamed of their weak bodies and small legs. They suffered in comparison with our race of natural athletes whose untrammelled life made them unequalled in fleetness of foot and in power of endurance.

Once a party of our young warriors were chased on horseback by a squad of soldiers and almost overtaken, when they jumped to their feet and outran the cavalry horses. In the flight the soles of their moccasins became slick from the prairie grass, so they kicked them off and in their bare feet escaped.

One thing which aided in keeping our men healthy, was the frequent use of the vapour bath. This was taken in a tepee pitched for the purpose. It was called the sweat-tepee and differed from the ordinary lodge in having no outlet at the top. Instead the poles were bent over and intertwined, and the rawhide was stretched tightly over them and fastened down securely.

Just outside the owner dug a shallow, crescent-shaped trench to hold the fire for the heating of the stones necessary to the bath.

Always he invited several friends to join him, and when the guests were seated in a circle inside the lodge, he brought in the hot stones and put them on the ground in the centre of the circle. He used sticks for tongs in carrying them, and before making the actual transfer he went through the process in panto-mime four times, in recognition of the four quarters of the earth—The Four Ways. When he had fastened

How We Took Care of Our Bodies

down the flap of the lodge, he poured water on the stones.

In the big steam that filled the tepee the men stayed until they perspired freely. Then they went to the stream for a cool plunge. Religious ceremonies frequently accompanied this custom, which insured more than cleanliness. Often it meant considerably more. For, when the young men, off the war-trail or the hunt, were idle, this vapour bath got rid of a surplus energy dangerous to self-control.

The hair and the scalp of every man, woman and child received special care that kept the scalp healthy and the hair glossy. We used a hair-wash made from a root dug from the prairie, and frequently we rubbed our scalps with black river-mud, and plastered our hair down with it. Then we wound a piece of cloth or deerskin about our heads. A day or two later we rubbed and combed out the dried mud. For combs we had spears of joint-grass tied in little bundles.

Our women rarely knew other than perfect health, for their duties kept them out in the pure air and sunshine the greater part of the time. So, when motherhood came to them they did not experience long, cruel suffering. It was not an uncommon thing, when we were on the march, for a woman to drop out alone, and on the second day ride up in line with her new-born baby in her arms.

We needed little medicine, but what we did need was gathered from forest and prairie or dug from the earth.

Once in my childhood I ate some poison berries.

55

Tahan

They made me burn as though on fire and caused me to break out in a red rash. A medicine man took me into his tepee and bled me. He scratched me all over from head to foot with the teeth of a garfish, after which he smeared my body with the juice of an herb. Then he buried me up to the chin in black mud. He finished his treatment by dancing around me, shaking his gourd rattle and singing his Medicine Song to chase away the evil spirits. I soon fell asleep and when I awoke the fever was gone. Remained only the discomfort of the scratches with which my body was covered.

The medicine man had a sure antidote for snake bite. They gave it internally, just before applying to the wound the still warm flesh of a freshly killed prairie dog. Sometimes, instead, they used a plaster of blue mud.

We drank from mud holes full of disease germs, we ate putrid meat, we were drenched by rains, burnt by summer suns and bitten by winter frosts, but a healthier people would be hard to find.

CHAPTER X

MORAL CODE—MARRIAGE CUSTOMS

THE moral code of our people was strictly observed by both sexes. There was but one standard of morality. That which was right for the man to do was also right for the woman. The Scarlet Woman was unknown among us before the advent of the white man. Many an Indian maiden has been wooed and wedded by the paleface only to be left unprotected, unprovided for, and thus to become an outcast and a prey to the unholy.

It was the Kiowa law that every woman should have a husband to provide for her. Therefore, when war had made the men fewer than the women it naturally followed that a man must take more than one woman to wife. So the Kiowas were polygamous. It was the custom where a man married the oldest of a number of sisters, for him to take to wife every one of them as soon as she arrived at marriageable age. This, however, was a privilege, not an obligation. There was no ceremony at a Kiowa wedding, but the wooing was done after a fashion long observed.

When a young man arrived at the marriageable age, he usually found opportunity at a feast or a dance to whisper into the chosen maiden's ear his mating hopes. Followed always the presentation of robes and horses to her father and sometimes the giving by the maiden of a buckskin shirt beautifully beaded—her handiwork—to her lover.

If the father did not look with favour upon the offer of marriage, it was not exceptional for the wooer to carry off by force the denied object of his affection.

One of the marriage customs, peculiar to the Kiowas only, I believe, was the prominent position accorded the mother-in-law—the bride's mother, by the way—immediately after the wedding. For four moons the newly married man was not allowed to speak to an unmarried woman. If any communication was necessary, it was carried on through the mother-in-law.

Owing to our strict adherence to the single standard of morality, the Kiowa mother was able to bear children sound in body and mind. Before the coming of the white man we were not afflicted with the loathsome diseases that make for blighted offspring. Never do I remember seeing in our tribe a child deformed or even birthmarked, and an idiotic infant was an extreme rarity. It was a rare occurrence, too, for any of our people to become mentally unbalanced. In such event the person was looked upon as possessed by overpowering spirits and was treated with respectful consideration.

The orphans of the Kiowas never lacked for loving care. They were adopted by parents who gave to them attention fully the equal of that bestowed upon their own flesh and blood.

Mutual interests made of us a true brotherhood. Since the members of the tribe were brethren, there was no incentive for any one to take advantage of another. So, there was no thieving among us. To be sure, the property of a hostile tribe might be obtained in any way possible. For a man to enter the enemy's camp, outwit him and escape with his horses, was not only right but honourable.

A man with the forked tongue, a man with the coyote heart, could have no standing in the tribe.

It was not long after our first intercourse with the white man that this saying originated:

"The pale-face writes his words on paper and forgets them; the red man does not write his words. He remembers them."

I have known Indians to travel many days and to undergo great hardships rather than break their word. The characteristic prevails even in these degenerate days.

Not long ago a party of Seminoles living in the Everglades of Florida agreed with a white man to go with him as guides on a bear-hunt. Before the day set, some white men who wanted the job, told the red men the hunt was off. When the Indians learned they had been victims of the forked tongue, they were nearly a hundred miles from the white man's place. They covered the entire distance afoot. Finding the man at home in the yard, they stalked silently to him, and without salutation the leader spoke:

"Injun come. Injun no lie."

Then apparently deaf to the response the little party stalked away on the homeward trip.

Affairs of honour in the long-ago time were often settled face to face and foot to foot. One such affair was connected with the romantic mating of my foster parents, Zepkhoeete and Tsilta.

CHAPTER XI

THE MARRIAGE OF ZEPKHOEETE AND TSILTA*

THE trees had leafed sixteen times since Tsilta first opened her eyes in her mother's tepee. In her full rounded form was the sprightliness of a young antelope that dances in the sunshine when the grass is green and tender. In her face was the freshness of a morning when the prairie flowers bloom and breathe their sweetest perfume. Her eyes were those of the fawn, her hair the veil of midnight. When she opened her full red lips and spoke, there was music of the rill which laughs its way among the flowers on the hillside.

Red Scar was gaunt and wrinkled and ugly, and had two wives. He was a warrior unafraid, and in other days was good to look upon until his face became a target in a fight with soldiers, when a bullet struck the end of his nose, plowed a furrow across his cheek, and left a trail easy to read. Under the stress of excitement the scar would turn a deep crimson colour, hence his name.

Red Scar's visits to the lodge of Tsilta's father were frequent and prolonged and he always lost in the

* This account of the mating of my foster-parents is introduced by permission of *Pearson's Magazine*, where the story first appeared in the August issue, 1905.

gambling, for he saw nothing but Tsilta. He made many raids on the herds of the Cheyennes and therefore was rich.

One day the maiden saw him of the red scar point her father to a herd of fifty ponies. Her father wagged his forefingers across each other, and her heart sank. She knew she was given to ugly Red Scar in exchange for the ponies.

Zepkhoeete was young and handsome and brave. Tsilta had danced many times with him. The hug of his arms was strength and his touch made glad her heart. In him was enough.

When Tsilta passed his lodge, with hair veiling her face, Zepkhoeete understood she was no longer his for the winning. But the young warrior told her in strong words what he would do. That very night there would be two swift horses under the big tree at the crossing of the river. And then away—and away!

With lightness of step and brightness of eye, Tsilta returned to her father's lodge.

When she looked into the face of Red Scar she shrank back as from an old lean coyote and would have fled. But he caught her by the wrist and in a voice like a bear's growl, said:

"My wife."

She turned an appealing face to her father, but he nodded and said simply:

"His wife."

Obediently she followed Red Scar to his new tepee, passing his old, weather-stained lodge before the door

The Marriage of Zepkhoeete and Tsilta

of which sat his two hag-like wives. They turned their faces from the passers.

Inside the new lodge he had erected for her Tsilta crouched down at the farthest side, like a wounded deer shrinking from the hateful fanged wolf.

At night Red Scar made a peyote feast for his friends. He ate so many of the spirit buttons that he slept a long time, and his lodge was empty for the whole night.

He awoke to find Tsilta sitting meekly by the fire.

Zepkhoeete had not been seen in the camp since the going down of the sun.

When Red Scar sat down to gamble, one of the men looked at him slyly and said,

"Red Scar has a wife."

The bullet's trail became a flame, but the wrinkled lips made no reply.

A company of young bullies passed by. One of them in a voice filled with ridicule, cried,

"Red Scar has a wife."

In answer there was a glittering of the eyes, a flare of the scar, and that was all.

After dark, when all was still in the camp, there came the call of a whippoorwill in the brush.

Red Scar saw his new wife raise her head with a quick start.

Again and again there was the call.

The tall, gaunt man rose, seized a rawhide lariat, clutched her arms and bound them behind her back.

"Red Scar has a wife," he snarled in her ear, his

63

face like the western stormcloud when the sun is setting.

When he had bound her feet together, he made the lariat fast to a lodge-pole overhead. Then, buckling his knife to his side, he lay down to sleep.

The night walked on. There was silence save for a sound like the breeze in the bushes near where Tsilta lay against the wall. Outside there came again and again the call of the whippoorwill, plaintively insistent.

Roused by a slight noise at the doorway of the lodge, Red Scar crept like a shadow across the floor. A moment he listened, then hurled back the flap and leaped outside.

There was the sound of scuffling feet, a blow, a low gurgling, then quiet.

The jealous husband returned to the fireside, threw on a handful of bark and sat down.

The wife lay with her face to the wall. As the light grew stronger she saw a tiny stream of red creeping under the edge of the lodge, and slowly making its way toward her face. A foot from her eyes it formed a little pool.

The sun had walked up above the treetops when the husband and wife stepped outside the tepee, she following, as do all obedient wives. The blanket about the man's tall form hid his marred visage and reached to his moccasined feet. The face of his wife was veiled by her long black hair.

The whole camp was astir, for a big thing was to be done that day.

The Marriage of Zepkhoeete and Tsilta

Red Scar strode on up the rise with long, purposeful steps. Behind, in a straggling procession, came men, women and children. On the summit of the hill the man halted and faced the slight girlish figure. About them gathered the expectant people in a circle.

Red Scar let fall his blanket. A knife glittered in his hand. He took one step toward the shrinking girl. The women shot glances of approval at one another, then drew their blankets more tightly around their faces. The man stood straight as the arrow in its quiver, his great chest drinking in big gulps of the morning air, the scar on his face a prairie fire on a distant slope when the ground is wet with rain. Tsilta stood as does the bruised flower wilting under the fierce glance of the summer sun.

"Tsilta!"

The voice of Red Scar was harsh, guttural, vulture-like. It grated upon the perfumed breeze of the morning.

"Tsilta, is it forgotten—the law of the Kiowas? The wife whose feet walk in the crooked trail, what she shall suffer? One of two things shall she suffer. She shall die by the hand of her husband. He may cut her nose from her face. Choose!"

The girl stood like an image of stone. The man seized her dishevelled hair and raised it from her face. Her soft eyes looked unflinchingly into his own. From the proud lips there came no sound. The knife glinted close to her face.

"No, not that! Let Tsilta die!"

65

Tahan

The quavering, plaintive voice had in it the shudder of autumn winds when the leaves are falling. She could not, she *would* not live to bear always the badge of dishonoured wifehood, undeserved as it was. The gibes and sneers of the women would be worse than death.

Red Scar thrust his knife into its scabbard and drew his bow from its panther-skin cover. Placing one end upon the ground, his knee in the middle, by a dexterous movement he slipped the noose of the string into the notch; then, with well-accustomed hand, fixed a barbed arrow to the string.

The sun was flooding hill and valley with rare radiance; but darkness was upon the faces of the women who looked upon the maiden. A flock of crows wheeled down among the trees near the river, and their cawing was the funeral chant of Tsilta. The mockingbird's song from the thicket was the taunting voice of dying hopes. A butterfly, like a piece of a rainbow that had slid off the edge of a cloud, floated gently between the fierce-faced, relentless man and the defenceless girl.

Red Scar thrust his left foot forward, the muscles of his right arm swelling into ridges as he drew the arrow to the head.

Came a clatter of hoofs and the flash of a horseman.

Red Scar was hurled backward to the earth.

There was a shout of triumph from the rider as Tsilta was swept from the ground by his circling arm —and they were gone.

66

The Marriage of Zepkhoeete and Tsilta

"Zepkhoeete!" shouted a hundred voices as the daring horseman whirled away. On and on, across flower-decked prairie and grassgrown rise and through wooded streams they sped.

On a high hill the young warrior halted and faced the back trail. In the distance were two oncoming horsemen. He dropped his precious burden to her feet.

"Tsilta will wait here," he said, the battlelight gleaming in his handsome face as he strung up his bow.

In the lead of the rapidly approaching horsemen rode a tall gaunt figure with a blood-coloured scar on his face.

Straight toward him rode Zepkhoeete.

As they met the young warrior's horse swerved to the right. As they passed there was the twang of a bowstring.

Red Scar's horse reared and plunged headlong to the trail-edge where he lay with an arrow sticking in his side.

Zepkhoeete rode back to the waiting one. Placing one foot upon his she sprang lightly up behind him, and again they sped onward, the remaining pursuer nearer than before.

In a brushlined ravine Zepkhoeete whirled out of the trail and waited.

Through the bushes the fast-riding warrior came. As he drew abreast, there was the well-timed music of a bowstring. From the horse's side came a spurt of blood and he floundered among the bushes.

67

Tahan

With a merry whoop that echoed among the canyons, the young warrior with the maiden at his back rushed on.

Night came, and they were alone in a wooded dell where a bubbling spring refreshed them. The tired horse cropped the tender grass. The stars kept watch.

"One sleep, and then Zepkhoeete will go back and fight," he whispered, as they sat with his one robe around both their bodies.

"But Red Scar is strong—cunning—— He has had much fighting—— If—if—he should kill Zepkhoeete——"

The young brave laughed scornfully at her fears.

"Zepkhoeete is a man. How won he his name! What did he when the scarfaced one would have driven his arrow through the body of Tsilta? Back must Zepkhoeete go. To all the men must he prove his right to call Tsilta wife."

The day was yet young when a man and woman on a single horse halted before the lodge of Setayte, chief of the Kiowas.

"By the law of the Kiowas, Zepkhoeete asks fairness in fight with Red Scar," said the man.

"It shall not be broken—the law of the Kiowas," answered the great chief.

There was the beating of the council drum. The warriors quickly assembled. The aged Medicine Man rose and made known the law of the Kiowas touching the case of Red Scar and Zepkhoeete:

Should a warrior steal another's wife and remain

68

The Marriage of Zepkhoeete and Tsilta

away one sleep—a White Night sleep—and then return, he would not have lost his warrior's place nor right—the right of a fight to the death with the offended husband. But—should he not return, or should he kill one who pursued him, or should he be caught, he should be looked upon as an outlaw and therefore worthy of death, which he must suffer as a criminal.

"Zepkhoeete stands ready to meet in mortal combat the aggrieved Red Scar," the speaker went on. "Red Scar must fight if he would stay a member of the tribe. To stay without a fight Red Scar must cease to be a warrior. He must fight to the death Zepkhoeete."

"Now," commanded Setayte, when the Medicine Man had finished, "let the warriors meet in fight."

A prolonged "ho-oo-o-oo-oh!" from every throat announced the universal approval.

It was Red Scar's right to choose the weapons. He well knew the skill that had given the younger man the name Big Bow, so he chose the knife.

That fight lingers yet in the memory of the Kiowas, and the prowess of one of the combatants is still sung by the campfires and at the feasts.

The men faced each other, stripped to the skin save for a bit of buckskin about their loins.

Red Scar seemed to have the advantage in brawn and weight. His muscles gathered in hard bunches and stood out in ridges with every movement of his seasoned body.

69

Tahan

Zepkhoeete was the superior in strength and agility. He stood still as a sapling.

The people gathered in a big circle about them.

Tsilta was seated upon a robe beside the aged Medicine Man. Her alert eyes, quick-heaving bosom and expectant attitude told the tale of her deep concern.

The scar flamed out the deadly hatred in his heart as its owner fastened his piercing eyes upon the face of his youthful antagonist, who stood in easy attitude waiting for the word.

A knife was handed to each one.

Red Scar took his with a savage grab, and the fight was on.

Zepkhoeete went with a rush, but halted just out of reach of the other's knife, as it swept in a circle towards him.

Again the young warrior approached, this time carefully, inch by inch, body crouching, every nerve and sense alert. Almost within reach of his tall foe he halted and gave a backward spring—none too soon. The other stood in his tracks.

Zepkhoeete must go to him. He did go, this time erect, feinting, sidestepping and dancing away, elusive as a shadow. The gleaming knife of Red Scar played in circles and thrusts above and around face and body but it never touched the agile youth, who twisted, ducked and glided in and out, now leaping high into the air, now backward and again forward, almost within the embrace of his enemy, always his taunting face not far from the glistening weapon.

The Marriage of Zepkhoeete and Tsilta

Red Scar, with great self-restraint, waited for the favourable opportunity for one good thrust. Not for a moment did he take his gleaming gaze from the face of the youth.

"A stiff-legged buffalo is Red Scar," laughed the young warrior tauntingly, as he straightened up out of reach. "He stands in the place his blood shall make red."

There was no reply.

"He fights not well in the daytime. He stuck a knife into his best friend's back. He crept out into the darkness to do it. He is a coyote."

Still no reply from the grim warrior.

The supple youth lurched back just in time to avoid a vicious stab as Red Scar took one quick advancing step.

Then Zepkhoeete thrust out his face while a sneering smile played over it, and hurled the deadliest insult known to a Kiowa warrior:

"Red Scar is a woman, he——"

He did not finish the sentence.

He of the marred visage bounded forward. There was a swish of his knife which the other narrowly escaped. But before he could recover, the fingers of Zepkhoeete closed upon his throat, the leg of Zepkhoeete met his in a grapevine twist, and with a thud on the ground Red Scar lay upon his back with eyes starting from their sockets as he gasped for breath.

The knife of Zepkhoeete was poised for the home

thrust. It hung for a moment as an eagle hangs before it swoops upon its prey.

"If Red Scar say he is a woman, Red Scar may live," hissed the voice of the victor.

Came no reply from the fallen man.

"Let Red Scar say he has the heart of a woman, Red Scar shall live," repeated the triumphant youth as he planted his foot upon the heaving breast of the vanquished warrior.

The reply came guttural and firm:

"Red Scar is a man. He can die."

Zepkhoeete lifted away his foot. Admiration mingled with his smile of triumph. He threw away his knife and beckoned to Tsilta, who went directly to him. He took her by the hand and drew her to the centre of the circle. Then he turned defiantly to the assembled warriors.

"Men of the Kiowas," he said, "this woman has not violated her wifehood. She is true. For three winters I have planned she should kindle the fire in my lodge. Red Scar had ponies. He gave them to her father. Her father gave her to Red Scar. I have kept the law of the Kiowas. I have spoken no word to her to shame a Kiowa warrior. I love her. Dare any one of you say she shall not be my wife? Let him who dares, step out. I meet him here and now with the knife."

He paused for the answer. A shout of applause burst from the men. He strode toward his lodge.

Tsilta with light step followed, her black hair float-

The Marriage of Zepkhoeete and Tsilta

ing like a soft cloud behind her. At the door she turned in time to see Red Scar leap upon a horse and dash madly across the prairie.

Red Scar never returned.

CHAPTER XII

THE tribe was divided into bands with a chief for each band. These prairie people had not yet developed the clan system. A man rose to the position of chieftain by force of personality, by prowess in war and by wisdom in council, and he stayed in power until death unless he proved himself unworthy. Then he was deposed and another put in his place, by common consent.

In the faraway time the Kiowas did not have a head chief. The leaders of the several bands were guided in their important affairs by the medicine men, who believed that in dreams and visions they received revelations from above. And since these men spent their lives in fasting and praying, we felt them to be especially fitted to listen to the Voices of The Above-Ones.

There were five orders of warriors. Into some one of these the boy—the "rabbit"—was initiated when he reached the proper age. He then chose another newly promoted "rabbit" for a life-and-death friend. Each took a vow to stand by the other even unto death. If one was killed in battle it was the sworn comrade's duty to avenge his death.

74

Orders of Warriors—A Warrior's Joke

The fifth order—the Kho-ee-tsay-ko—dog soldiers —was composed of members of the other four. These men had distinguished themselves in battle and were known to be men of exceptional worth. Their badge of distinction was a belt of skin painted red. To them were assigned the most dangerous duties. Also they had oversight of the tribe when it was on the move—a sort of police escort.

When the various bands were together in camp, which was always pitched in a circle, the tepees of the Kho-ee-tsay-ko were on the eastern edge—the place of honour.

In the old days when a party went upon the warpath, they rode one sleep from camp. On the morning of the second day the chief of the band asked of each man: "Is your wife soon to become a mother?" If answered in the affirmative, the man was sent back home.

The return of a war party was an occasion of deepest grief or of wildest joy. If it had met with defeat and had suffered loss of warriors, there was a slow approach to camp amid the wails of the women. If it had met with success, a warrior was sent on ahead with the news. Shortly followed the victors. Near home they lashed their horses into a run and dashed into camp to the delight of the whole village. Then followed scalp dances, feasts and a time of general merriment.

One summer two of the chiefs with their followers went upon the warpath against the Utes. One of them shot a Ute chieftain near his tepee, scalped him

and returned to camp. The other Kiowa happened
along soon after, gave his warwhoop and charged
toward the Ute's tepee. At the approach of the enemy
the dying chieftain's warriors propped his body up
against the lodge and placed his warbonnet upon his
head and his bow and arrows in his hands so he might
die like a man. Then they fled.

The Kiowa sent an arrow through the body of the
supposedly defiant Ute, then jumped from his horse
and jerked the warbonnet from the enemy's head to
scalp him. The scalp was gone! The Kiowa was certain he had killed the chief, and the missing scalp
brought terror to his heart. He leaped to the saddle,
called to his warriors and they lashed their horses
madly homeward. The party arrived at the camp
while the other chief was celebrating his victory by
dancing around the scalp he had taken.

The frightened chief, whose heart still trembled with
fear, dismounted and told of his adventure. With the
warbonnet in his hand as evidence, he explained, in
terror-stricken tones,

"I took this from the head of the Ute. The scalp
was gone. Where did it go?"

Amid shouts of laughter from the victorious chief
and his merry-makers, he soon learned the truth. He
didn't appreciate the joke. Downcast and ashamed,
he remounted his horse and headed alone for the Ute
country. When he returned the scalp of a Ute was
dangling from his belt. So he regained prestige in
the eyes of his warriors.

CHAPTER XIII

PRAYER was important in the life of every Indian. Every act of his life was an act of prayer.

Song was one of the most habitual methods of appeal. An Indian never sang for the purpose of entertaining an audience. He sang to give voice to his feelings and to convey his hopes and desires to that invisible power permeating all things. He chose the unseen voice as the best means of communication with the unseen Mystery. Whether in a religious ceremony or while gambling, before starting on the war-path or while dying, he supplicated the Invisible in song. His death-song was a call to the Mysterious One for strength to meet the unknown, unflinching and unafraid. It was also an appeal to The Above-Ones to witness his dying like a man.

Often when the men were on the war-path, the women gathered about the tepee of the chief, fixed their minds on the absent ones, and sang heart-cheer. They believed this would fill the warriors with renewed strength and courage.

Some of these songs were individual, and no one ever thought of using one of them unless it was given

77

him by the owner. The gift of a song to a visitor from another tribe was not an infrequent occurrence.

To us God was everywhere. The life in a tree, the beauty in a flower, the curative properties in an herb, the gorgeous-hued cloud, each was the Great Mysterious One. We worshipped Life.

There was a messenger of the storm, of calamity, of prosperity. Every mountain and valley and plain had its guardian spirit. And frequently, moved by a sense of gratitude, a warrior would leave beside a spring or upon some spot where he had been successful in war or the chase, a votive offering.

Often have I known my father to rise before the sun walked up and go down to the stream to worship. He would dip up a handful of water and present it to Him, face turned to the east until the sun looked over the shoulder of the hill. After a prayer of gratitude to the Spirit of Light, he would return to the tepee and Mother would go alone to worship.

As we children grew up under the example of our parents, our minds and hearts were open to the Four Winds. When we drank from a clear bubbling spring, we could not help thinking of its mother and of the Spirit which watched over it.

When I was thirteen or fourteen years of age and I knew that it was about time for me to stop thinking of myself as a child, there came into my heart a yearning for something—I knew not what. So I went away into a place of silence where only the sighing of the breeze and the songs of the birds could be

What Prayer Meant to Us

heard. There my soul answered to the mysterious calling of God as the flower sleeping in the earth answers to the voice of the sun in the springtime.

I became so exalted in spirit that I lost all sense of place and time, and in my ecstasy fell into a kind of dream.

I saw in my vision a rattlesnake. The snake glided near and coiled as though to strike its fangs into me. Then it turned from me, still coiled, and struck at some object invisible to me.

I heard a voice.

"The rattlesnake is your friend," it said. "He will be your defender."

Afterwards I had a medicine man put the figure of the rattlesnake on my left breast with unfading dye. I did not tell him why I wished it. He seemed to know. While engaged in the work he remarked that the rattlesnake is the fairest enemy in the world; that before it strikes it always gives warning with its rattles; that henceforth I must be like it.

So the rattlesnake became my "medicine." Later I acquired an additional medicine—a bear's tooth.

When I awoke from my trance I found myself physically weak. I returned to camp and learned to my surprise that I had been gone three days and nights.

One of the older men who must have been through a like experience, quietly said that I had come to myself.

The place of my spiritual ecstasy became my sanctuary. Often I stole away to it to pour out my soul in gratitude to the Mysterious One for His goodness.

This experience, or something like it, was that of every Indian youth, I believe. We never talked much of such occurrences. They seemed too holy. But what any man did say of them was listened to with deep respect.

We never mentioned the name of God except with reverence. Indeed there were no words in which blasphemy could be expressed; and this is true of every Indian language of which I have any knowledge. "The fire burn you; the water drown you; the cold freeze you," were our curse words. Before the Indian could blaspheme he had to learn the white man's tongue.

He had to learn of the white man, too, of a devil and a hell. In the old Kiowa belief there was no devil and no hell. The white man brought the Indian the devil and has given him hell—I might add ever since—to-day the aborigine's religious belief is greatly modified by contact with the white race.

We believed in evil spirits, but we also believed they could be propitiated. We did not locate them in a single place of origin, nor give power to a chief bad spirit. Indeed, heaven and hell were together on The Other Side of Darkness. Thither, with the righteous and respected went the coward and the liar— these latter *to become eventually brave and truthful.*

The Kiowas had their unwritten scriptures which gripped their minds and hearts and influenced their

What Prayer Meant to Us

lives more strongly, I believe, than do the sacred writings of any other people. Because of a lack of knowledge of this in detail, many earnest folk who have sought to enlighten them, have made most woful mistakes. It is folly to attempt to change a people's ideas suddenly, and the Indian's religion is strongly interwoven with every fibre of his being.

CHAPTER XIV

OUR IDEAS OF CREATION AND OF THE ORIGIN OF OUR TRIBE

OUR belief concerning the creation of the world and all things therein, was this:

The He-Who-Makes wished it and the earth and the sun and the moon and the stars came. Then he caused our father the Sun to send his warmth into the heart of our mother the Earth, and she gave forth all living things, vegetable and animal.

And this was the origin of the Kiowa tribe:

The Great Mysterious One sent down a special messenger to Earth. He tapped upon a hollow log, calling to the inside:

"Teh'pdha!" *   ("Come out!")

People immediately began to emerge. They kept on coming out and coming out until there were many of them. Came to the opening a pregnant woman. She could not get through, so no more people could get out. This is the reason the tribe is no larger.

The Messenger stayed among the creatures who

---

* This was the name of the tribe until the death of the great chief Teh'pdha. Since he had never given his name to any one, according to custom, it could never be mentioned again. So the tribe was called Kiagu-dal-taga—People—Who—Came-Out—becoming Kiowa in the white man's tongue.

Our Ideas of Creation

had answered his call, and taught them how to kill animals and how to prepare their flesh for food and their skin for clothing. When he had showed them all the vegetables that were good to eat, he disappeared.

One day a girl was playing in the woods. Looking up into a tree she spied a porcupine. She determined to catch it. When she began to climb the tree it began to shoot upwards. It grew so rapidly that it soon reached the sky. Punching a hole through it, it went on growing until it carried the girl into the upper world.

There the porcupine revealed himself in his true character as the Sun Boy—the son of the Sun.* He married the girl and in due time a man-child was born to them.

Came a day when the three were out on the prairie. The Sun Boy discovered a prairie turnip, the top of which had been bitten off by a buffalo. He said to his wife,

"You must never touch a prairie turnip if the top of it has been bitten off."

He wouldn't give the reason for this command. The woman wanted to know, so one day when her husband's back was turned, she pulled the turnip up by the roots.

It left a big whole in the ground through which she could look clear down to this world.

* The Sun itself we commonly called Grandfather, a name also applied to the Great Mysterious One.

83

Tahan

She had been so happy in the upper world with her husband she had forgotten ever having been elsewhere. But now she became heartsick for her old home.

She waited until her husband was not looking. Then to a bush near the hole she tied a rope, and with her boy in her arms let them down upon it towards this world.

She had almost reached it when her husband discovered the escape. Picking up a stone he threw it through the hole, struck the woman's head and killed her.

Her boy dropped to this world unharmed.

The Old-Woman-Underground took care of him until he grew to manhood.

One day while he was playing a game with other young men, a sharp, flat stone thrown into the air fell on his head and split him in two. That made twins out of him.

Shortly afterward one of the pair walked under a lake. As he was disappearing, he said to the people:

"Some time I will return. I will stand upon a high hill. I will stamp my foot and cause the earth to tremble. I will cry with a loud voice and all of the dead Kiagus will come back and with their weapons drive their enemies from the land. And the Kiagus shall again occupy the world in peace."

The other twin changed himself into the Great Medicine of the tribe, to whom he gave himself as a pledge of their future existence.

Our Ideas of Creation

"But should you ever lose me," he warned, "the tribe shall cease to be."

Thenceforth this mystery—the Great Medicine— which was about eighteen inches in length, was kept in a buckskin bag in possession of the medicine men. In the front of battle it was always carried by a warrior, shotpouch fashion, to insure victory.

Once a warrior did not carry it in the right manner into a fight. In consequence the triumph went to the enemy who carried the Great Medicine away.

Then the Kiowas became disheartened. The horses died and the dogs would no longer bark in the nighttime.

The warriors looked toward the earth and cried,

"Eeah, eeah! The time has come when the tribe shall cease to be."

Came Strong Medicine, a young warrior, who had been praying in solitude. He said to the people:

"While I fasted and prayed The Great One spoke to me. He said: 'I will tell you a way whereby the Sacred Thing can be recovered and the tribe saved from destruction. Over the hill toward the sun-rising are men with hair on their faces. They have horses which whoop loudly. Capture those whooping horses, make shields out of their hides and war clubs out of their legs. Let the warriors arm themselves with them. Let them go toward the direction from which the shadows come when the sun walks down. There will they find the enemy who have the Sacred Medicine. Let the warriors charge unafraid upon them and they shall recover it.' These are the words which were spoken to me."

The warriors considered this. Then they said, "Let Strong Medicine lead and we will follow."

Strong Medicine led and did the things directed.

When he and his band arrived at the village of the enemy, they gave a mighty warwhoop and charged upon them, wielding their war clubs.

When the sun hid itself and the stars looked down and the prairie wolves came out and sang their night-song, all stiff and stark and bloody lay the mighty men of the Land of Shadows.

CHAPTER XV

THE Kiowas had a pretty accurate idea of the size of North America. This knowledge was obtained partly from members of other tribes and from white men. However, our people had travelled extensively when the country was mapped only by the trails of unshod feet.

I have heard the old men tell of a time when the tribe lived in the far north. This is not tradition alone. It is also history recorded many generations ago on skins and carried down by the hands of those fitted for such work. From time to time these records were transferred to fresh skins.

I remember an old man spreading upon the ground a large skin covered with lines and queer-looking figures. Pointing to certain spots upon it he talked about the places where the tribe had camped and of the happenings therein many, many moons ago.

Judging from these maps of their journeyings, their first habitat must have been between Hudson Bay and the Rocky Mountains. Indeed I have heard them tell that their forefathers left the land that was covered with snow nearly all of the time, and came to a land where no snow ever fell, where it was always warm and where the Indians lived in houses which were very much like those of the white men. Forced out of this country they had made their way back to the cold north, and had been driven south again.

It is quite certain that they reached the Gulf of Mexico, for I recall their having taken a captive—a blond-haired white man—on the "edge of a big water which the eye could not go across," and by the location on the skins the "big water" must have been the Gulf. I have also heard them talk about the "big water where the sun walks down"—the Pacific Ocean.

But they had little knowledge of the white man's way or of his complex civilisation.

They had no adequate idea of the value of money and didn't even know what paper money was. In my childhood's time a number of our most restless young men raided a store and among the plunder they brought home were some pieces of paper queerly coloured and cut into uniform shape. Ignorant of its value they used it for "smoke paper." I now know that it was paper money. A bale of such money wouldn't have appealed to them as a substitute for a twenty-five-cent silver piece—a fact of which the white man was never slow to take advantage.

Some of the chiefs had visited the national capital and other cities, but nearly everything they saw they found very confusing.

As I now recollect their talk concerning these visits, they must have been in churches and in other places

Our Ideas of the Continent

where large numbers of people congregated. But connected with these places were many things which they did not understand and for which they could see no use.

Altogether there were so many useless things everywhere, even in the houses where the white people slept and ate, that a strong contempt for the dominant race was begotten in their minds.

The things the white men ate—white man's food—made the Indians sick in their "middles," they said; the way they ate them; the soft beds they slept in; the things they did and did not do; the way the women, especially, dressed—all left a very unfavourable impression upon the red men of the plains.

Neither could these sons of the free life understand why there were white men compelled to work from morning to night, or all night long, for those who did nothing but ride around wearing fine clothes.

The savage Indian placed no value upon his property or his services but gladly helped his fellows in need without thought of material reward. He was naturally courteous. Many years ago when the men of the camp were in council, a warrior belonging to a tribe but recently at war with the Kiowas, suddenly appeared in the tepee. He stood silently erect until invited to speak. The men were even then laying plans for a campaign against his tribe. When the visitor told of a strange sickness of which many of his people had died, of the poverty and starvation from which they were suffering, he was given food

Tahan

and allowed to depart in peace. Afterward the two tribes became friends.

Once a stranger from some other tribe came into our tepee. His moccasins were worn out, and Father gave him the only pair he had. And when Mother learned that his wife and children were sitting on the ground outside, hungry and almost naked, she brought them all in and provided for their necessities.

The Indian is a natural socialist. Before his faith was modified by contact with the white intruder, he believed that The-One-Who-Makes created the earth and all things for all of the people. Private ownership of any part of the earth was entirely foreign to his mind. Although any one might occupy a place as long as he wished, no one could sell any of it any more than he could sell the air. He believed there should be no rich and no poor. As long as he had anything anybody was welcome to share it.

Trained by the inheritance of centuries to feel himself equal with his brother-man in the ownership of the mountains, prairies and forests he roamed and hunted, the streams he rode and fished, is it strange that he has little understood the white man's greed? Strange that he has resented the white man's encroachment on his primitive rights? Strange that that resentment should have smouldered and burst into the flame of warfare?

CHAPTER XVI

THE records of the white man's history make small account, if any, of the injustice meted the red man. Its "talking leaves" are nearly always those of the forked tongue. Many and many an Indian battle has been misrepresented in the narration of the details and in the account of the cause. I personally know this statement to be fact. I have particularly in mind the events that led up to the so-called "battle" of the Washita:

In the autumn of 1868 a band of soldiers in Kansas raided a peaceful village of Cheyennes. The women were forced to endure the most fiendish treatment before they—like the children and the men—were horribly mangled. They were attacked and killed simply because they were Indians. This is the truth.

When the news of the massacre reached the tribes camped at Fort Dodge and Fort Larned, they were so filled with rage and resentment they started immediately on the warpath—quite as the white men would have done under like circumstances.

It was just before the time of the big buffalo hunt, when General Philip Sheridan, Commanding Officer of the Department of the Southwest, sent a Caddo Indian—Caddo George—with a message to the Cheyennes, Arapahoes, Kiowas, Comanches and Apaches.

The message said that it was the wish of the Great Father at Washington that there should be no more war, and that if they would come in and camp on the Washita River, there would be peace.

At this the people were glad. They had been chased across the plains for several successive summers by the soldiers, and at the prospect of living in peace, undisturbed even for a season, there was general rejoicing among the tribes.

So, after a successful hunt, they went into camp on the Washita. Everything was made snug and comfortable before the approach of cold weather, and without fear of disturbance from the soldiers—for had not the messenger brought the word direct from General Sheridan?

There was nothing to do but to enjoy. The young men gave themselves up to singing and dancing at night and to dreaming in the daytime; the old men to telling stories of the days before the intruding white man came, and to playing their games in the fireglow; while the merry laughter of children at play and the voices of happy women at work, all spoke of peace and good will. Even the savage dogs became amiable from much feeding, and the boniest ponies grew fat from plenty of grass.

In every tepee were fire and meat and merry hearts.

Came a north wind. It made the water of the

The Injustice of History

river hard. It shook snow from its wings. But the fires burned the brighter, the robes were drawn the closer, and the laughter was all the cheerier.

My foster-mother, whose mother was a Cheyenne, had taken us children on a visit to the Cheyenne camp but a short distance up the river. There was a feast in Grandmother's tepee while the wind howled and the snow swirled and drifted and the sparks flew upward.

It was far into the night when the camp grew quiet and the fires grew dim and I snuggled down under the soft robes close to Mother. I fell asleep thinking of the fun I would have with the boys on the morrow, when the sun should reach the place of short shadow.

Crack! Crack! Crash! Crash! came shots and volleys mingled with strange shouts. The warriors in our tepee sprang up, with ready guns in hand. Their practised ears told them at once the dread meaning of it all.

Hastily buckling on their belts, they gave their war cries and plunged out into the snow to meet the invading enemy. For a little while the women remained with us children in the tepee. But guns and voices grew louder, came nearer, and the shouts of soldiers and the screams of women and children mingled with the flash and crash of guns, the clatter of horses, the twang of bowstrings and the defiant whoops of the surprised but stout-hearted warriors. The camp was in the death grapple. The soldiers fought for glory; the Indians for home and loved ones.

93

Tahan

Bullets whizzed through the tepee and Mother pushed us children out of it ahead of her so that none should be left behind.

In the snow, which was waist deep to me, I became separated from her and the others in the confusion, and I lost my robe. A soldier on horseback came dashing toward me, and I dived under a pile of brush. His gun blazed as he passed me. The noise was carried on farther down the river but I lay still, shivering from the cold—I was naked but for a small piece of blanket about my loins.

Calling to the women and children came an old warrior with his arm dangling at his side. I crawled out to him.

"Come on, boy," he said, "we'll go yonder with the women and children and die with them."

He took me to Mother and the other children. He had gathered a number of them into a little clump of trees. I huddled down between Mother's knees and she wrapped the bottom of her robe about me. I was just beginning to feel warm, when little See-Seh —Arrow-head, my foster-brother—fell limply against me. Mother took him in her arms. The blood was trickling from his breast. As he was dying she called to the other women,

"The soldiers are going to kill us all. Let us go upon the long trail with a song."

They joined in the death chant while women and children were struck down all about us.

The few survivors were finally driven off like a

The Injustice of History

herd of animals. A man on muleback drove us, and he swung and lashed out at us with a lariat all the way to the place where Custer sat upon his horse and waited.

My own father, California Joe, was General Custer's chief of scouts in that fight, and I believe it was he who drove us.

We huddled down again in the snow, and watched the smoke and fire coming from the tepees. The soldiers were destroying them, together with the provisions and the winter robes.

After a while there was the sound of many guns at some distance from us. We thought the soldiers were killing the warriors whom they had taken prisoners; but they were only shooting the horses. They killed nearly a thousand.

It must have been in the afternoon when the soldiers started us down the river. I walked a while, but my feet were frozen and my whole body was so numb, that I fell down in a snowdrift. My older brother, Tsaeepahgo (One Horse), took me upon his back and carried me. When Mother saw how cold I was, so cold that I could scarcely cling to his neck, she took the robe from her shoulders and wrapped it around me. Otherwise I might never have come through the suffering.

In history—the white man's history—the "Battle of the Washita" is called a great victory. But that is always the way. White men's massacres of Indians are always victories; Indian victories over white men

95

always massacres. Indian strategy is treachery; white men's treachery, strategy.

Eight years later General Custer led the Seventh Cavalry into the Sioux country to do to them what he did to our people. The outcome of that raid is alluded to as "The Custer Massacre." It was not a massacre. It was a battle and an Indian victory. Chief Gaul simply outgeneralled Custer, and in defending their families and their homes, the warriors did to the invading white men exactly what the invading white men would have done to them.

But if ever there was a massacre of human beings under heaven, it was in our camp on the Washita, on November 27, 1868, when one hundred and three men, women and children were killed, *after being promised peace and safety*. But one side of the Indian's story has been told, and that side the white man's. So it is my belief that the foregoing true account of the facts has never before been written.

We had nothing to eat on the day of the battle and at night we slept in the snow without fire. On and on the soldiers drove us through the snow while the children moaned and the women bit back their grief-cries for the sake of the men, who walked along, grim-faced and silent.

My frozen feet were so sore and swollen, I could not stand. The older boys carried me until finally we reached Fort Cobb. Here we remained all winter closely guarded by soldiers.

Spring came and my feet were well. One day as

TAHAN (LEFT), AT THE AGE OF FOURTEEN. PHOTO-
GRAPH TAKEN AT FORT COBB JUST AFTER RESCUE
FROM THE INDIANS

The Injustice of History

I was playing in the warm sunshine, two white men came along and looked at me fiercely. One of them grabbed me by the arm. Wolf-like I snapped my teeth upon his hand, and bit and scratched with all of my might, until with an exclamation he gave me a slap and let me go. I ran into the brush and hid until darkness fell, then crept to Mother and told her what had happened. She cautioned me to keep away from the white men. They would either kill me or steal me, she said.

Instead, they caught me one day, took me to an officer's tent and brought Mother there. After a long talk between the Indians and the officers, I learned that I was to be taken away among the white people, for it was felt certain I was a captive. Finally they found Indians who told of the Kiowa raid and of the death of my own mother. From their description of our cabin and its location, an old scout identified me. Then I was told that, within a few days, I would be handed over to my own father—California Joe.

I did not know my father. I did not want to go. I could not find my foster-father, Zepkhoeete. I seemed to belong nowhere, to nobody. I wanted to creep away like a wounded coyote, and die.

When I again saw my foster-father, I was no longer a child; and never, since the day they took me from her, have I seen my good foster-mother who sacrificed so much for me.

At the ranch to which they took me, I soon grew

heartsick for the camp. It was with great difficulty that they could make me understand them when they talked to me, and I could not make them understand me.

I slept out by the corral. One night the call of the camp was too strong. I mounted a good horse and hit the trail leading northward.

On the second day I fell in with a number of Indians returning from a raid with several good horses and other booty. They were the most peculiar looking lot I had ever seen. They called themselves Estizeddelebe—Brave, Dangerous People.

At first they did not seem inclined to allow me to stay with them, but one of the young warriors whose language I did not understand took my part. As I was not particular where I went, so long as I did not have to return to the white people, I accompanied my new friends to their camp. It was at the foot of some big mountains.

A glad surprise awaited me there. I found the parents of Nacoomee and Nacoomee herself—the little playmate of my childhood days.

CHAPTER XVII

THE BEGINNING OF A TRIBE

THOSE with whom my lot was now cast were composed principally of men who had been undesirable members of their own tribes. These, of course, had been put out. Others left of their own will.

As I now recall it, there had been a council of many of the tribes. A few of the men quarrelled with their respective leaders, and left.

Zakatoh, the Kiowa chief of the Estizeddelebe, was one of these. He and several of his brother-warriors had refused to give themselves up when the Kiowas surrendered to the United States authorities. Afraid of being imprisoned or hanged for their raids upon white settlements in Texas, they had fled westward.

It was not long before they were joined by other stragglers, and Zakatoh, by force of his personality, had become their leader.

There were a Comanche or two, several Cheyennes and Arapahoes, at least one Osage and a Cherokee, and some from other half-civilised tribes, the larger number being Seminoles—a most peculiar combination. They had some difficulty in understanding each other clearly as they had not been together very long, Each man was compelled to use his own language at first, but always the sign language helped.

The Seminole came to predominate. I learned it rapidly, for I made my home in the tepee of Zakatoh whose wife, Tosopahehle—Pretty Face—was a Seminole. She could not learn his language, but he found hers easy for him. So the tepee-talk was Seminole.

In the new tribe there were, all told, about thirty men, women and children, when I first met them.

There were more men than women. But it was not long before there were more women than men. For these freebooters of the plains went on frequent excursions, and when they returned their arms were not empty.

They made a most picturesque appearance. Some of them wore the costume of the prairie tribes—the long-fringed buckskin shirt and leggings, and the moccasins with rawhide soles and shape peculiar to these tribes. Others wore the short-fringed shirt and leggings, and the soft-soled moccasins of the forest dwellers. There were two Mexicans, with their ornamented short jackets, slit bottomed trousers and high-heeled boots; and one white man in the dress of his civilised type.

The Indians wore their hair in the style of their respective tribes. The men of the prairie braided theirs on each side of their heads, and around each braid rolled a piece of otter skin or red cloth. The Kiowas fixed the hair on the left side in this manner, but cut the right side even with the lower part of the ear. Like the other prairie tribes they braided the scalp lock, and let it hang down the back.

The Seminoles wore short hair, with the exception of the scalp lock which they braided as did the others, while the Osage cut off all of his except the scalp-lock and a roach running along the top of the head.

The two Mexicans and the white man let their hair hang loosely about their shoulders.

The band increased in numbers. Forced by the same causes which led Zakatoh and the original members to throw off their tribal allegiance, malcontents from various tribes kept coming in.

The primary reason for their banding together was that of self-protection. The weaker of the plains people were always in danger of being robbed or slain by the stronger, so loyalty to each other was the first law of existence.

When a straggler was met on the prairie by any of our tribe, or when any one appeared in our camp for food and showed a disposition to join us, the question was not what he had been nor whence he had come, but whether he was willing to become one of us for good or for ill. If any such showed a spirit to the contrary, his property was taken and he was left on the prairie to become food for the wolves.

Our chief was very suspicious of any member of the band whom he deemed a rival for his position.

The white man whom we called Kithlucks—Don't-Know—from the fact that he could hardly understand the mixed dialect we spoke—led a party of the warriors into Texas, plundered a Mexican settlement and captured two women.

Zakatoh, who had not been consulted in the matter, looked upon this as insubordination. Moreover, as the white man might be looking forward to deposing him, he took him on a hunt one day, and the white man never returned.

Notwithstanding Zakatoh's strict discipline, there were desertions from the band from time to time.

Zackoyea, an influential Kiowa chief, was with us until after a fight with soldiers during which he with several of us became separated from the main body of our people. For several days we were without water, in consequence of which I became completely exhausted. And he, believing that I was dying, left me. He returned to his own people and reported that I had died. But they believed for many years that he had killed me.

With the feeling that there was not a single tribe friendly to us, a vigilant watch was kept against surprise. We never felt safe.

Zakatoh devised a system of signals by which our warriors could communicate with each other when separated. In case any of us wished to notify the others that an enemy was in the vicinity when we were scattered on the prairie, we went to the top of the highest hill, kindled a small fire and put some damp grass on it to make a dense smoke. Then we spread over it a robe which we jerked away deftly.

The Beginning of a Tribe

This made a puff of smoke. The number of puffs conveyed certain things to our friends.

At night fire-arrows were shot into the air as signals, and the cries of the screech owl and the bark of the coyote were imitated for message-carrying purposes.

CHAPTER XVIII

CHOOSING A MEDICINE MAN

IN such a motley company as that of the Estized-delebe, there was naturally a wide difference in religious ideas and ceremonies. But no one interfered with any other one's belief—an affair looked upon as wholly individual.

Still the Indians all felt the need of a common ground upon which to meet and worship.

The Cheyennes and Arapahoes had their peculiar kinds of Sun Dances, as did the Kiowas. But the Seminoles, for instance, could not celebrate the ceremonies of the Buskita, or Green-Corn Dance. They lacked both the corn and the Black Drink necessary to the rites. Could they have got the corn, the Black Drink would still have been wanting. Only their Medicine Man knew how to make that, and they had no Medicine Man.

Indeed, for the matter of that, our tribe had none. This caused most of the men grave concern.

The Seminoles, strange to say, were the least disturbed over the matter. They held that the most necessary things to have were a wise chief, good guns, plenty of ammunition and watchful eyes.

But the others talked a great deal about it. They

Choosing a Medicine Man

argued that without some one to listen to the voices of The Above-Ones to tell us what to do and how to do it, we could not hope to survive.

There was an old Pueblo, Quohahles, who did not have much to say. He never said much, but when he did talk it was with wisdom. And he lived apart from the others.

Always he kept a piece of buffalo meat hanging on a pole back of his tepee. This, he told me, was an offering to The Above-Ones. He had, moreover, a large mystery bundle.

Some one thought of him as the most likely one to meet the need and fill the place of Medicine Man.

One night, as the men sat in talk, he quietly entered the circle and remained standing in silence for a long time. Finally he spoke.

"We must move. The warning has come in a dream. Before the sun walks up, we must move."

His manner was so impressive the men thought it wise to do as he counselled.

Before daylight the next morning we started. Just at sunup, when we were on a hilltop on our way westward, Quohahles called attention to a low, rumbling sound like distant thunder. This increased in volume until we recognised the noise.

It was a buffalo stampede.

As we stood there on the hilltop we saw the buffaloes coming from the north—a great brown mass as far as the eye could reach. It looked as if the hills were moving. We saw them sweep over our

Tahan

camping place which we had left but a few hours before. Had we remained there we would have been trampled into the earth. Quohahles's dream had saved us. This placed him still higher in the estimation of the entire band.

Then the warriors began to talk of the way they had seen men tried or tested as to their genuineness before they were received as medicine men by their tribes.

One of them said that among his former people a man used to go away and fast and pray for three or four years in order to fit himself for his' office. Then he came back and announced himself qualified to cure diseases and to hear the voice of The Great Mysterious One.

Thereupon some one of the tribe killed a prairie dog and took out its liver, while others found a rattlesnake. They made the snake bite into the liver until it was black with poison. After dipping their arrows into it they returned to camp.

The chief called for the claimant. He came, naked body painted red, and took his stand opposite four waiting warriors—a few steps away. They fired the poison arrows at him.

If an arrow so much as scratched his skin the man would die of poisoning and thus be proved an impostor. But if he was truly prepared, the arrows would fall harmlessly to the ground.

Our men did not try Quohahles in this way. But they saw him scoop his hands full of red coals of fire and rub them over his body without injury. So he became our Medicine Man.

As I watched the holy man with his quiet dignity which nothing could ruffle, and as I witnessed the wonders he performed at times, the desire took possession of me to become like him, a Medicine Man.

When I told him of my desire, he thought it over for several days. Then he called me into his tepee and asked me if I fully realised what it meant to fit myself for one through whom The Great One could speak. He informed me that it would take years of prayer and fasting and thought and great self-denial; that if I had the desire to become a warrior I would have to give it up; and that I would have to fulfil every vow that I had made before beginning my novitiate.

After that, I sought seclusion away from camp to meditate upon the goodness and power of God, who was in every tree and leaf and flower and breeze, and whose messengers watched over every stream and valley and mountain.

Sometimes on such occasions I fell into a kind of sleep in which I seemed to be awake, and to feel a presence which I could not see.

When I told Quohahles of these things, he advised me to continue my devotions and in due time he would give me further instructions.

He laid down certain rules of conduct for me to follow. Among the number were these warnings—not to look at my reflection in the water nor to enter a tepee if there were dogs in it; to keep away from the fire when meat was being cooked; and to abstain from certain kinds of food.

Once Quohahles fell into a trance in which he remained two days as one dead. When he revived he told me that his spirit had left his body and travelled great distances; that he felt neither hunger nor weariness; and that he had learned mysteries of which as yet he could not speak.

This wonderful man possessed a working knowledge of the laws of the human mind such as I have never found in books. He could not explain how he performed his wonders, but he knew what to do in order to produce certain definite results.

Often, for instance, during religious ceremonies, I have seen men fall to the ground in a deep sleep and become rigid and stiff, after Quohahles had waved his sacred fan of crow feathers before their faces.

On a time when the moon looked like a buffalo's horn—far gone in the last quarter—Quohahles, who had been engaged in prayer since the day before, called me to him. At his word I laid aside my robe so that I was naked save for the breech-clout.

"You have been earnest and diligent in seeking the mysteries," he said, "I will now prepare you for the office of Quo-dle-quoit. Your medicine shall be strong. For four years nothing can kill you."

Then while he prayed to The Above-Ones and to the Four Ways, I almost held my breath in awe.

The prayer finished, he painted my body white

Choosing a Medicine Man

from waist to feet, which he made black. From waist to neck he smeared me with yellow. Around my forehead at the roots of the hair he drew two streaks of black, which he extended on each side of my face down to the chin. On each cheek bone he put the shape of the crescent moon. On each breast he drew a picture of the sun in white. To each wrist, which he coloured red, he tied a bunch of leaves.

During the ceremony he chanted a prayer; also, while painting the crescent-shaped moon, he explained that among his own people—the house dwellers—it was sometimes cut into the flesh. Which was not necessary in my case, since I had followed his instructions in every particular.

The painting finished, he put on my head a cap made of jack-rabbit skins with the ears sticking up.

Believing as I did, without doubting in the least anything he told me, after this ceremony I was ready and anxious for the most dangerous duties. But according to his instructions I was always as careful and discreet when in danger, as though The-Ones-of-the-Four-Ways did not insure my safety.

I shall not tell of narrow escapes I had, lest they pass the bounds of the reader's belief.

Quohahles also taught me several secret and mysterious things.

Once when the camp was very quiet he had me stand before him in his tepee. He approached me with his sacred fan of crow feathers in his hand and began to wave it in a circle before my face.

Tahan

"You shall now see many things," he said.

And after an interval of silence, during which I kept my eyes fixed on the circling fan, he spoke again.

"Look at that herd of deer running across the hill, yonder. See those buffaloes—those white men on horseback—that beautiful valley—that camp of painted tepees."

All of these things I did see very distinctly, although we were shut in by the walls of the tepee.

Afterwards he taught me how to cause others to see what I wished them to see.

The days that I passed with the Medicine Man were wonderful days to me, and I hoped to continue to learn many mysteries. But there came a sudden change in the life of the tribe, and my studies ended.

Much of what I did learn, however, has been of practical use to me in the years that have followed.

CHAPTER XIX

MY BROTHER-FRIEND AND BUCKSKIN

ONE of the young warriors, Efawhahcho—Crazy Dog—and I became fast friends. He was a remarkable young fellow, several years older than I, and a usual doer of unusual things. When the other men sat down to gamble, he would go aside and pray. When they feasted, he would slip a piece of wood under his belt against his stomach and declare that he enjoyed it more than a stomach full of meat. In a storm when the rest of us sought shelter he would stand out in the drenching rain or driving hail listening to the voice of the thunder-bird, while fire-arrows pierced the clouds and the wind howled around him. Yet with all his oddities, he had great good-nature.

He was tall and athletic, with the tread of a cat and the heart of a lion; with eyes that could see what others could not; with ears that could hear where others were deaf.

His left eye had a most singular appearance, for it was never closed. In battle an arrow had struck in the corner of it, leaving a deep scar which kept the eyelid fixed. There was a constant sparkle in the pupil, which at times seemed to blaze as with fire. The women were afraid to look at it, for it was a magic eye, they said.

Tahan

He was a sure shot, which was remarkable, for in firing he never raised the gun to his shoulder. He held the breech at his belt.

I asked him how he could take aim in that way. He put a short stick into my hand and told me to strike the pommel of my saddle with the end of it. I did so.

"That is how I aim," he said.

He possessed a strange power over animals and could "feel" the nearness of an enemy. With this "feeling" came always a sensation like the rising of bristles between his shoulders.

Once when we were riding down a tree-covered hill —I behind him—he suddenly held up his hand in token of silence and motioned for me to turn round and go back. I did so without question. He followed.

After a while he rode up to my side, and told me that a war party of Utes were camped at the foot of the hill—that he "felt" them.

The next day we crept down afoot and found it to be as he had said.

On a hunt one day, we came upon a young buffalo calf under a shelving bank where its mother had hidden it and then gone to graze with the herd. It was lying flat on the ground, which was about the colour of itself. Efawhahcho gave it a kick, but it didn't move. He lifted it and let it fall. It seemed only to spread out the more thinly like a robe. But for the twitching of an ear and the blinking of an eye,

My Brother-Friend and Buckskin

it looked dead. Its mother had taught it to play 'possum as a protection against enemies.

My companion finally declared he would bring it to life. He made passes over its head with his hands, whispered in its ear and blew in its face. The calf got up instantly, and followed him like a dog.

Efawhahcho had been restless for several days. He walked about in a lost way, and kept looking off across the prairie, a faraway expression on his face. When I tried to engage him in conversation he would answer absent-mindedly and abruptly.

At last I insisted upon his telling me his trouble.

"I don't know what ails me," he said, "I seem to want something I haven't got."

"I know. You want a wife," I told him teasingly.

"You are my brother-friend. How can you make fun of me?" he asked sheepishly.

He looked all around to make sure we were out of earshot of the other men. Then——

"I believe that's just what ails me," he agreed.

And he brightened up at the thought.

"But," he went on, "I have never spoken love in the ear of a woman. How am I to begin?"

This was as much a conundrum to me as it was to him. Nevertheless I suggested that we might go some night and steal him a wife.

Efawhahcho at once took to the idea. So after carefully laying our plans we set off for the nearby Ute country.

Arrived there, we had no difficulty in locating a

camp. We hid in the brush on a neighbouring hill and watched to find out where the women went for water. Several days passed, and we were none the wiser.

One night we crept into the camp around among the tepees. But there came no chance to seize any one of the pretty girls and carry her off. Then we decided to lie in wait by a water spring.

Accordingly, the next night at dusk found us flat on our faces near the water hole, our horses tied in the thicket near by.

As we lay there several girls came for water at different times, but always some old woman came with them.

Above the voices of children and the barking of dogs, the sound of a tom-tom and of singing floated down from the camp. Night was coming on, and we were almost ready to give up, when two girls came tripping down the hill. Still an old woman followed closely.

The girls filled their vessels and started away. One loitered.

Without warning Efawhahcho sprang up, seized her and threw his blanket over her head. It completely smothered her cries. But our captive did not give up without a struggle. The bridegroom-to-be bore witness to this in the ugly scratches that covered his face.

We had a lot of trouble getting her up on the horse, but once in the saddle, with Efawhahcho behind her, we were away, with not a Ute the wiser.

We made a brief halt the next morning. Efawhahcho lifted the girl to the ground. She sat down sullenly. Efawhahcho offered her food. She refused to eat. Her language was not his, so he used the sign talk. With ungentle gestures he commanded her to obey. This made her only the more sullen. He threatened her with the lariat.

I interfered.

"That's not the way to use a woman," I argued. "My Kiowa father used to call my mother nice names, and make her beautiful presents. Try that way with her."

Efawhahcho sat thinking a long time. Then he took a string of beads from his neck and put it around hers.

"Mahye Gaitike," he coaxed, "I give this to you."

With this he got under headway, and by the time we arrived at our camp he had succeeded so well in his love making that his bride took her place in his tepee, a most obedient and dutiful wife. Mahye Gaitike—Good Woman—remained her name.

Efawhahcho and I were on the scout together one spring. Away on the edge of the Navajo country we surprised a man in the chaparral. The fellow jumped on his scrubby-looking little horse and dodged around the bushes so that even Efawhahcho could not get a shot at him.

We chased him out onto the open prairie. Here he put his horse to such a rapid pace that we were soon left far behind. After a while he halted on a little knoll and waited until we were almost within gun-shot, then sent his little animal across the prairie at a most amazing speed.

He repeated this performance several times, before we finally gave up the chase through fear of being led into a trap.

My brother-friend and I could talk of little else but the way that horse could run, until nothing would do but to possess him. Our own horses were far from being stiff-legged buffaloes, but the Navajo's mean looking creature was brother to the wind.

We examined his track and found we could trail him easily, for his right fore hoof had a piece broken off. We tracked him to a water hole, and from our hiding place near it spied a number of Navajo quogans, or houses. That night we visited the herd, but the little horse was not in it.

Next morning we made a wide circuit before we picked up his trail again. All day across the desert we followed it, but not a glimpse of that horse did we get.

Night after night, in camp after camp, we prowled in search of him—with no better success.

The longer the search the more eager we grew to get what we wanted.

Came a day when our stores failed us—when our supply of dried meat was exhausted; when the punk-fire in our buffalo horn died out; when our water-bottle—a buffalo's stomach—swinging from the pommel of my saddle, was pierced by a cactus thorn, and sprung a leak.

116

My Brother-Friend and Buckskin

Yet this did not swerve us from the trail. The horse we must have, we told each other.

One evening when the long shadows had faded, came the reward.

In the rear of a shack, in a little log pen, we found him. Against the pen leaned some long poles, hung with fresh sheep meat. Featherfooted we went, helped ourselves to a piece of the meat, and slipped away to our horses in the chaparral to wait for the right time to help ourselves to the horse in the pen.

At last the dogs ceased their barking and only the night noises of wild things could be heard.

Now came the question whether my brother-friend or I should go into the pen and come out with the coveted prize. The little corral was within a few feet of the shack where the owner slept, and we knew that he as well as his dogs had sharp ears.

The matter was decided with a pebble. After tossing it from one hand to the other for a while, Efawhahcho asked me to guess the one that held it. The right guess gave me the right to go. I won.

I handed him my reins, tightened my belt and slipped noiselessly to the back of the quogan, my ear strained for signs of wakefulness.

From the distance came the staccato bark of a coyote, and the quavering notes of a screech owl shivered through the darkness. Not ten feet away a dog uttered a low growl, but a little whine following it, told me that the dog was asleep, dreaming perhaps of a fight with the wolves.

117

Tahan

I crept to the pen and carefully lifted the top poles of it to the ground, fearful the while that the horse would snort and all would be lost. Stooping low I caught sight of him outlined against the dull sky.

Inside, I managed to drop my lariat over his head and to spring to his back. While trying to make him jump out I made so much noise that the dogs awoke and began to bark. I heard the Navajo speak to them, and in sheer desperation I lashed the horse with the rope until he leaped the fence and we were away.

I shouted to my comrade as I passed him. A gun blazed holes into the night, but that was all.

As the distance opened up between us and the Navajo, I gave back defiant whoops which were echoed by Efawhahcho.

My new steed carried me over the ground at such a rate that I soon lost my comrade in the darkness. When I reached our camp I was nearly spent with weariness and hunger. A bit of food first, then I slept the sleep of the utterly worn from sundown till sunup.

I had been back a day before Efawhahcho came in.

My ugly little horse's makeup was one big laugh in itself. He had a short body, dun, dirty and flea-bitten; a big long head, short ewe neck, and no tail worth speaking of. His legs were long, crooked and shaggy with black stripes running around them. He was about the colour of well-smoked buckskin, so I called him Buckskin. His makeup was one big laugh, as I said, but when he showed what he could do, the ridicule quickly turned to respect.

He and I soon became true friends with an understanding of each other such as seldom occurs between man and beast. I could go to sleep anywhere knowing that he would waken me if any one or thing came near. He would lie down or get up at my command, would run like the wind at a word or touch, and in time learned what I meant by the pressure of a leg on this or that side of his body.

Once he stampeded with the other horses in a hailstorm, and I feared he was lost to me forever. But with the passing of the storm he came back, and always, as long as he lived, played an important part in my life.

CHAPTER XX

I WAS now able to take my place as a hunter and warrior with the other men, and with my wonderful little horse, I felt that I was bigger than anything that could happen.

In the first days of my warriorhood, came a big buffalo hunt. We prepared for it as usual by an all night of prayer and left camp at daylight.

The herd was out on the plain not far away, but we all led our horses so they would be fresh for the work. I didn't have Buckskin. I had loaned him to Efawhahcho.

It was after sunup when we arrived at the stamping ground, and the signal was given for the dash. We mounted quickly and went at the prey in a mad rush, each of us singling out his buffalo.

I picked out a nice fat bull, as the herd went lumbering off across the prairie, and was soon at his side. I sent a shot into him, and whirled my horse to avoid the expected charge.

Again I came up beside him, and again I fired, but this time I didn't whirl soon enough. I didn't have Buckskin to work with, and it nearly cost me my life. The buffalo charged and upset my horse and me.

120

I Become a Warrior

The enraged animal was about to stamp my life out with his forefeet when one of the passing hunters killed him.

When I came to myself I was sitting on the prairie and wondering what had happened. I soon found out, for beside me my horse was lying, so badly gored he had been shot.

That night in the camp, the other hunters sat in the fireshine and told of their exploits.

I had no good thing to tell of myself, so I sat in the darkness with heavy heart, and heard how one of the young fellows had ridden up behind his buffalo, grabbed him by the tail, jabbed him with his knife, and had hamstrung him; how another had jumped from his horse to the back of his prey, spurred him with his knife and, after riding him a while, had driven the knife into his neck again and again until the blood spurted and he fell dead.

The recitals furnished a very entertaining evening for everybody except me.

The next day and for several days and nights, there was fun and feasting.

It was the women who brought the skins and meat into camp, and who took great pride in roasting just right the choicest bits—the luscious humps and marrow bones—for their hunter-and-warrior men.

After a hunt like this, when there was plenty of food in the camp, there was little to do but to think and dream. It was then that the warriors would meet in talk over the condition of their race, compare it with the past, and bewail its prospects for the future.

What rankled in their spirits worse than thorns in the flesh, was the way in which the white intruders had treated the Indian from the time they first set foot on the continent.

"Had the paleface been fair," they argued, "we would have been brothers. There would have been no war. Always there would have been peace, had they been just. They not only have taken our land, they have killed off the buffalo, the deer and the turkey. What is there for us to look forward to? In a little while their iron-shod horses will be trampling down the grass here where our tepees stand."

Their faces grew sad as they thought and talked about it. They could see nothing for themselves but extermination.

But they always ended the talk by declaring they would fight to the last and die like men.

Then one by one each warrior rose and went silently away.

Our wild prairie men were real patriots, for they loved their country with a fervour that could not be surpassed.

As the years went by the buffalo became fewer and fewer, and our wide range smaller and smaller. So our raids grew more and more frequent. This, too, in spite of the fact that we were bent on keeping our tribe's existence a secret. But we always took pains, on returning from our raids, to cross the reservation

I Become a Warrior

of some tribe, if possible, and lose our trail in a beaten track.

Thus, I am sure that the Comanches and other tribes were blamed for the killing and plundering done by our warriors.

Our men had long wanted to make war upon the Apaches in return for what they had done to us on one occasion. When Quohahles, the Medicine Man, declared that the medicine was strong, we set out toward their country under a leader appointed by the chief.

After several days' ride from our camp, each warrior got a stone about the size of his fist, and we put them all in a heap in a secluded spot. Then each of us promised, in case we met with defeat and were scattered, to make his way to the rock pile, remove one of the stones, and wait in hiding nearby for at least one sleep; then to throw the stone away, and take a trail previously agreed upon.

Following this custom of the prairie tribes, a separated band was able to get together again.

As we went on our way, one of the warriors in advance came galloping back to report that he had seen a bear cross our course with his head toward the wind.

This was a bad sign, for crossing the bear's trail would surely bring us defeat and death. The sign was never known to fail.

As all of us believed the bear had come to warn us,

most of us were more than willing to go back. But not Efawhahcho.

"You who turn back are afraid to die. You are not men," he scoffed. "As for me, I started upon this war trail as a man. I will go on. All of you who are not afraid, come!"

Five of the men paid no attention to the taunt, and went back.

"Come on," I shouted to the others.

There was no reply.

"I will go on," I cried. "My medicine is strong, I go if I go alone!"

Then the five who were left joined Efawhahcho and me. The leader was not among them. So I became leader and the seven of us went on towards the Apache country.

We had not gone far, that same day, when we sighted a number of Indians. They proved to be an Apache war party, and a war party we did not want to meet. We wanted to surprise their camp at night and get away with booty. But now that we were in sight of the enemy we would fight, no matter what the consequences.

The Apaches, uncertain of our intentions, halted on a ridge and stood looking at us.

We turned into a hollow, out of sight of them, dismounted, stripped, and tied our clothes to our saddles, ready for the fray. Then we rode boldly out to meet the enemy.

I Become a Warrior

The Apaches greatly outnumbered us, but this did not daunt us in the least.

. As we rode slowly towards them, Efawhahcho came up beside me.

"Tahan," he said, "this is my last war-trail. You will remember your vow, my brother-friend, and when you go back to camp, tell the warriors I died like a man."

He well knew I would do this and that I would not forget my vow, made when we became brother-friends. We pledged ourselves to everlasting friendship, to die, the one for the other, if necessary, and to avenge the death, should one of us be killed.

This was a custom of the Kiowas and also of the Dakotahs, with whom my comrade had lived a while.

When he had spoken, he gave his long war whoop, whipped his horse into a run, and sped ahead of the rest of us.

The Apaches, now aware of our intentions, came full tilt towards us. As we neared them our warriors separated. Some circled to the right, others to the left, our enemy between. We all fired at them as they passed. They kept together, turned and came at us again.

Exhilarated by the excitement of battle, I became careless of what might happen. Buckskin seemed to share my feeling. With ears laid back on his short neck he responded to the pressure of my knees, dashing to the right or left at my will, as I, with my warriors, fought the enemy almost hand to hand.

125

Tahan

I saw Efawhahcho fall slain from his horse. It maddened me, I started after the exultant and yelling Apache who had killed my brother-friend. Several of my warriors helped me cut him off from the rest——

I pass over what followed.

But I came out with a buckskin shirt and leggings of beautifully beaded workmanship and a certain other thing with blood on one end of it dangling from my belt.

True to my vow, I had avenged my brother-friend. From that day the warriors began to call me chief.

When the Apaches were completely routed and we were assembled, we found that three of our men were slightly wounded and one other besides Efawhahcho gone on the Long Trail.

CHAPTER XXI

ADVENTURES

OUR chief kept warriors scouting around on the prairie nearly all of the time. Hence, it came about, in the autumn of this same year, that I was chosen one of two to go out toward the northeast to watch the movements of some cattlemen.

Separated from my companion, one day, I unexpectedly ran onto a bunch of cowboys. As they saw me about the same time that I caught sight of them, it was too late to retreat and too dangerous. So I decided to meet them boldly and offer signs of friendliness.

I found them a jolly lot. They took me to their camp and finally to their ranch at Paladora Canyon.

I was with them for probably three months, and with my small stock of Mexican words was soon able to hold conversation with them in a kind of jargon. It was there I learned some English, too, and it afterwards stood me in good stead.

When I left the cow-punchers and went back again to Zakatoh, he acted as though he believed I had given the white men information hurtful to his welfare and I was constantly on my guard. I determined that if I saw signs of danger from him, he shouldn't be the one to get the first shot.

Tahan

Came a day when we heard there were big doings between the Indians and soldiers at Fort Sill. So Zakatoh took our whole band near that post. We made our camp on Cache Creek.

All along the stream were Kiowas, Comanches and Apaches. We mingled freely with them and found that a number of the chiefs with their bands had been rounded up by the soldiers. The chiefs were in the guardhouse and their warriors in bad humour. A big fight was a likely thing at any time, and the soldiers kept close watch.

There were heroes among those wild savages of the plains. One of the chiefs who was at Fort Sill at the time, was accused of leading a raid into Texas, where a number of white men were killed and horses run off. An officer ordered his soldiers to seize the accused. Although guiltless of the charge, he readily surrendered.

Shortly the man who had led the raid stalked majestically into the officer's presence. It was Setayete (White Bear) a chief of most striking and noble appearance. In the fearless grandeur of his manhood, he faced the soldier and bent piercing, unflinching eyes upon his face.

"I talk straight. I am the chief who led that raid," he proudly said. "If you take any man and hang him like a dog, take me."

He was taken to Texas where he was tried and condemned to be hanged. While attempting to escape he was killed.

128

Adventures

We all wondered if the Kiowas might not have been accused of making a raid which we ourselves had made, so we were careful not to let a word drop which would cause anyone to suspect us.

There were not more than six lodges of our band at this time, and no one paid us much attention. Besides it was difficult for outsiders to understand the language of the Estizeddelebe. That they all believed we had been brought in by the soldiers we knew, and we wisely allowed them to keep on thinking so.

One day there was an unusual stir at the post and we found out that the soldiers were about to start with several of the Kiowa chiefs to Texas. We found out, too, that the white men intended to hang them.

That night the Kiowa warriors mounted their horses and circled round and round singing their war songs. They rode up close to the barracks and called to the soldiers:

"Come out and fight us like men."

In this Zakatoh and the rest of us joined. We hoped there would be a big fight.

The next morning we saw near the guardhouse a number of wagons and squad of soldiers. They were closely guarding the noted war-chief Setankyea (Sitting Bear).

When they ordered him to get into one of the wagons, he refused. The soldiers seized him and threw him in with brutal force.

About a mile from the post Setankyea rose to his

129

feet and called to a number of his warriors who were following on horseback.

"These soldiers think they are going to take me to Texas," he cried, "and hang me like a dog. I will show them! You young men go to your camp and say to the people that Setankyea died to-day, the first day out."

He drew himself up proudly.

"Now I will show you how a chief can die. And I call upon Those-Above to witness that I die like a man, unafraid. But I do not go alone," he finished fiercely, "I take with me upon the Long Trail one of these soldiers."

At this he tore off the handcuffs, the flesh coming with them. He put his bleeding hands to his mouth. When he took them away, they held a large sharp knife.

There was a flash of the steel, a piercing war whoop and the blood spurted from the side of one of the guards sitting nearby.

Seizing the guard's gun Setankyea snapped it at another soldier. There was no cartridge in the chamber.

The soldiers fairly riddled the chief with bullets. He fell out of the wagon to the ground and sang his death-song while the soldiers continued to send their bullets into his body. At last he gnashed his teeth, gave one long defiant whoop and fell back dead.

The old chief was half Cheyenne and had the reputation of being a Mystery Man. One of the strange

Adventures

things which his people believed he could do, was to cough up a big knife at will. It was in this way, they claimed, that he obtained the one with which he stabbed the soldier. How else he could have got it was as much a mystery, for the officer * in charge had searched the chief before taking him from the guardhouse.

That night our chief got us together and we speedily slipped away to the westward, taking with us several additions to our band. These were Indians who were glad to escape from the restraint of the soldiers.

Far into the southwest we went.

While crossing the Staked Plains we rode into the teeth of a terrific wind which lasted several days. So dense was the cloud of fiercely driven sand and dust it nearly stifled us. Blinded and choked we were compelled to huddle down together with our robes wrapped around our heads to keep off the stinging particles.

With several others I was lost from the main company, and but for the plains-craft of one of the older men we would have perished. He went groping along the ground, feeling of every weed and sparsely scattered grass-bunch until he found a plant, the leaves of which always point directly north and south. By it he got the points of the compass.

That country of the southwest was new and strange

* Lieutenant (later General) Pratt, of the Tenth Cavalry, was the officer. He told me many years after that he himself stripped the chief and thoroughly examined his garments; that there was no knife about him and no way for him to get one before he left the cell.

to nearly all of us and new emergencies frequently arose, but some one of the men always proved equal to them.

One calm evening a scout came into camp and reported the discovery of a tepee village. Looking forward to a scrimmage and booty, we quickly made our way to the place. It was in a deep rocky canyon. We cautiously neared the edge and dismounted.

As we peered down at the weather-beaten tepees, some three or four hundred yards below, we noticed there was no smoke rising from them. Stealthily we watched for the signs of life usual in an Indian village, but neither to our eyes nor to our ears did there come sight or sound of them. A strange something seemed to spread over the place, to become a part of it and to hold us in its uncanny embrace.

Silently, from behind the rocks, we peered down at the tepees in the canyon. The sun died out like a coal of fire on the edge of an ash-heap. The shadows faded into purple gloom. Stars pricked the sky with pin-holes, through which The Above-Ones looked down. The moon, a huge, pale-faced war drum, showed itself on the rim of the world and walked up the sky, sending down its soft light to uncover the jagged rocks of the canyon and bring the tepees out of the darkness like ghosts. They grew whiter and whiter, and held our eyes in strange fascination.

The silence was like that which must have been before anything was. It was so intense, so ominous, so awful, we seemed to hear it. We were scarcely able to breathe as the soundlessness settled down upon us. Our straining senses were ready to break.

Suddenly, a piercing scream, sounded far down the canyon.

As one man we dashed to our horses, sprang to their backs and sped away from the awful place.

In camp, we sat huddled together in the moonlight talking over the strange thing, when some one noticed that Quohahles, the Medicine Man, was absent. The next day he came in. He had visited the silent village and found the skeletons of the inhabitants, who must have been carried off by a pestilence. He found also the body of a horse which had fallen over a cliff. He said the scream which had brought terror to our hearts must have been the animal's death-cry; that once before he had heard the same kind of a cry, and it came from a dying horse.

In that strange land we crossed a desert which was so naked there was not so much as a stick of wood for a picket pin. But nevertheless, when night came, we were able to tie our horses to the ground.

Each man took his knife and dug a hole about twelve inches across at the top and twice as wide at the bottom, pulled up an armful of bunch grass, tied the end of his lariat around it, stuffed it into the hole and stamped the earth down upon it. So our horses were literally tied to holes in the ground.

It was on this desert trip that one of the men discovered huge tracks in the sand. They looked somewhat like a buffalo's, but were of greater size. No one had ever seen anything like them. We followed them day after day, and at night thought long over them.

At last, soon after we broke camp one morning, we saw the trackmakers away out on the plain. There were two of them, great, long-legged creatures with high backs and crooked legs.

One of the older men tried to account for them through an old legend which says that the first buffaloes were light in colour and very large and that they came from a wide desert across a great water. At sight of us the creatures took fright and ran away at a rapid pace, swaying from side to side like mountains about to topple over, but undecided on which side to fall. We stood gazing at them in wonder until they disappeared in the distance.

They gave us much talk for many moons.

Years afterward I saw a circus parade in one of the great cities. Among the animals were several of these "about-to-fall-like-a-mountain buffaloes." I learned they were camels.

Since then I have often wondered how the two we tracked ever got into the Great American Desert.

CHAPTER XXII

WE drifted from the desert country back eastward until we reached the Wewoka River in the Creek Nation, Indian Territory.

The Creeks were advanced in civilisation. True, there were among them those not far removed from our condition, but many possessed a culture equal to that of the highest type of the white man.

They were engaged in farming and other industries, and often held fairs to exhibit their products.

We had not been long with them when they had one of these fairs in Muskogee. We learned there were to be horse-races. This alone was enough to draw our whole band to the place.

On our way to the town we saw many things which interested us, and certain it was that we with our wild appearance and our peculiar costumes were of no less interest to the people we passed. Many of them were of the white race.

Arrived at the fair-grounds, we left the women to pitch our tepees and we looked around the town.

We had heard of the railway train with its "Smoke-Horse," so we went to the station to see it.

With roar and clash and clatter, hiss and shriek,

the huge monster came dashing in. Its ear-splitting war whoop startled us. Its blazing eye, like a camp fire in the middle of its forehead, astounded us. When it stopped and the "Smoke-Horse" stood panting and blowing its breath out in great clouds, we stood aloof with our blankets over our heads and talked it over.

The thing itself was far beyond the thing we had pictured.

We wondered what made it go if, as we had heard, it was not really alive.

One of the young fellows declared that the next time it came, he would ambush and lasso the monster so that we could examine it.

We noted its speed; and I for one, felt certain that if it would leave its smooth trail and come out on the open prairie Buckskin could outrun it.

For want of a better name, we called the train the "Big Noise."

The exhibits at the fair-grounds came in for their share of comment and criticism.

We found the bed-quilts of many pieces and colours most attractive. We thought the big pumpkins and the potatoes might be good eating and we knew the corn was excellent. But when we learned that it was necessary to toil all summer to raise them, we lost all interest.

We liked the looks of the fat hogs and the cattle and the chickens, but it was beyond our comprehension how people could be content to live in one spot and work all the time and feed them every day. We

Visit to the Creeks—My Horse Race

greatly admired the horses, but in our judgment the care they required overbalanced their worth.

Contrasted with our free life of the plains this "white man's road" in which these Creeks were going was unlikable to us. We could kill enough game in a few days to last us for months, and have more fun doing it than they could have in years. We could go and come as we pleased, untrammelled by hog-feeding and rubbing-down horses. And the excitement we had in creeping into an enemy's camp, outwitting him and getting his horses, was more fun in our opinion than any that the white man could get out of a life-time.

As we walked about the place with eyes big and ears wide, we saw much which excited our curiosity.

We saw white men and Creeks gazing at wide sheets of paper so intently we thought they were praying to their medicine.

We observed when they ate they used little iron forks. Surely not to keep their fingers clean!

We were struck with the war-bonnets the women wore! Truly these were a queer people.

We noticed how loudly people talked to each other, even when standing or sitting close together.

The plains Indians habitually talked in low tones. Indeed this was necessary when in camp, if we were to enjoy privacy, for the walls of the tepee were thin.

As compared with the white man the Indian is a man of silence. When on a hunt he seldom speaks lest he scare away the game; when on the warpath, he keeps still lest by speaking he discover himself to enemies. Besides, when one is talking neither his eyes nor ears can do their duty.

We were sitting on the ground in a circle talking over the many odd things, when a man on a velocipede went pedalling past. Not a man of us gave so much as a hint of the astonishment we felt, but the wag of the band finally broke the silence caused by the strange sight.

"Ugh. The white man is very lazy. He straddles a wagon wheel and sits down on it to walk."

He spoke in an undertone, without so much as a ghost of a smile on his stolid face.

No one laughed at the time, but when we entered a tepee and were sure that no strangers could see or hear us, we stoics of the plains were suddenly transformed into the most hilarious of laughers.

Came the day of the big races. A white man approached our camp and told us if we had any horses that could run, to get them ready. Also that we would have to pay him so much money as an entrance fee.

This was another new thing to us. Of money we had not so much as a single piece. Had we possessed any we would not at that moment have had empty stomachs. We had had nothing to eat that day.

We talked a good deal about the lack of courtesy shown us by these Creeks of the white man's road. If they had visited us in our country, not only food

Visit to the Creeks—My Horse Race

but presents of clothing and other things would have been placed before their tepee doors.

We satisfied the white man by giving him two ponies so that my horse could enter the race. When he saw my little steed he broke into most astonishing roars of laughter and called his friends to see the grotesque thing that we called a race-horse.

"And they are to run him in the big race!" they cried between roars.

"All right, my son, but it's darned tough on you," called the chief man of them to me as they took their departure.

Many white men and others came to our camp and offered bets.

Some of our people threw robes on the ground and asked the white men to throw their silver on top of them. This every man refused to do. They were afraid the money would be stolen, we were told.

Another strange situation! Men in their own camp afraid that friendly visitors would steal from them!

Some of them offered paper money against our beautifully tanned and painted robes. With this we would have nothing to do. We did not know the value of it. But silver money would make good ornaments. We would accept it.

Finally, we came to terms with the white men.

When the sun passed short-shadow time, I got ready for the race. I stripped to the skin except for the breech clout, and painted face and body, my legs, with their stripes—red, yellow, white and blue—looking like

139

barber-poles. Then I unbraided my hair, except the scalp-lock, in which I stuck a beautiful eagle feather.

Buckskin was lazily cropping grass at the end of a rawhide lariat. I tied it around his under jaw, and he was ready.

The sun was sliding toward the place of long shadows when I mounted and rode toward the judges' stand.

The faded and frayed fringe of humanity which bordered the southwestern frontier was surging toward the track and chatting in the many tongues.

Big, clean-limbed horses with shining skins and small gaily jacketed jockeys on their backs, were out on the track warming up.

As I watched those horses, noted their greyhound build, and contrasted them with Buckskin, my heart became a mudhole full of frogs.

In slovenly, loose-jointed gait and with drooping head, old Buckskin, like a bundle of loose-hung accidents, carried me on toward the starting-place.

Near it a young girl stepped out from a tepee and coyly approached us. I brought my horse to a standstill.

How pretty she looked with the little circle of red in the centre of her forehead!

That little circle of red meant much to me because it betokened the fact that she had not yet been taken to wife, and I had asked her the old, old question.

Her name was Nacoomee—Handful-of-Flowers.

She stepped modestly around to the side of my

horse, her eyes two camp-fires in the dark. She was barefooted. She had bet her moccasins on Buckskin. The only clothing she had on was a piece of faded red blanket wrapped about her. She had bet her dress of finest doeskin against a handful of lump sugar with a Cherokee woman.

Confused, she turned quickly away, but not before I had caught a flash of the dark eyes, and the music of the words—

"Go, Tahan, and win."

The mudhole full of croaking frogs in my heart became a sunlit green place in the woods with laughing water and bordering flowers and singing birds. In the midst of it all was a new tepee and Nacoomeè, no longer in the rag of a blanket.

At the starting-place Buckskin stopped, put his hindfeet and forefeet close together, humped his back like a buffalo in a storm, hung his big head still lower and lopped forward his long ears as though he was so ashamed of himself he was ready to fall down and die.

"Git that old jack-rabbit out of the way! We're going to have a race," yelled a white man at me.

"Y'd better do y'r hair up, sonny, 'er yer bronch'll git his feet tangled up in it," gurgled an old cowboy.

At this I took fire and felt like getting my gun and filling his big mouth full of bullets.

The hardest thing for an Indian to bear is ridicule.

But fire burn them! what cared I for those barking coyotes?

Tahan

Over the fence the crickets were singing their prairie song beneath the dust covered flowers, and yonder stood Nacoomee—the "world"—barefooted and in a strip of red blanket, and her words, "Go, Tahan, and win," still sounded their sweet music in my ears.

Yonder, too, sat my people, naked and bronzed like statues, indifferent as statues, apparently, as though they had not wagered everything they had on my horse.

I was going to win that race. Buckskin, my good old friend, would that day prove to the howling wolves about us, that he was indeed brother of the wind, and I would ride him as light as a feather in an eagle's wing.

And at the end of the race there would be more than glory.

All the fine horses came up in an even line abreast of us.

Buckskin was quietly dozing. A flag dropped in the judges' stand. My naked heel went into Buckskin's flank. He was off like an arrow from a bowstring and soon caught up with the "greyhounds." They had a running start. I had asked for a standing start.

We were to go twice around the big circle—a distance of probably two miles.

The first time we came round it, the horses were strung out and Buckskin and I were at the tail-end of the procession. But at a word from me, he began to creep up and up.

We passed horse after horse until at the head of the home stretch, with but a short distance to go, only two horses were ahead of us. But they were going in their long level leaps like greyhounds. Their riders glanced back and began to whip.

I didn't have to whip Buckskin—he knew as well as I knew. I lay down flat upon him, patted him on the neck and began to chant a wild song.

"Now, Buckskin, you can beat them. You must win. Now, Buckskin, now—go!" I sang.

He understood. He went. When we flashed under the wire all of those fine horses were still coming.

And now the joy, the ecstasy, the glory, of it! The crowd surged around us to get a closer look at good old Buckskin. We got rich on that race. But by far the most precious of all the prizes that Buckskin won for me, was Nacoomee, Handful-of-Flowers.

CHAPTER XXIII

MY MARRIAGE

IN the crowd at the race-track was Colonel Clayton, commanding officer of Fort Gibson. He wanted to see the boy and the queer-looking animal that had won the race against some of the best horses in the southwest, so I was introduced to him.

After I had told him something of my life, he induced me to go with him to his house at the post. Here he told me of the advantages which would come to me and the service I might render by connecting myself with the army. But just then I had far more important business on hand. Promising the officer to return and enlist, I went back to Muskogee to find that my people had gone. They had packed up the booty won on Buckskin, and headed westward.

It was several days before I located them. I found their camp at night and they were having a feast celebrating my little broncho's victory.

They were overjoyed at my safe return. They thought I had been arrested, when they saw me start to Fort Gibson with the officer, and not knowing how to find me or to give me help, had hastily decamped.

While they sang a song in my honour, I looked for Nacoomee. She was taking no part in the festivities.

My Marriage

I found she was in her father's tepee, and before it a Mexican was sitting.

I gave him a quick glance of contempt, then grabbed his scalp-lock and jerked it fiercely. Like the coyote that he was, he sneaked into the darkness.

"Ee-e-mah, Nacoomee!" I called.

She came and followed me to the feast.

The next day I lost no time in giving her father the costliest trophies I had won in the race. They won. Nacoomee was mine.

I was ready. Close at hand stood a mule with a large pack on his back, and Buckskin and another horse beside him.

Nacoomee and I mounted and started on the old trail marked out by the first man and woman—a trail just wide enough for us two. According to the custom of the tribe, we needed no wedding ceremony.

That evening we stopped in a sequestered spot beside a little stream. We were in an unfriendly part of the country, but we gave the matter little thought. The future was held captive in the now. The present was all.

My bride pitched our tepee. When she was busy within, I went to loosen the rawhide ropes that bound our food-pack to the mule.

Nacoomee called to me.

"What are you doing, Tahan?"

She ran to me and pushed me away.

"Have you forgotten so soon you have a wife to do that?" she pouted.

Tahan

Confused, I replied somewhat sheepishly,
"There's no one but you to see me do it."
She burst into a ripple of teasing laughter.
I took my gun and scouted around our camp.
In a short time I came back with a fat young buck on my shoulders.
I skinned it and Nacoomee helped me cut up the meat.
She chattered gaily as she worked.
"I am glad you got this fresh meat, Tahan. The tenderest piece we shall give to the Spirit of the place. I am sure it will please better than the dried meat we brought."
I gave her the piece.
She laid it carefully aside, and went to look for the sticks to hold it. She chose three about the size of my wrist, and cut them some longer than my length. Tying their tops together, she fixed the meat on them and set it up at the back of the tepee.
This was our offering to make the Life of the place our friend.
Her sacrifice was a string of beads placed on a little bush beside the brook.
Mine was a beautiful buckskin bag filled with tobacco. After I had scattered part of the contents to the Four Ways, I laid the bag on a stone on the hillside. I chose this spot because the stone was shaped like a bear.
The days that followed were dream days.
Birds, like flowers made alive by the breath of the

146

My Marriage

prairie, darted about in the sunshine and among the yellowing leaves; or swung in the tops of the tall cottonwoods to sing their feast-songs and chirrup to us their welcome from the Everywhere.

Great eagles stretched their arms and swam in the blue, far overhead.

And over all came floating now and then a snow-white feather-cloud from the Spirit of Peace.

The nights came and brought cool breezes, but no darkness.

Owls called and answered one another in stately voice through the starlight. Our brother-wolves sat on the hills and sang us their night-songs. The horses cropped the rich pasture. And all was contentment.

Each day I left Nacoomee alone with her bead-work, while I scoured the prairie to see what food it held for us.

Afoot, one day, I wounded an antelope. It gave me a weary chase before I downed it, and it was no light burden to carry homeward.

I was late, but the fire burned bright in the tepee, and savoury odours met me.

Over the coals hung broiling meat on the skewers, and in the ashes yam-like roots were roasting.

The roots Nacoomee had found on the flat near the creek.

How good that supper tasted, as we sat on the robes and ate it in the bright light of our tepee fire.

So—came and went away again and again the

nights with their voices and their stars and their thin-bent moon in the west.

We changed camp many times—just to be doing it, seemingly. But often I believed it was because of some dream or some warning of bird or of beast that had come to Nacoomee.

For it was in the constant presence of Intelligent Life we were living, and to us everything around us was interested in our welfare.

One day, while on the move with all our belongings, we idled about on the prairie. Our shadows began to grow long before we thought of a camping-place. But we found one not far away.

It was beside a little stream of sweet water, where grew good grass and tall trees.

When the tepee was pitched and the horses hobbled, I stepped across the little stream and stood listening to the whisperings in the tree-tops.

From the other edge of the stream spoke Nacoomee:

"How pleasant this place is! Always and always I could stay here."

"Every place is pleasant," I replied. "Come to this side."

I stretched out my hand toward her. She took it but did not cross. Her face was bent down towards the water.

"Look!" she exclaimed joyfully, "both of our faces are there close to a flower. It must mean that always and always we shall be together."

She had hardly finished speaking. A brown and

148

My Marriage

withered leaf floated down between us, fell into the ripple, and drifted away.

With a startled look on her face, Nacoomee raised her eyes to mine. Our hands fell apart.

A squirrel whisked up a nearby tree, where he sat chattering.

A red bird—like a spray of blood—dashed out of the bushes with a plaintive cry.

I leaped across the stream. Silently, and together, we hurried to the tepee.

Something, we both knew, had startled the wild things.

I took up my gun.

A short distance up the stream, a trail crossed it. I went cautiously towards it, until I saw coming a small party of warriors. At first I took them for enemies, but I soon learned they were of our own people—the Estizeddelebe—and were headed for Zakatoh's camp.

Back in the tepee I found my woman waiting—her gaiety changed to sadness. I asked her nothing. She told me nothing.

So I can only guess at the message the brown leaf brought to Nacoomee.

She asked to go back to Zakatoh's camp. We went back the next day.

In the winter that followed the white hunters had a big buffalo kill.

We came upon the signs of it—a wide, level stretch of prairie covered with the bones.

Tahan

We could have walked across the littered space, almost without setting foot on the bare ground.

The white men wanted only the skins. They left the meat for the wolves.

This made us feel much as cattlemen would have felt if their herds had been treated in this way.

And this was not the only slaughter-ground we came upon that winter.

This caused much serious talk among our people.

If such work went on, we knew that starvation lay in wait for us. Even then, at times, our meat-poles were bare for days.

That winter and another passed.

Our lodges became fewer and fewer in number. By ones and by twos and by families our people went away and did not come back.

The prairies were empty of game. Not even a jackrabbit could be found. And the children cried from hunger.

Came the First Green Grass. And one day I came into camp with a lean antelope behind my saddle.

I dismounted in front of my tepee. The flap was closed, and two sticks were crossed before it. This meant I must not enter.

No one ever thought of going into a tepee if crossed sticks were before the door.

As I stood deep in thought, a woman passed me.

She didn't speak. She simply looked at me. But I knew from the look why the sticks were crossed before my door.

150

My Marriage

I went a little way off to cut up the antelope meat. But my eyes didn't leave the sticks very long at a time.

Not until the next day were they taken away.

Then I entered my tepee.

Nacoomee was sitting on a robe, with a limp little creature in her arms.

I made the fire brighter so I could see it better. And I looked at it a long time.

Nacoomee broke the silence.

"Is he not wonderful, Tahan?" she exclaimed joyously.

"He is wonderful," I agreed, "the most wonderful child in all the world!"

A little later while I was broiling strips of the antelope meat, Nacoomee suddenly cried out:

"Oh! now I have it! His name shall be Tapahyeete."

So our child was given his name—Big Boy Antelope.

· I had often thought of the promise I had made Colonel Clayton to return to Fort Gibson. I felt the time had come for me to keep it. But it was not until the leaves began to fall that I started, with my little family, in the direction of the fort.

CHAPTER XXIV

MY ENLISTMENT—IN THE BARRACKS

TRUE to my promise, I went to the colonel, and enlisted for special duty as a scout. I was attached for the time being to Company K of the 16th Infantry.

Thanks to the intelligence of Colonel Clayton, I enjoyed far greater liberty than did the other men. I knew intuitively that he had given the first sergeant instructions with regard to me.

The sergeant, whom we familiarly knew as "Old Jock," was a veteran of the Crimean War—a member of the Light Brigade which made the famous charge at Balaklava. We never tired of hearing him tell of this event. He always wound up with what I then knew as "Old Jock's piece" and recognised years after, when I had learned to read, as Tennyson's poem— "The Charge of the Light Brigade."

We also enjoyed hearing Old Jock make the barracks ring with his two songs—"When the corn is wavin'; H'annie dear, h'o meet me by the stile" and "H'it's 'ard to give the 'and where the 'art can never be."

Once the men got me to drink too much "firewater" and I performed a war dance in such realistic fashion that the men skipped out, missing roll-call in consequence. Old Jock caught me looking for them with my gun and promptly locked me in the guard-house.

The next morning he released me and took me to the colonel.

The good old greyhaired officer gave me such kindly and fatherly advice that for his sake—as long as I belonged to his command—I did not taste again the "water-that-makes-foolish."

I gave to Colonel Clayton the love of a son to a father. He understood me through sympathy and was unfailing in his kindness and consideration. Never through it did I escape any necessary discipline, but he always befriended me when I stood most in need of it.

One day a United States marshal came and arrested me for an offence committed in the Creek Nation.

It was many moons past and had to do with a trick played on Buckskin. Our wild band of the plains was on the way to Muskogee and had camped overnight near a house occupied by white men. One of them caught Buckskin drowsing and cut off what little hair there was on his tail. I caught the man and when I left him he was in no condition to play any more tricks. It was for this I was arrested.

The marshal started to take me to Fort Smith, Arkansas, to answer the charge in court, but before he got me off of the military reservation, Colonel Clayton sent a file of soldiers to arrest him. He was locked in the guardhouse and finally sent away under guard.

As a recruit I was quick to learn the drill. The old sergeant would order me to stand out in front of the company and as I was straight as an arrow, he would call the newly enlisted men's attention to me and bid them note how a soldier should stand. Then he would march me up and down, calling to the soldiers,

"See how a soldier should carry himself! He walks with his legs, not by swinging his body."

This fostered my pride and made me determined to be the best soldier possible.

Within a few months I was transferred to a troop of the Fourth Cavalry, then at Fort Sill. My troop commander was Captain Harry Crews—"Handsome Harry," the men called him—and he was every inch the soldier. I tried always to imitate his manners and those of the best men in the troop, and to speak the English language as those men spoke it.

In my spare moments I learned the bugle, became a bugler of the troop, and chief trumpeter of the post. Then the men gave me a fine trumpet of special make.

My position was similar to that of first sergeant of a company and I had in my "command" twenty musicians.

I had just dismissed them one morning. We were all on parade ground, when an officer passed.

One of the men didn't salute him.

"To the guardhouse!" was the order I looked for.

My Enlistment—In the Barracks

It wasn't given. Instead, the lieutenant let the offence pass, seemingly without the slightest notice.

I couldn't understand this.

"Why didn't you salute?" I demanded of the offender.

"Why! *Me* salute a d——d nigger!"

The reply was emphatic but not enlightening.

At the post were other negroes—"buffalo soldiers" we Indians called them. Some of the whites mingled with them. Some didn't. Why?

Lieutenant Flipper was a fine specimen of physical manhood and a good officer. An enlisted man refused to salute him. Why?

The lieutenant didn't punish him. Why?

For the answers I went to an old soldier. He praised the officer for ignoring the slight, and introduced to me the race problem.

Always, afterwards, I took pains to offer the negro the most punctilious salute, for I myself knew something of how an outsider felt.

Conditions finally grew unbearable for the lieutenant. He deserted, went to Mexico and became a general in the Mexican army.

I found that the monotony of military life was irksome for the soldiers who had seen years of service, as well as for the recruits. Many of the latter had been used to such things as the Bowery of New York City afforded, and when the novelty of frontier experiences wore off, they sighed for the flesh-pots of their Egypt.

But with me the matter was different. To leave the wild free life of the plains for the discipline of a military post was to confine an eagle in an iron cage. My captain seemed to understand this and gave me frequent furloughs. Then I would go to my tepee on Cache Creek above the post, where stayed Nacoomee, my wife, with our baby-boy, and take them for a trip across the prairie.

The men of the troop were always complaining about the food. And indeed there was just cause. For breakfast we had coffee, "skilly"—oatmeal mush with syrup—and bread; for dinner, a small piece of beef, varied with pork and beans once a week, and sometimes potatoes; for supper, nothing but bread and coffee.

There were loud rumours to the effect that the commissary sergeant was industriously engaged in feathering his nest with proceeds from the sale of the company's rations. But the rumours didn't help matters any, and if it hadn't been so far to civilisation many of the men would have taken "French leave," so poor in quality and so small in quantity was the food.

Entertainment was almost as meagre. We had little to colour the daily routine of barracks life, so we made the most of old happenings.

There was one that varied as to time and place but never as to actors or performance. Of actors there were but two—Captain Davis and Private Rankin. Regularly every pay-day when Rankin had drunk

My Enlistment—In the Barracks

enough of the sutler's whiskey, he would have an interview with the captain.

"Davis," he would begin, without saluting, "do you remember when you were a private in my Company?"

The captain would nod his head in acknowledgment of the fact.

"And, Davis," he would conclude, "do you remember you were such a dirty soldier that I had my men forcibly scrub you with soap and water?"

At this the captain would march Rankin past the barracks to the guardhouse, and the next day release him.

We always looked forward to the "piece," which seemed never to grow stale.

CHAPTER XXV .

A N hour came when news ruffled the routine.
Men were to be picked for an important mission!

Both Captain Davis and Rankin were among the lucky. So was I.

The captain was leader. This man had risen from the ranks during the Civil War and was noted for his fearlessness. He had, besides, two other marks of distinction—a commanding presence and a great length of whisker.

I was detailed to act as special scout and interpreter.

Our business was to round up a half-breed, Tom Starr—the worst man, it was said, that ever rode the crooked trail in Indian Territory. People believed him to be in league with the devil who gave him protection for his evil deeds.

On numerous occasions he had been surrounded by marshals and all chance of escape cut off, apparently. But every time he got away—led into safety by a bird, red as a spurt of blood. It would dart from the brush, utter a peculiar cry, circle around his head, flit before him, and——

All that the posse would find would be the head

of one of its number impaled on a stake by the trailside.

When we arrived near the desperado's stamping-ground on the edge of the Creek Nation, the captain sent me ahead to locate him.

I was dressed as a cowboy, armed with a Winchester and a white-handled Colt's sixshooter, and mounted on Buckskin.

As I jogged along the trail I talked with everyone I met to get the desired information. Finally I learned that a party of horsemen was in an abandoned log-cabin which stood in a clump of trees just off the trail, and but a short distance ahead of me.

I rode leisurely along waiting for darkness.

Arrived at the cabin, I dismounted before the door and was about to knock, when I was startled by a voice close behind me. It asked in the Creek language what I wanted there. I replied that I wanted something to eat.

Though it was too dark to see his face, I felt sure that the speaker was Tom Starr.

The man reached over my shoulder and knocked. The door swung open. Keeping behind me he followed me into the cabin. It contained but one room dimly lighted by a flickering fire in a large fire-place. It was light enough, however, for me to see five men with their sixshooters swinging at their belts, and their Winchesters leaning handily against the wall.

I sat down on a bench near the door.

Tahan

The man who followed me in sat down on another bench, behind me.

This made me feel somewhat uncanny, but I dared not look around at him lest I unduly excite his suspicions. That he was already suspicious I judged from his actions. Such men are always on the tiptoe for their natural enemies—the representatives of the law.

I knew that a false move on my part would mean my death, that my hide would not hold bunch grass when the gang had finished with me.

On the floor across the room was a bucket of water. I got up, got a drink, and turned around.

The man who sat behind me was gone.

My eyes and ears had been on the alert, but when and how he had disappeared I didn't know.

The men in the house did not seem inclined to talk, but in answer to my questions they told me they belonged to a cattle outfit. Of course I knew this wasn't true.

After eating some osaufkee out of a gourd, I bade the men good night and sauntered out.

They had not asked me anything concerning myself. This made me feel that they knew what I was, and it took a good deal of self-control to keep from looking back as I went out of the door. I more than half expected a shot in the back, and it felt as if ants were crawling up and down on it.

Buckskin was gone from where I had left him, but some distance up the trail I found the old bronck headed toward the place where I had tied him. As I coiled the rope in my hand I found damp sand on it. This told me that he had been dragging it through dew and sand, and for some considerable distance.

Hoofbeats came to my ears. I led Buckskin out of the trail into a clump of bushes.

Soon a horseman galloped past and dismounted at the door of the cabin. He held a conversation with the men inside, then mounted and rode swiftly past me up the trail. I knew him to be the one who had so mysteriously disappeared and the one who had failed to get away with Buckskin. I also knew he was looking for me, and being firmly convinced that this man was Tom Starr, I rode back to our outfit.

As soon as Captain Davis received my report we started for the rendezvous of the outlaws.

We reached it at daybreak. The captain hammered on the door with the butt of his revolver and commanded those within to open.

After a short wait the door was flung open and a man asked what we wanted. The captain ordered him to strike a light. I translated this command into Creek.

The Indian soon had a bright fire burning in the fire-place. To our disappointment it revealed but the one man.

After a short conversation through me, we were on the point of leaving. But I had noticed the Indian glance at a corner of the room from time to time and I told our leader.

The floor was made of split logs, the ends of which

were laid on the sills loosely. The captain easily lifted one end of a puncheon.

Instantly the muzzle of a gun was thrust almost into his face and discharged.

Every man of us fired several shots in quick succession at the place, and then tore up the floor. There in a shallow cellar sat three men.

I heard a horse gallop past the door. I reached it in time to catch sight of a fleeing horseman. He fired several shots, one of which struck the door jamb, knocking the flying splinters in my face. I fired repeatedly at the fugitive in the dim light. He sent back several defiant whoops and disappeared at the bend in the trail.

When we had handcuffed the four remaining, they acknowledged that it was the much-wanted desperado Starr who had given us the slip.

All that was needed to complete the traditional picture was one of our heads impaled on a stake by the trail-side.

As we stood in the bright firelight, after the fray, old Rankin exclaimed:

"Davis, you're shot!"

"Shot!" echoed the captain, "shot! where?"

He ran his hands up and down over his breast.

"Wounded in the whiskers, Davis," replied Rankin.

The desperado had discharged both barrels of a shotgun at the captain, and the long whiskers, with the exception of a few strands, had been mowed off.

Service as Scout and Interpreter

Tom Starr had got away again.

But we rode into Fort Sill with his men as our prisoners, and placed them in the basement of the guardhouse.

CHAPTER XXVI

I ACCOMPANIED nearly every scouting party which left the post, whether in pursuit of desperadoes or of Indians.

To be in the saddle on the wide, sweeping prairies was to be like the prodigal returned to his father's house—fatted calf, best robe and all—for on such occasions I dressed and lived as an Indian, and the prairie furnished the calf.

One day I went, with a small detachment of soldiers, after some Comanches. According to the report, they had run off with a lot of Texas cattle.

I struck the trail, but the officer in charge was never the wiser.

It was Zakatoh's.

And far from me was the thought of betraying the men whose fasting and feasting and fighting I had shared for years.

Indeed, I was often tempted to try to find the doughty warrior, and once more cast in my lot with him.

It was on an expedition in the panhandle of Texas that I made my first open rebellion against discipline.

We were camped on the Sweetwater, just below

164

TAHAN IN THE COSTUME OF AN APACHE CHIEF
WHOM HE KILLED AND SCALPED

Scouting in the Southwest

Fort Elliott, and orders were issued prohibiting any of us leaving camp.

No sooner did taps sound than every man of us, except the guard, slipped away by twos and threes.

As we had left Fort Sill on the evening of payday, we had not had our bi-monthly blow out, so we intended taking it in the drinking and gambling places near the post.

There was a genuine rampage that night, and the next morning there were consequences. Every man of us was ordered to walk and lead his horse.

I bucked. I was no dough-boy, I was a cavalryman.

I sat down on the ground and declared I would sit there till the Sweetwater froze over before I would walk.

Finally I was ordered to get into the ambulance. In this, under guard, I rode all day.

During a scout in this part of the country, we ran across a war-party of Apaches. In the scrimmage with them, a bullet took the big toe-nail off my left foot. This was the nearest I ever came to being wounded in my war-days.

But it was the last fight for my faithful Buckskin. The bullet that glanced off my foot went through his body.

He was human to me, my comrade in peril, sunshine and storm; with a heart beating steadily strong and true; with feet sure, tireless and fleet—my Brother-to-the-Wind, indeed.

I left him lying where the coyotes fought, but he

has never been forgotten, nor will he be so long as my faithful memory brings me the pattering hoof-beats of his unshod feet.

As we were returning eastward, the troop was ordered down the North Fork of the Canadian River. We went into winter camp near where Oklahoma City now stands.

The winter furnished a few of us with at least one memorable experience. On a scout we were caught in a blizzard and snowbound.

The storm lasted over a week. We ran out of provisions. For several days our only food was parched corn and little of that. Our horses lived on the bark they gnawed from cottonwood poles.

When we finally got back to our quarters camp-fare, meagre as it was, was a feast for a while.

In the spring I went with the troop on an expedition intended to quiet the restless Cheyennes. We camped at Bent's Ranch.

There a scout came in with despatches from Fort Reno.

I had left my wife and child at this fort, so I went to him for news of them.

He took me aside and told me that a certain officer had basely insulted my Nacoomee.

It was this same officer who had once ordered me to perform a menial service for him, and had struck me with the flat side of his sabre when I refused.

166

Scouting in the Southwest

I vowed at the time to get even with him. Now I had double reason.

I could not get permission to go back to the post and protect my wife.

I determined to go anyhow and deal with that man in my own way.

I told two of my soldier friends of my intentions, and as each of them had grievances, real or fancied, against their officers they decided to leave with me.

One of the soldiers went by the name of Jack. The other one everybody called "Gee Whiz," because of his frequent use of that expression. He had been a lumber-jack in Michigan and in a fight had bitten a man's ear off. To hide away he enlisted in the army. In this he was not singular. More than one man enlisted to escape penalty for crime. Enlistment in the army in those days was in many instances like dropping through a hole in the ice.

One day Gee Whiz was on herd guard when a hail-storm came up and the wind blew his hat off. He was bald as a billiard ball, save for a little fringe of fiery red behind his ears; and when the hail-stones pecked him on the naked pate his voice was heard shouting, "Gee Whiz," above all the roar of the storm.

Gee Whiz was his name from that time on.

CHAPTER XXVII

MY DESERTION AND CAPTURE

THE horses of the troop were hobbled near the camp and we foresaw no trouble in getting ours.

With our arms and some food from the chuck tent we were ready to start just after tattoo.

We found the herd too well guarded, so we decided to go afoot.

It was a foolhardy undertaking, to say the least, as it was some three hundred miles to the nearest settlement, to which my companions expected to make their way.

For myself, that which overshadowed all else, was the scout's news concerning Nacoomee. To get to Fort Reno and settle matters with that officer and protect her, was to me the most important business in this world. My plan was to take her and our child and try to find Zakatoh. Then we would be free again!

There was no moon that night and the clouds in the west betokened rain. We hoped for it, as it would blot out our trail. But the rain didn't come and this doubtless contributed to our undoing.

Guided by the North Star we travelled northward,

My Desertion and Capture

making as rapid progress as possible until sunup. Then, to the southward, we distinguished a bunch of horsemen coming swiftly.

We crouched down in a shallow buffalo wallow, hoping they had not discovered us.

On they came.

I counted them when they were near enough. There were eight of them—Indians. We believed them to be scouts attached to the command we had left.

We flattened out against the ground, making ourselves as nearly invisible as we could.

On came the Indians, directly toward us.

About a hundred yards away, they swerved aside and might have passed on without seeing us but for the fellow Jack. In his excitement he raised his gun and fired. An Indian threw up his arms and toppled to the ground. His fellows scattered to the right and left.

I deeply regretted Jack's action, and Gee Whiz cursed him roughly for the fool he was. But we were in for it and knew we might as well get all of them we could.

Gee Whiz and I fired two shots apiece at the fleeing Indians. A horse fell and its rider went running across the prairie. One of his party took him up on his horse, and away they all went westward, disappearing in the distance.

When I examined the Indian Jack had shot, I was astonished to find him a Cheyenne. There were no Cheyenne scouts attached to our outfit.

Tahan

Expecting at any minute to sight pursuers, we hurried on. About a mile from the Cimarron River we hid in a brush-lined ravine. Here we remained until the sun was low in the west.

Then Jack, who seemed to have no more sense than a rabbit, slipped away from us and shot at a deer. Running toward it he stopped suddenly and pointing toward the south, yelled:

"There they come!"

And sure enough they were coming—a squad of cavalry and Indian scouts, besides McKusker, the white scout.

The three of us made for the river, agreeing to get behind some cottonwood trees on the bank and fight it out. For, since the death of the Indian, to surrender meant death to us anyhow. If we could stand them off until dark we then had a chance, slim though it might be, to get away.

I got behind one of the scattered trees. Gee Whiz and Jack did the same.

Our pursuers numbered twelve, including the lieutenant in charge. They halted about a quarter of a mile away, and the officer sent McKusker to take us in.

When within shouting distance, he drawled out,

"Come on in, boys, we got yeh!"

"To hell with yeh!" bawled Gee Whiz. "Yeh haven't got us, not yit! Ef yeh want us bad enough, come on en' take us!"

The scout returned to the command, and they did

My Desertion and Capture

come on, with drawn sixshooters, the officer in advance.

"We might as well die right now as any time, boys," muttered our bald-headed comrade, cocking his gun.

Like a frightened coyote Jack slumped down at the root of his tree.

For a moment I was an aspen leaf in a storm. Never before had I experienced such a feeling.

Came words which had been often repeated to me —words of the old Medicine Man:

"When the time comes for you to die, die like a man. To die is nothing. I know what it is to die. It is to go to the Other Side of Darkness."

At once I was myself again. And I remembered the old man's advice:

"Fight to the last gasp and die without a whimper."

I *would* die like a man. But to leave my dear ones——

I cast out the thought in a moment and became exhilarated. Stepping out from behind the tree, I shook my fist at the swift-coming enemies and gave my war-whoop in sheer joy.

"Now, boys, hold your fire till they git to the little bunch of mesquites," counselled Gee Whiz.

He pointed to a clump of bushes about two hundred yards distant.

"Kid," he commanded, "when they git thar, take the lieutenant. I'll plug old McKusker. Jack, take an Injun!"

He dropped to his knee behind his cottonwood.

Tahan

A little stormcloud decked in gorgeous hues swept across the face of the sun. To me the cloud was the robes of the Sun Boy trailing behind him on his way to our rescue. A butterfly came floating past on gauzy wing. It was a piece of the Sun Boy's rainbow robe he had torn off and thrown down to encourage me. I heard the chirrup of a cricket behind me, and the ripple of the stream as it ran laughingly on.

It came to me that I must get all the enjoyment I could out of life while it lasted.

I sent out a long defiant whoop.

The lieutenant deployed his men in a skirmish line, came on at a gallop and soon neared the bunch of mesquite.

I glanced at Gee Whiz. He was caressing the breech of his gun with his cheek and softly swearing. His lips were drawn back from his set teeth and his face was not good to look upon.

I drew a bead on the lieutenant and was looking through the sights of my rifle at the officer's breast. My finger was vibrating against the trigger.

Suddenly Gee Whiz grabbed hold of my gun.

"Boys," he choked out, "they're too many for us. We'll give in en' then we'll have a chance to git away."

He had weakened under the strain.

I was mad enough to kill the bald-head.

The words of the officer came sharp, short and decisive:

"Throw down those arms! Sergeant, take charge of them!"

172

My Desertion and Capture

Disgusted, I threw my gun into the river.

Not a dozen paces away the men were sitting on their panting horses.

The lieutenant's gun covered us.

By the time we got our belts unbuckled, McKusker . had dismounted and was approaching. He was always drunk while in the post, and his big nose reminded me then, as it always did, of a camp fire on the side of a hill. His bristly hair stuck up like a bunch of black jacks on a knoll. When he opened his mouth to speak, it was a dark chasm edged with blackened snags over which fire had swept.

He approached Gee Whiz, stuck his red nose up into his face and wheezed out:

"Well, we got yer, didn't we!"

Out shot bald-head's fist to the red nose and down went its owner.

Then Gee Whiz charged upon an Indian scout lolling on the neck of his pony. He grabbed him by the hair and thumped him on the ground. For a while there was an emphatic vocal and physical mixture of Gee Whiz and redskin.

The soldiers tore them apart as they were about to roll over the edge of the bank into the river.

Our captors camped there on the river that night, and our legs were tied together with a rope when we went to bed.

During the night we got our legs free, and in the darkness would have escaped but for the vigilant Indian scouts, one of whom was aching for an excuse to puncture us with bullets for what Gee Whiz had done to him.

The next day we were taken to the camp from which we had deserted, brought before the officers and questioned as to our reason for leaving.

When the sentry took me back to the guard-tent, he said to me kindly,

"I'm blamed sorry for yeh, kid."

"Yeh needn't worry about me. But why are yeh sorry?" I asked.

"Why, don't yeh know? They've drumheaded yeh —given yeh a drumhead court-martial. They're goin' to shoot yeh!"

"Well, I'm not dead yet," I replied, more bravely than I felt.

The fellow Jack began to whimper, whereupon our bald-headed companion gave him a round cursing.

"As for myself," he growled, "all I ask is one more good crack at old McKusker." *

* Phil McKusker had been a deserter himself, and had lived for years with the Kiowas. He was pardoned and became a valuable man to the Government, notwithstanding his liking for strong drink. Eventually it was the means of his death. While on courier duty, and drunk, as usual, he fell from his horse and was devoured by wolves.

CHAPTER XXVIII

IN CHAINS UNDER SENTENCE OF DEATH

C OME, men, get ready!" ordered the sergeant of the guard.

He looked in at us through the doorway of the guard-tent.

We thought the time had come for our sentence to be carried out. But a wagon was driven up and we were ordered to get into it.

"I'm goin' to take yeh t' Fort Reno," the sergeant informed us.

I emphatically declared my lack of faith in his ability to perform that bit of duty.

"Looka here, Kid," said the sergeant, "yeh're a-goin' t' Fort Reno. Yeh'll be full of holes, mebbe, when yeh git thar, but yeh're a-goin' t' go thar."

And take us there he did, not allowing us so much as the shadow of an opportunity to escape.

Arrived at the post, we were taken to the blacksmith shop to have the shackles riveted on our ankles. Obediently I held my leg up against the anvil for that purpose. I knew old Chris, the blacksmith, and as I looked into his good-natured face, I whispered,

"Make 'em big, Chris, won't yeh?"

He glanced at the sentry in the doorway.

Tahan

"By gum, Kid, I'll do it!" he replied.

When we got back to our cell we found the old blacksmith had been as good as his word. We could slip the chains off easily.

With our shackles clanking at every step we were set to digging drainage ditches around the post.

The sentries were supposed to guard us closely. As certain bottles with loosened corks were not infrequently slipped to us from the sutler's, the degree of strictness may be guessed.

On one occasion a sentry took too long a pull at the bottle, and we had hard work to revive him in time to take us to the guardhouse when recall from fatigue sounded.

There were many good opportunities for getting away easily, but we made no attempt to escape.

We had learned from some of the old soldiers that there was a chance of our sentence being commuted or set aside entirely.

At last a friend told us that the papers concerning our case had been returned.

We began to lay plans for escape should the findings prove adverse.

There was another prisoner in the cell with us now, so four were included in the plans.

One morning at guardmount a friend who had knowledge of things in the adjutant's office, whispered a few words to me as we stood in line for inspection. That day, as we worked in the ditch with picks and shovels, we decided upon the time for an attempt to get away.

More than a week before Gee Whiz had started to cut a hole in the ceiling of our cell. It was soft pine, and he cut through it with his pocket-knife and a saw made out of a piece of tin. We drowned the noise of the work by singing and rattling our chains, and hid the track of the saw with soap the colour of the ceiling.

On the evening before our escape Nacoomee came to the guardhouse as usual.

She lived, with our little Tahpahyeete, in a Cheyenne camp across the river. It was near the post, so she came to the guardhouse every day, when I was called in from fatigue. The sergeant allowed her to talk with me through the grated door.

Now I told her of our plans in which she was to aid us—just Gee Whiz and me.

Jack, the craven-hearted, had backed out. We were glad he was too cowardly to join us.

As for the other fellow, his chains fitted him so tightly he couldn't get them off, and he refused to let us cut them. He said he'd rather serve his two years and a half in Leavenworth than the same length of time in the army at Fort Reno.

Nacoomee promised to come, with arms and horses, to the post side of the river, and to be in a certain place at eleven o'clock on the following night. Gee Whiz and I expected to make our escape immediately after that. He had decided to go eastward to the railroad. I intended to take my wife and child south-westward, and try to find Zakatoh and his band.

The next morning at guardmount I was more than pleased to see that the officer of the day was the man who had insulted my Nacoomee. It was no uncommon thing for soldiers of his type to do, for, in the eyes of such men, she was "only a squaw."

The sergeant of the guard was a big negro of the Tenth Cavalry.

For these two men above all others my love was not great and if we could get safely away, these two would be held responsible for the escape.

That evening at our interview Nacoomee informed me she had everything in readiness. The river was high and still rising, but she thought there would be little or no trouble in getting the horses across, as she had a Cheyenne woman to help her.

At retreat our chains were examined as usual by the sergeant of the guard as we prisoners stood in line during roll-call. We always had a good laugh over this after returning to our cell.

At last taps sounded—ten o'clock. We had just an hour to wait.

Gee Whiz got up on the bunk and tore loose the ends of the boards which he had sawed off in the ceiling. What we most feared then was the negro sergeant. It was his duty to come in and examine us and the cell. Usually this duty was considered done in simply seeing that the four of us were on the bunk. It was a kind of sloping platform, common to us all.

If he should come in and examine our chains or the ceiling——

If he should, we were agreed to spring on him, knock him down with our shackles, and take our chances with the guard outside.

We took off our shackles and lay down on the bunk.

CHAPTER XXIX

'LEV'N o'-clo-o-ck en' aw-l-'s we-ll!" drawled the sentry on Post Number One.

This was echoed around the garrison by the other sentries.

We were in the act of rising to our feet.

There was the grating of a key in the door.

We lay down quickly, shackles in hand, and drew our blankets over us.

The black face of the sergeant appeared in the light of the lantern he held aloft.

He took a couple of steps, flashed his lantern over us and up to the grated window, and turned his eyes slowly up toward the hole.

Another instant and that negro would have earned a mighty sore head. But he turned, went out and locked the door.

Up we got. Gee Whiz climbed into the loft. I quickly followed.

On the comb of the roof there was a lattice-like ventilator. From the ground it looked like an easy thing to break through, but now the slats seemed to be of iron.

Escape—Death of Nacoomee

Gee Whiz whispered down to Jack for the old pocket-knife which he had left on the window-sill.

After what seemed like hours we got it, and my comrade went to work on the slats like a beaver.

The night was very still, the faintest noise carrying a long distance. The sound of the whittling seemed to my tense ears loud enough to be heard all over the post.

The walls of the guardhouse were made of scrub-oak logs, two rows of which were set into the ground six or seven feet deep and about two feet apart. The space between was filled with gravel and cement. So, the only possible way for us to get out was the way we took.

At last enough of the slats were cut. We crawled out and straddled the comb of the roof. It was very steep, and as we looked down we could just see the top of a sentry's head on either side of the guard-house, as he paced his beat. They met at each end of the building.

As my comrade and I sat there astride the roof I lifted my eyes toward the northern sky. Across it flared a long serpent-like streak. I had never seen anything like it. It was an awesome thing. I pointed it out to Gee Whiz. He took one good look at it over his shoulder and whispered:

"That's a comet, Kid, en' it means good luck."

There was no moon that night, but the stars looked down out of a clear sky. The eyes of Those-Above were giving us just light enough.

Tahan

Gee Whiz took my hand in a grasp of true fellowship.

"Now, Kid, we'll go together, er we'll die together," he whispered.

The sentries passed around the corners of the building, and stood, as we thought, talking in low tones.

We slid down to the edge of the roof at the back of the building and dropped together.

We had scarcely struck the ground before both sentries were blazing away at us.

My feet balanced on the edge of a gutter and threw me backward against the wall. Gee Whiz was well away when he discovered I wasn't with him.

The sentries blazed briskly, but he came back.

Grabbing me by the throat, he shook me hard.

"Damn yeh, air yeh hurt?" he breathed huskily.

"N-no," I gasped.

"Wal, come on then!" he growled, and jerked me on.

Away we went together.

The sentries blazed busily. Their fire burned holes only in the night.

Soon pandemonium broke loose. Bugles blared. The long roll sounded. Orders were shouted.

We reached the Cheyenne camp down by the river. I spotted the horse I wanted. He was picketed. I pulled up the stake. With the rope in one hand, I laid the other on his withers, ready to leap to his back.

182

Escape—Death of Nacoomee

An Indian's head rose on the other side.

"My horse!" he grunted.

I didn't wait to argue the point.

Gee Whiz also failed in his quest.

The camp was in an uproar. Wild whoops filled the air.

But neither Indians nor soldiers knew what the rumpus was all about until we had made a good start.

We neared the place where Nacoomee was to be with the horses. A figure started up from the roots of a tree. It was an Indian woman with a bundle in her arms.

It was not Nacoomee.

The woman stood in silence for a time, despite my anxious questioning. Then she told me simply that in trying to bring the horses across the river, Nacoomee with the horses, had sunk in the quicksand.

Nacoomee!——

But a few hours ago she had left me at the iron-barred door of my cell.

Nacoomee!——

The Great Silence made no answer to my silent call.

I was left alone on the trail too narrow for two to walk abreast.

When I came to myself Gee Whiz was shaking me and trying to pull me away from the place.

There were shouts and yells up toward the post, and the sound of running horses coming nearer.

Tahan

I had my child in my arms. I begged my comrade to leave me.

The woman spoke.

"Go, and some time come back," she advised. "I will care for Tahpahyeete."

I knew she would.

"Come, be quick, Kid!" urged the man.

I put my child into the woman's arms and darted away with Gee Whiz.

It is wise for the hunted to do what the hunter least expects.

We went around the post, once narrowly avoiding a squad of soldiers, and started south parallel with the road toward Fort Sill. The officers would be least likely to look for us in that direction.

How good it was to feel the springy turf under my feet and the cool breeze in my face!

"Think of it, Kid, it's jes' thirty days since I took a good full-sized step," exulted Gee Whiz.

He stretched his long legs into increased speed. But he soon slowed down. We had a long trail before us, and we needed to save our strength.

It was coming daylight when we arrived at the South Fork of the Canadian River.

For the first time I was aware that Gee Whiz was in his stocking feet. He had left his shoes in the guardhouse. I made him take off his socks. His feet and ankles were bleeding. The prairie briars had torn away the skin and flesh.

184

Escape—Death of Nacoomee

My ankles were fully as bad. My moccasins had kept my feet in better condition.

Before we started across the wide stretch of sand on the river's edge, I showed my comrade how to walk as an Indian walks, with his toes turned inward, so his tracks would not be so easily recognised.

When we had crossed the river he sat down and tenderly nursed his feet. The sharp clinging sand-burs had been torment to him. It was quite a while before he yielded to my coaxing to go on.

Before the sun came up we had found a hiding-place in a fringe of bushes by a little stream. Here Gee Whiz buried his feet in the cool mud all day, while I alternately slept and watched for signs of pursuers.

CHAPTER XXX

ON THE WAY TO CIVILISATION

WHILE I was watching the trail that day I saw a detachment of cavalry gallop past toward Anadarko. Likely they purposed heading us off should we appear there.

When the sun went down and we were ready to start, we were so stiff, footsore, weak and hungry, we could hardly walk. The month of confinement in the guardhouse had told on our physical condition. Gee Whiz tied his ragged socks on his sore feet, and after we hobbled along for a while we limbered up and made good progress.

It was not yet midnight, but dark as pitch, when we came to the outskirts of Anadarko on the Washita River.

In the woods we ran onto a party of cavalrymen—the same, we were sure, that had passed us during the day.

We crept around the camp, and waded across the river to the Agency.

There was a light in the store. I walked in boldly and bought a can of meat. The clerk I knew. He did not recognise me. But I was on the alert when I left the place.

CHIEF TAHAN FROM A DAGUERREOTYPE TAKEN IN TEXAS
JUST AFTER HIS BAND HAD ENCOUNTERED A HOSTILE
TRIBE, AND, STARVING, HAD BEEN CAPTURED—
BY SOLDIERS.

On the Way to Civilisation

About a mile on the road to Fort Sill we sat down by the trail and feasted. Gee Whiz was complaining of his sore feet when he suddenly forgot them.

Came the clickety-click of shod hoofs and the noise of wheels on the hard-beaten road.

We knew it was time for the mail from Reno to Fort Sill.

Close enough for us to see in the dim starlight, we made out the familiar buckboard. We saw also that the driver was alone.

When the rig was within a few steps of us, my comrade jumped up.

"Hold up thar!" he commanded.

The frightened driver jerked the mules to a standstill,, dropped the lines, and reached up toward the stars.

"All right, boys, all right," he quavered. "Here it is right behind me. Don't shoot!"

"Put your hands down. We don't want the mail-pouch," my comrade assured him. "We don't want nothin' but a ride."

The driver grabbed the lines and steadied the shying mules. Then, on his very hearty invitation, we got into the buckboard.

We were glad of the chance to ride, yet uneasy in the knowledge that the mail-carrier had come from Fort Reno. He was certain to know all about our escape and therefore certain to report it. With the whole garrison awake to it, our chances in avoiding arrest would be slim.

Tahan

We rode for a while in silence. The driver broke it.

"Travellin' some?" he inquired.

"Down to Sill," I replied. "Had a little hard luck. Horses pulled their picket-pins. But we'll find some o' th' outfit at Sill. Punchin' cattle f'r old Goodnight," I lied. "Yeh know his ranch—out at Paladora Canyon."

I knew the ranch. Years before, it will be remembered, I had spent some time there when for a season I had left Zakatoh.

The driver abruptly changed the subject.

"Thar was partic'lar hell t' pay at Reno last night," he said.

His passengers paid "partic'lar" attention.

"Yep," he went on, "two gin'ral pris'ners made their git-away. Th' most darin' d'livery that any set o' convicts ever made in these parts. One of 'em had a squaw wife, en' he is hidin' around th' camp thar somewhar I think. They found th' squaw on a sand-bar in th' river though. Got drownded. Th' whole garrison's scoutin' after 'em, en' if they git away, they'll have to go some."

Our host was loquacious and apparently friendly. Whatever suspicions he might have entertained concerning us seemed allayed.

He went on to say that the negro sergeant was under arrest in the guardhouse, and that old "Pussy Foot" was in trouble because of the escape.

Old "Pussy Foot" was the other man whom I hoped to see suffer.

On the Way to Civilisation

This news was a source of no little satisfaction to me.

It was near sunup when we arrived at the crossing of Medicine Bluff Creek above Fort Sill. We left the buckboard, thanked the carrier for the ride, and struck off into the woods.

We made for Cache Creek and soon reached it.

On the bank, just back of the officers' quarters, stood several large water tanks, unused and empty.

Gee Whiz thought one of them would make a good hiding-place.

We chose one and climbed in. It was within forty yards of the back door of an officer's house. Soldiers passed and repassed all day long. They were so close we could easily hear their conversation. We probably could not have chosen a safer retreat.

At dusk we crawled out, went down to the post gardens and bought food and clothing of the man in charge.

Up to this time my attire had consisted of a shirt, a pair of overalls and moccasins. I had no hat.

Gee Whiz was not only hatless and bootless, but also sockless by this time. He had so often tied and retied his stockings on his sore and swollen feet, that they had become frazzled beyond use.

I was greatly tempted to seize a government horse and hit the trail for the west where I was sure of falling in with some wild tribe. But Gee Whiz kept picturing the wonderful things of the white man's country in glowing terms, so I stayed with him. That night we set out for Caddo—the nearest railroad station—one hundred and sixty-five miles away.

It was daylight when we arrived at Rush Springs.

From time immemorial this had been a camping place, so we looked for soldiers here. We found a body of cavalry camped on one side of the spring and a wagon-train of freighters on the other.

We hid in the grass until the former started toward Fort Sill, and lingered with the latter long enough to learn that both soldiers and Indians were scouring the country for us.

We left the bullwhackers and the trail, but still headed for Caddo.

During the day, as we made our way along a wooded stream, a posse of marshals suddenly dashed out of the timber and surrounded us.

It was all up, then.

Not yet. The marshals were looking for a gang of train robbers. Our descriptions tallied with none of them, and as Gee Whiz lied so earnestly and so well about having lost our horses, the men let us go.

We took the train at Caddo for Denison, Texas. As we left the train I lost Gee Whiz in the crowd, and out of my life.

I went out of town.

Ten days and nights had passed since my escape from the guardhouse, and I was utterly worn out. I lay down in a fence corner and slept.

When I awoke, the stars were fading out of the eastern sky. I had slept all day and nearly all night.

CHAPTER XXXI

WITH A GANG OF OUTLAWS

THAT morning I opened my ears and eyes in a new world. Around me were farmyard noises and the bustling back and forth of the men at their early tasks.

There was nothing in this country life for me.

I had little real knowledge of civilised ways. The highest type of culture with which I had come into contact, was that of the semi-civilised tribes of Indian Territory. I could not call cultured a large percentage of the soldiers with whom I had associated. They were of the lowest stratum of civilisation.

I gravitated to the edge of the underworld. In time I went to the bottom of it.

The Denison saloons invited me. The day soon found me among their idlers. They were very kindly disposed when they found I had money. My clothes belied the fact.

I loaned my two months' pay to my easily-made friends. They promised to pay it back the next day. The next day never came.

Money gone, friendship vanished, and no one to give to me either!

The night noises of the town bothered me. The

roar and shriek of a train, the rattle of a wagon, even footsteps on the sidewalk would awaken me with a start. So way out of town I found a camping place.

Came there always numbers of travellers with their wagon outfits. They readily offered me the hospitality of their kind. To accept this, I soon became a regular visitor.

One night I was talking with a Choctaw Indian when he spoke of the notorious outlaw—Tom Starr.

I vividly recalled the time I tracked him and his gang and he got away.

His permanent rendezvous, the Choctaw told me, was in the Creek Nation, east of Eufaula, only a few days' ride from Denison.

I now became obsessed with the idea of meeting the bandit of whom I had heard much.

With this end in view I went with the Indian when he left for his home. I travelled with him for several days, then struck out alone in my search.

I learned that any stranger seen by Starr in the vicinity of his home would probably receive very ungentle treatment. But as I felt in constant danger of arrest, I reasoned that no matter where I was or in what company, my situation could be neither better nor worse.

I presented neither a formidable nor a creditable appearance. I wore an old suit of clothes much too large for me. I was penniless and unarmed.

This, I reflected, might be in my favour should I meet the much feared man.

With a Gang of Outlaws

I had no difficulty in finding food. It was given me by the poor but kind-hearted Indians whose houses I visited on the road. A gourd of osaufkee—a food made of corn—was the usual offering.

Arrived at a place in the Creek Nation called Hickory Ground, I met with a large gathering of Indians.

The occasion was the whipping of a horse thief. According to his promise, the culprit was on hand. He had been free from the day of his sentence to that set for punishment. This was a privilege not unusual among the Creeks.

The crier called out that the time had come.

The culprit stripped to the waist and took his place on the spot indicated by an officer.

He drew himself up proudly and called out so all could hear:

"Hononwah do-e-escha!" (I am a man.)

He would show he could suffer as a man should.

The officer then gave him twenty-five hard lashes with the thonged whip. It brought the blood, but he did not so much as flinch or shrink under the punishment.

This seemed to settle the matter entirely. Having paid the penalty, he regained his standing among his fellows.

I had reached the vicinity of Starr's place when I was taken sick of a fever.

At a little distance from the road I lay down under a tree and became unconscious.

Tahan

When I awoke I was lying on a blanket in a house. A short man with long straight hair and face black as charcoal, was cooking something in a big iron kettle which hung in the fireplace.

When he found I was conscious, he told me how I came there. He had found me. Tom Starr had brought me to the cabin. My utter helplessness had appealed to the outlaw. I was in Tom Starr's house.

The desperado proved to be entirely different from what I had imagined.

He was of fine appearance, spoke to me kindly, and did everything he could for my comfort. He asked me no questions about myself.

I volunteered the information that I was from the West and was just wandering through the country when I was taken sick.

Starr would often be gone from home several days. Sometimes when he returned he would have a new horse; sometimes two—always good ones.

When I grew strong enough to go outdoors I began to yearn for the saddle.

The black man—Kahjolustee (Blackberry)—told me there were good horses all around us; if I wanted one to go and get it.

Late one night four tired men arrived at the cabin in company with Kahjolustee, who seemed always to be on the watch.

The men threw their heavy saddle-bags on the floor for pillows, spread their saddle-blankets, and lay down in their clothes. They were soon asleep.

With a Gang of Outlaws

The next morning the men were up bright and early.

While they were cleaning the mud from their out-fits, I walked up behind one of them. His sixshooter was lying on the ground. I picked it up.

Quick as a flash the man snatched it out of my hand and angrily asked what I meant.

I was so surprised I didn't reply. I walked away wondering at his conduct.

Kahjolustee informed me I must be very careful how I acted when this man was around. He was a very great man—greater in fact than Tom Starr him-self. The whole country everywhere was against him. Nearly everybody wanted to kill him.

His name was Jesse James.

I had never heard of this most notorious bandit of the United States. At the time he meant no more to me than any of the other riders of the crooked trail.

As I remember him, he was a rather genial fellow with a full beard of a reddish colour and very peculiar eyes that seemed to be in constant motion.

He and his men stayed with us for more than a week. I helped them break a rather wild horse, and one of them gave me a white-handled Colt's six-shooter.

I soon became fully equipped with horse and saddle, and with my complete recovery from the effects of the fever, began to feel ready for anything.

Our visitors fully rested, went on their way to Texas. Indeed Starr's ranch was a half-way place for such men, as they ranged between the north and south.

There were a number of visitors at the rendezvous while I was there. Among them was a Creek Indian by the name of Ed Grayson. I took a great liking to him. He and a cousin by the name of Tom Grayson, were "on the scout." Which means they were under the displeasure of the law, and were dodging around for hiding-places among their friends.

The Indians in this locality always did this, instead of leaving the country, although it was a pretty sure thing they'd be caught or killed some day.

One day I went with Ed Grayson to Eufaula. Several United States marshals were there looking for him, and the reckless fellow said he wanted to have some fun with them.

As we rode into the little town he advised me to wait at one of the stores while he rode around to find what he could scare up.

In a little while there were whoops and shots up the street. He had found the marshals lurking in some of the stores, and he was trying to get them started.

As he rode down the street he looked the incarnation of fearless manhood.

Tall, lithe and alert, he sat his clean-limbed sorrel horse, a part of it.

He came at an easy canter with his long black hair floating around his square shoulders and whipping into his clear-cut face.

The bridle reins hung loosely on his horse's neck.

With a Gang of Outlaws

He had a sixshooter in each hand. At intervals he fired into the air and gave his piercing yell of defiance.

This was his challenge to the marshals to come out into the open like men and try to take him.

Not one of them so much as made himself visible.

It was but a short time after this that Ed Grayson's career came to an end.

We were in town one day when he spied an enemy entering Crabtree's store. Drawing his gun from its holster he left me with the remark that he would go across and settle with him.

As he passed through the doorway, he cried out,

"I am ready to die right now!"

This was a challenge often used by the Creeks.

Grayson was an expert with the revolver. With the gun, he had a serious fault. Instead of bringing the muzzle upwards and firing at the same time, he had the habit of raising the muzzle, cocking the gun with the motion, and firing as he brought the muzzle downwards.

This time the fault proved fatal to him. It gave his foe but a moment's advantage, but it was enough.

He fell with a bullet in his head.

That night Tom Grayson and the rest of us rode through and through the town shouting out our vengeful defiance.

Shortly afterward I saw Tom Grayson fall into the Big Sleep on the porch of Crabtree's store. He went down under a charge of buckshot from a double-barrelled shotgun in the hands of an enemy.

Well equipped with horse and guns, I began once more to lay plans. I told them to some of the young fellows of my acquaintance. I had vengeance to wreak on the man against whom I had a just cause. They agreed to go west with me to do this and— other things.

But one day there was a mix-up with the marshals, and one of our men was fairly riddled with bullets.

I counted myself lucky to get out of the Creek country afoot and as poor as when I went into it.

NACOOMEE (TAHAN'S DAUGHTER, RUTH GRIFFIS)

CHAPTER XXXII

ON THE TRAMP

SO I became a tramp. I was not fit for anything else.

Not caring where I went, I beat my way on cartrucks, and landed in a railroad construction camp west of San Antonio.

The superintendent gave me a job as a nightguard. Thieves had been running off the mules, and my instruction was to shoot the first night-prowler in sight.

A night-prowler appeared.

I shot.

My victim proved to be a gang boss who had been visiting a nearby Mexican ranch. He had gone against orders and was trying to sneak in unobserved. The bullet struck him in the shoulder. The wound, though painful, was not dangerous.

Shortly after this, the superintendent got drunk one night, and came reeling into camp in his night-shirt. He wandered around among the mules and ran afoul of the guard.

I was the guard.

He began cursing me. When he called me a vile name I promptly knocked him backward with the butt of my Winchester.

Tahan

He fell into a bunch of cactus.

His yells woke up the camp and the men took him to his tent.

The next morning he ate his breakfast standing.

It takes time to extract cactus thorns.

I lost my job.

I went back to San Antonio.

Near there I got a job picking cotton. I liked the work, so before dawn next morning I was in the field. It wasn't light enough to see. Even the snowy bolls of cotton didn't show up against the darkness. But I wanted to make use of the first streak of light.

When the breakfast bell rang, I had my bag filled so full it was too heavy to drag with ease.

I ate hurriedly.

I was drenched with dew, but I lost no time in getting back to the field.

Again I worked alone. I couldn't understand why the other pickers didn't come.

The sun had walked well up in the sky when they did come.

The whole crowd—blacks and whites—had been having a good time somewhere. Their minds stayed full of it, for frequently they broke out in chuckling and laughing.

Weighing time came.

My cotton was thrown out. It was too heavy!

Dew-drenched it had to be spread in the sun and dried.

Truly, the pickers had had a good time somewhere!

200

On the Tramp

A fortnight finished my labours in the cotton field. I went back to town.

I wandered into "Hart's Gold Room," and soon became engaged in losing my lately earned money at a game of monte.

Somebody started something. Shooting began and the lights went out.

When the merriment was over and the lamps relit, the monte-dealer's neck was bleeding from a bullet wound, and my shirt was open at the throat. My collar-button had been shot away.

I hit the ties again, my back to the west.

Soon I met with a wrecking gang of negroes at work. I needed a job. In order to get it I told the boss I was a negro. I got it.

The fellow was insolent and blasphemous. When I couldn't stand for any more of his foul talk, I threw down the shovel. I had worked but part of a day.

The railroad owes me for that work yet.

Again I headed eastward.

One day I started through a large pasture toward a big ranch-house where I hoped to get something to eat.

As I strolled along I saw in the trail a lariat which some cowboy had lost. I coiled the rope into my left hand and with the other unconsciously began, through force of the old habit, to swing the noose around my head. This startled a bunch of horses and they went galloping away.

Tahan

A cowboy came tearing through the brush, six-shooter in hand.

I earnestly explained how I came by the rope, and how I happened to be swinging it around my head.

The cowboy wasn't to be taken in by any such tale. No, indeed! He made me carry the rope ahead of him to the house.

After he had talked with the other men of the ranch, they all cursed me for a horse-thief and locked me in a smokehouse. They intended taking me to jail the next day.

But there was a small window in the little building near the roof, and through this, during the night, I squeezed myself to liberty.

Innocent though I was, there was evidence enough to send me to prison for a long term. I counted myself lucky when I found myself aboard a flatcar on the way to Houston.

When I arrived in Houston the church-bells were tolling out the sad news of President Garfield's death.

In the market-place I was attracted to a stall of eatables in charge of a fat negro woman. At the sight of a large "Washington pie" my mouth began to water. But, alas! I hadn't the wherewithal to make it mine.

After pondering the situation, a brilliant idea occurred to me.

I had seen railroad men present pieces of paper with writing on them and get in return goods and money. I looked carefully along the street until I discovered a piece of paper which appeared to resemble what I had in mind. I got it and took it to the negress.

"Auntie," I said, "I want some of that Washington pie. I haven't got any money, but I've got this. I'll take four bits worth of pie and the rest in money."

She took the paper, scrutinised it and handed it back. But her face was one broad grin.

"Lawd bress yo,' honey!" she chuckled, "I cain't spah de money, but yo' all c'n have all dat Wash'ton pie yo' wants to eat. En' when yo' all gits de money yo' c'n come back en' pay me fo' it."

The old black woman never got the money. But many and many a time have I wished I could have paid the trustful soul.

I had a good time in Houston, even though my sentence hung over me like a black storm-cloud. I was always afraid of the policemen I met on the street, for I had heard soldiers say they had a mysterious way of detecting men who had broken the law.

My fear was less at night, and I usually slept well. My bedroom was a hogshead partly filled with shavings. It was located near a warehouse where I felt comfortably secure.

One night I awoke with the feeling that the world was coming to an end. My bedroom was rolling and tumbling downhill over the rough pavement. It finally landed with a tremendous shock against a building.

Tahan

As I crawled out, I heard a maudlin song in the distance. I gathered that a company of young rowdies had given the hogshead a kick and started it rolling.

After that a cowstable was my sleeping-place and I "boarded around."

In my aimless wanderings came now and then a chance to do work that I liked. In passing a big pasture one day, I stopped to watch some men trying to ride a wild unbroken horse. The men were not good riders and the horse was a first-class bucker. He had little trouble in freeing himself of everyone that managed to mount him. They gave it up and were leaving the animal to the enjoyment of his victory.

I offered to ride him, and did so, to a standstill. For this the owner gave me five dollars.

It didn't go for board. I lost in a game of chucka-luck.

Every morning, after I had cadged my breakfast, I strolled along by the shops and stores as they were being opened and swept. I pitied the men who were content to do that kind of work morning after morning. They possibly pitied me. But I was free—free to go out into the woods; to stay and watch the birds and animal people and listen to their voices.

At such times I was carried back to the wild, un-trammelled life of the plains and I lived over again its experiences. Memories of my lost Nacoomee then led me to upbraid myself for leaving my son. Followed always the resolve to go back and train him to be a great warrior.

On the Tramp

With this consoling vision I usually fell asleep, only to awaken as a lone scrub oak in a clearing, after the wood-choppers have done their work.

When I began to notice the apparent happiness of the gay young people of the town, I felt more lonely. I was apart from them. A great gulf lay between their world and mine. I could not cross it and they would not.

The white man's country was a place in which I didn't seem to fit anywhere.

I watched the children playing in the schoolyards. Their games puzzled me. I wondered how, when they were grown up, they would make a living at such things as "blind-man's buff" and "drop the handker-chief." The hunting-game and the war-game, and such like, of my savage boyhood days were the very things that we played in earnest when we became men.

One night I wandered up a fashionable street. I was stopped in front of a large house by the most wonderful music that I had ever heard. A woman was singing, accompanied by a piano. I stood rooted to the ground fascinated, enthralled.

On many a night afterward I sat on the curb before that house, my feet in the gutter, my soul revelling in the glory of that exquisite voice.

As it floated out to me through the open window, it soothed my bitter, turbulent spirit, charmed me into better thoughts and left lasting impressions. The sweet singer never knew of her holy ministry to the heartsick, lonely outcast of the street.

Tahan

I used to sit there when the music ceased, and think of the voice that had been hushed by the treacherous sands of the river, and of my child, and blame myself for acting like a coward in saving myself and leaving him. Then I would make a new vow to go back to him.

It was the memory of Nacoomee, my wife, that kept me many times from doing wrong. To me the influence of a good woman is a wonderful thing. I have always believed and still believe that men will be as improper in their conduct as women allow them to be, whether they are savage or civilised, and as good as women compel them to be

CHAPTER XXXIII.

IT was in Houston that I met unkempt, cadaverous Jerry.

Jerry was a tall man when he stood straight up and down, but he usually resembled an interrogation point. He had no teeth when I first knew him, and his face crumpled up like an accordion, every time he shut his mouth tight. He was a typical hobo, but he proved to be the best friend I ever had. He was a philosopher, and he taught me some of the greatest and most important truths of human life, and he was good.

I never learned his full name, but I called him Jerry, and he called me Injun.

My unkempt comrade of the underworld had a song which he often sang after his inner man was satisfied. The words ran as follows:

> "We are two bums, two jolly old bums,
> We live like royal Turks,
> If we have good luck a-bummin' our chuck,
> To hell with the man that works."

We left Houston one night on top of a passenger coach bound for New Orleans, but we rode in box cars and on brake beams before we arrived.

Tahan

One evening at dusk we were put off of a freight train which we had ridden all day. We were hungry and thirsty.

We sighted a large house in grounds studded with shrubbery and flowers and surrounded by a high stone wall. At the back of the lawn was a well with an old-fashioned sweep.

Under Jerry's directions, I scaled the high iron gate, reached the well and began to lower the bucket. The sweep made a great squeaking, and presently I found myself surrounded by a lot of women in black dresses and white bonnets. They carried candles and chattered in an unknown tongue.

I was on the point of making a dash for liberty when Jerry at the gate spoke to the women in their own language. Two of them entered the house and returned with food in their kind hands. As we ate it on the curb, my comrade explained that the big house was a convent of French-speaking women.

When possible Jerry always cadged enough chuck for two, but there were days and days we didn't have enough to eat.

One of these times, I was grumbling because I was hungry. We were sitting on the curb, and a moving-van full of furniture passed along the street. After crossing an alley it stopped. On the rear end of the van was a large mirror.

A shaggy billy goat came out of the alley. He looked into the mirror and shook his head. The goat in the mirror did the same. That was a challenge for

Jerry, My Pal

a fight. The old billy began to back away. So did the other goat. Then there was a rear and a catapult-like movement, and a smash.

Old Billy had finished the other goat.

"Injun, yeh're that goat," Jerry declared to me. "This is a mighty good world," he went on, "as that was a first-rate lookin'-glass. But yeh're so durned mean y'rself, that yeh think everybody else 's th' same. Yeh jes' see a reflection of y'rself in other people."

I did. Every one does. And we only do the world and ourselves harm by bumping our heads against the fact.

At another time we were in the country sitting in a fence-corner by the roadside. A well-dressed young fellow with a beautiful young girl at his side drove past.

"Jerry, it's blamed tough," I complained, "I can't never do that."

"Growlin' again," said Jerry. "Why, Injun, yeh c'n do that ef yeh want t' bad enough, en air willin' t' pay th' price. Look't here!"

He held up before me a cocoon out of which a butterfly was struggling.

I knew he would draw some lesson from it, for he was always making me see the invisible in the visible.

"What about it, Jerry?" I asked. "That's only a bug."

"Yes, but watch that bug. Notice! He's a-tryin' t' git aout."

Tahan

"So I seè. Why don't yeh take y'r knife en help 'im out?" I asked.

"Worst thing I could do to it," he said. "Why, Injun, ef I'd help this pore little bug aout of its shell, it wouldn't be able t' fly. It's th' work en th' struggle t' git aout that makes it strong enough to go. En' besides, it wouldn't look like a piece of a rainbow a-floatin' around. It's th' trouble en' th' work en' th' agony it has in gittin' aout that paints th' beauty on its wings en' makes it strong enough t' fly."

He stopped a moment, smiled at me, and went on.

"Injun, yeh're that bug. Th' fact that yeh want t' git aout en' up into whar yeh belong, is a sure sign that yeh'll git there some day if yeh try hard enough en' air willin' t' pay th' price. Remember, Injun, yeh're that bug," he finished soberly, "en' yeh cain't git anything worth havin' without payin' f'r it."

I have remembered.

Jerry and I were content with each other, but sometimes we were forced to be more democratic and travel in other company.

One night we shared our box-car with a gang of tramps. The motion of the car jostled one of them against me. In this way he found out I was carrying a small bundle. It was bread and meat which my partner and I were saving for future use.

Guessing it was food, the hobo roughly demanded it.

Had he asked me for it in a different spirit I would have given it to him cheerfully.

I blankly refused.

Jerry, My Pal

The hobo fastened his fingers around my throat, choked me to the floor and robbed me of the precious stuff.

When Jerry learned the trouble and protested, several of the gang set upon him. It was pitch dark, but my friend struck right and left with his big bony fists and knocked two of the fellows through the doorway.

By this time I had got free from my assailant and was groping my way toward Jerry. His voice guided me. He was roaring out big oaths which sounded to me like prayers for help.

When I reached him his fist smashed me in the face and knocked me out of the car. The train was running at good speed, but I was unhurt by the fall.

Two days later I found Jerry. He was sitting on a fence watching a gang of men at work. They were clearing away the wreckage of a train. It was the train that had carried our box-car. There had been a collision and one of the tramps was killed. Jerry escaped without injury.

We drifted into Morgan City, Louisiana. We also drifted into work.

The roustabouts on the dock were on a strike, so together with a number of our kind, we got a job loading a ship with bales of goods.

As I was coming up the gang-plank with my truck for a load, a big negro raised a club over my head.

"Drap dat truck!" he ordered.

I dropped it.

Tahan

The same demand was made of each one of our gang in turn, and each made the same ready response.

But we were mad; not so much because we were forced to quit, but because that negro and his gang were, for the time, our masters.

And the captain of the ship was mad. For some reason he could get no protection from the officers of the law, and he was anxious to get his ship loaded.

We who had been forced out of our work held a council of war. We decided that if the captain would furnish us guns and ammunition we would load his cargo.

Jerry put the proposition to the captain, and he agreed to it.

He brought out three shot-guns and a sixshooter. At my earnest pleading he allowed me to take the sixshooter.

My brother "warriors" answered to my call and we charged the gang of blacks, cutting out from it the big buck who had made us surrender to his club. The rest of the gang found refuge behind the boxes and bales of goods.

Then I made the big darky dance. I cut the dust around his feet with my gun, and he went at it in good style. When he showed signs of letting up my gun would speak, the dust would fly up near his feet, and he would hoe it down in the double shuffle speedily if not gracefully.

The captain roared his laughter and shouted his

Jerry, My Pal

encouragement. Our fellows nearly choked with the fun.

I made that black bully dance until he was dripping with perspiration and was as gentle as a Jersey cow. Then I let him go.

We went back to work, but the negroes soon capitulated and we lost our job. However, the captain paid us handsomely for breaking the strike.

CHAPTER XXXIV

M Y comrade and I went on to New Orleans, and established winter quarters. We slept under the tarpaulins which covered the goods on the dock, and lived largely on fruit we picked up at the same place.

At Mississippi City we witnessed the fistic battle between John L. Sullivan and Paddy Ryan. We enjoyed it from a treetop where, hidden by the moss, we had a splendid view of it.

On our way back to town Jerry was enthusiastic over the champion, and he punctuated his praise with philosophical observations.

"Did yer notice, Injun, how th' big feller got it on th' jaw once in a while, en' how he kep' smilin' en' goin' back f'r more? That's th' way a man 'll win at anything. No matter what a feller goes at, ef he cain't take a jolt on th' jaw once in a while en' smile back at it, he'd better not climb through th' ropes."

We walked awhile in silence. I broke it.

"Jerry, I can fight," I said.

He looked down at me with an incredulous smile.

"Oh, I don't mean a big feller like the two back there, but one of my size. Find me a man of my

214

My Prize Fight

weight, and I'll do to 'im what Sullivan did to Ryan,"
I boasted.

Jerry grew thoughtful. Finally he agreed that I
might be made into a prize fighter.

By the time we had reached New Orleans our plans
were made. Then came the necessary preliminaries
—the finding of a place in which to train; the securing
of an expert boxer to instruct me in the art of fistiana;
and, last of all, the matching of a suitable opponent.
These details my partner arranged in due order.

My training-place was the back room of a saloon;
my trainer a down and out ex-pugilist, who agreed to
get me into shape for half of my part of the purse.

It taxed Jerry's wits to get suitable stuff for me to
train on, for our food was whatever my comrade
could get by hook or by crook. He found what I
needed, however. He said the "coming champion of
the world," as he frequently called me, must be fed.

I had plenty to eat, even when my appetite became
voracious.

Jerry, no doubt, went hungry many days.

Almost at the start, my instructor told me I was an
apt pupil, and after I had had about three weeks of
constant training, he judged me ready for an opponent.

Jerry matched me to fight at catch weights with a
fellow of some reputation—Bull Skillet by name.

The purse was to be whatever the spectators would
chip in.

Came the day of the fight.

Tahan

That morning Jerry took me to the French Market and treated me to a breakfast of wonderful coffee, fried steak, potatoes and rolls. Where he got the money is a mystery. He didn't join in the feast—wasn't hungry, he said.

I took but little exercise that day.

About the middle of the afternoon I had another beefsteak as thick as my foot. Ravenous as usual, I devoured the meal and all the other eatables Jerry had provided. All that he would eat was a banana which he dug out of his pocket.

I knew he lied when he said he wasn't hungry, and I noticed that his face had grown thinner and more seamy. I had grown robust and as hard as nails.

While I was eating greedily, Jerry's leathery old face twisted into a smile of pleasure as he pictured the good things we would have after the fight.

It was about nine o'clock that night when Jerry and I appeared in the back room of the saloon. The place was packed with a crowd of whites and negroes—as tough a crowd as one would care to see. My trainer elbowed a way for us.

A broken-down old fighter was chosen for referee, and after some preliminary talk Jerry passed a hat among the crowd. The vagabonds tossed their coins into it.

There were no dressing rooms in the place, so I undressed in the ring. As I stood stripped down to a pair of old swimming trunks, Jerry tied a bright American flag around my waist.

My Prize Fight

We looked across the ring at my opponent. He stood stripped and ready for battle. The sight of him made Jerry's hands shake as he fumbled with the flag.

Bull's appearance was sufficient cause for apprehension. He was thick-set and short-necked and his muscles stood out in bunches and ridges—a striking contrast to my slim physique. He weighed about one hundred and sixty pounds. I was fully twenty pounds lighter.

Each of us was furnished with a soap-box for a resting-place, and we sat while waiting for the word.

Jerry was nervous. When the word came, he whispered cautiously,

"Keep away from 'im, Injun!"

As we shook hands in the centre of the ring a smile of contempt spread over Bull's face, and his short pug nose turned up as far as it could go. A fire-flash of anger passed through me. The turn-up of that nose was a nerve tonic to me. I would make the pug point downwards very shortly.

During the first two rounds we sparred, each of us feeling out the other. I found he was much slower than I, but I also found I had plenty to do to keep clear of his tremendous swings. One catch, and it wouldn't be well with me.

In the third round he got to my jaw with a right-hand hook, and I went down. But I kept my head and rested on my knee while the referee counted nine.

As I regained my feet Bull came at me with a rush

217

and a roar. Down I went again under a sledge-hammer blow on the chin.

This time I did not wait for the count. I was up in an instant and like a flash shot my right to his jaw, and floored him.

Again I got to him with a left swing on that pug nose. He staggered and the pug nose bled.

Bull came at me with another of his rushes.

Above the raucous shouts of the onlookers, rose Jerry's voice.

"Keep away, Injun," he yelled.

But I swung.

Bull ducked, and my right fist came into contact with the top of his head. It was like striking a rock. My right hand was broken.

While I sat in my corner for the precious two minutes' rest, Jerry rubbed me down with a gunny sack.

"Keep away from 'im, I tell yeh," was all he could say.

My hand puffed up. It was all but useless, and we were fighting with bare knuckles.

We came together for the fifth round.

I silently prayed to win, and vowed, if winner, to devote to the Sun all of my food for two days.

As we toed the mark I noticed that Bull's lips were bleeding and his right eye bruised. But it was the pug nose that gave me encouragement. It looked like a piece of putty.

218

My Prize Fight

I went down with a clip on the side of the head. It made me see stars.

After that I lost consciousness. Indeed, during the next several rounds, I wasn't conscious of what happened.

I came to myself for a while just before the last round. Jerry was squirting water out of his mouth into my face and rubbing my skin almost off with the gunny sacks.

"Yeh've shore got 'im goin', Injun, en' yeh've got t' git 'im this round. Now, go to 'im," he ordered, as I rose from my corner.

That last round is a blank to me. When I woke I couldn't open my eyes; I couldn't sit up; I couldn't turn over; I couldn't remember anything that had taken place for a while.

I stretched out my hand and touched Jerry. He was blubbering at my side.

"Yeh got 'im good and plenty," he said, between sobs.

"I got 'im?" I repeated, as memory slowly returned, "but what did he do to me?"

"Not a thing but give yeh the damnedest lickin' a man ever got," he blurted. "But yeh knocked 'im clean aout—made 'im dead t' th' world—en' you, yeh pore little cuss! yeh was aout y'rself f'r three rounds. But I couldn't make yer quit fightin', en' yeh won," he concluded, with a triumphant burst of weeping.

Poor, tender-hearted old partner! He was crying because of the mauling I had received.

Tahan

Bull, who was in another corner of the room—the same in which we fought—was in no better plight than I. And he was swearing at his friend who was applying some healing lotion to his bruises.

When we parted he complimented me in most forcible language for my gameness. He had thought he could eat me up in one round, he said.

The purse, which consisted of four dollars and eighty-five cents, I never got. The rascal who held it vanished with it.

It was two days before I could get about. I was black and blue from the waist up, and the worst was —two knuckles broken and my nose flattened against my right cheek. Jerry didn't succeed in getting it entirely straight.

Neither knuckles nor nose ever regained their normal condition.

CHAPTER XXXV

WITH MEN OF THE UNDERWORLD

SHORTLY after the fight, Jerry disappeared for several days. During his absence I lived on short rations. It rained nearly all of the time and this, with the loss of my pal, made me desolate.

One dark night I left my shelter on the dock and, partly from loneliness, partly from hunger, went from one low saloon to another. My hope of snatching a handful of free lunch proved slim. Always the watchful eyes of the bartender were in the way.

Finally, rain-soaked and disheartened, I lounged into the back room of a low groggery. I sat down in a dimly lighted corner and fell asleep.

I was aroused by the voices of two men. They were seated at a near-by table talking in low tones. Evidently they had not noticed me.

What I overheard caused me to sit perfectly still. They were planning a robbery, and were waiting for a third person to join them.

One of them became very impatient at the delay. He flung himself away from the table and into the bar-room where he ordered a couple of drinks.

When he returned he discovered me. I sat with my arms folded on the table and my face buried in them.

Tahan

With a muttered oath he grabbed me by the neck and gave me a vigorous shake.

I pretended to be sound asleep.

After several shakes from his not gentle hand, I got up and started to leave the place.

The fellow forced me back into the chair.

Then he and his pal looked me over in the dim light, alternately plying me with questions and talking in a foreign lingo. Satisfied with my answers, they became decidedly friendly in their manner. One of them got me a drink of whiskey. Then the other, remarking upon my woe-begone appearance, got me a handful of bologna sausage from the lunch counter and another drink of whiskey.

I began to feel better under the stimulus. This pleased my new friends.

The larger of the two, whom the other one called Hank, declared I was the very chap they were looking for; that if I would join them in a certain undertaking I would never lack either drink or food.

They were going to "crack a crib" that very night, Hank told me. All I would have to do was to stand on a special street corner and give them certain signals in case of need.

"I reckon you're game enough to do that," he concluded.

I pointed to the signs of my late fight and told them about it in detail.

They laughed uproariously and slapped me on the back.

JOSEPH K. GRIFFIS AS A SALVATION ARMY OFFICER

With Men of the Underworld

"You're the stuff!" cried one.

"You'll do!" agreed the other.

Immediately Hank described the house they intended to rob and set the hour for doing it; named the street-corner for the "look-out;" and gave me the signal—whistling a few bars of "Yankee Doodle."

We all had another drink and left the saloon, one at a time.

On my way to the appointed place I turned the matter over in my mind.

To go on might mean serious consequences.

Besides——

Jerry, I knew, would have nothing to do with the kind of men I was now going to help. .

Jerry had told me——

But Jerry was gone. He might never come back.

To go on might mean plenty to eat and good clothes to wear, for some time at least.

Jerry was gone. Who cared what I did?

What was the world of men, anyhow? A pack of snarling wolves fighting around some carcass, each for the biggest share he could get.

I was one of them. I would get my share.

A clock in a church steeple boomed out.

One—two—three!

It was the hour set by the robbers to begin their "crib-cracking."

I had reached the corner.

I glanced up and down the streets. They were deserted.

Tahan

A feeling of aching loneliness came over me. Then——

"Injun, whatever yeh git aouten this world, yeh'll have t' pay f'r."

Jerry!

I turned and fled down Canal Street to my place on the dock. Jerry had not come back.

Alone, I crept under the tarpaulin, out of the rain.

CHAPTER XXXVI

DEATH OF JERRY

JERRY and I tramped together for nearly two years. We led a precarious existence, but I never knew a time when his fertile wit wasn't equal to every emergency.

We had tramped over a large part of the South and Middle West before the day came for the parting of our trails.

It was in a small town in Illinois. We were attempting to jump a freight one rainy night, and he fell under the wheels. Both of his legs were crushed.

Men carried him to the house of a physician.

They would not let me in. So I crawled under the verandah to keep dry.

When I knocked at the door the next morning a kind-faced woman bade me enter. She said my friend had been calling for me all through the night.

As I approached the bedside, a smile of recognition flitted over his homely, weather-beaten old face. He tried to raise his hand in greeting.

I took the clammy hand in mine and slumped down on my knees at his side.

"Injun," he whispered, "it's all up. I'm goin' aout. I don't know what'll become of yeh, chum-boy, but git aout o' this——"

Tahan

My old partner was breathing hard. My throat swelled so I could not speak.

"Come closter, Injun, pard," he whispered faintly. "I want t' tell—yeh—somethin'——"

His voice trailed away into silence.

Jerry was gone. And he went as he had lived with me, trying to help me.

Just before they nailed down the lid of the rough pine-box they put him in, I laid a crust of bread at his head, and at his side I left the only thing I had to leave—my knife.

The men smiled at what I did, but it was the Indian way and the best, the last, that I could do. It was all I had. And all I had was for Jerry.

There probably have been better men in the world than the old tramp. There never was a better one to me.

Rest the ashes of my princely old vagabond pal!

CHAPTER XXXVII

I MEET THE SALVATION ARMY

FOLLOWED a time when as a green leaf torn from its bough by the storm-wind, driven across yawning chasms and whirled through forests of fire-blackened snags, I lay flat in the mud, kicked and trampled under beastly feet. This was in London, Canada.

I was sitting on a beer keg one evening, when across the market square came surging the song:

> "We'll all praise the Lord for the victories we have won.
> The Salvation Army will make the devil run——"

"Make the devil run!" I echoed to myself. "Good! I'd like to be in the fight."

The men and women singers came round the corner. The red and blue of their jackets caught my fancy. They marched beneath their flag, keeping step to the drum tap and singing to the clash of their cymbals:

> "We'll fight beneath our banner till we die."

That, too, caught me. I drew near while they formed a circle and knelt down in the dust. I wondered what they had lost.

Tahan

Approaching one of the men I jabbed my thumb into his ribs.

"What yeh lookin' f'r?" I asked.

"Lookin' f'r bums like you," was his reply, "and we've got t' git down pretty low t' find some o' yeh."

I followed the soldiers to their barracks and enjoyed their meeting.

I had attended religious services before. While I was with the cowboys, years back, I went with them to a little church on the edge of a settlement. As usual, from every belt in the outfit, a sixshooter was swinging.

Something during the service made us laugh. This, with the comments of the cowpunchers, spoken in no still small voice, brought a tall, red-whiskered person down the aisle.

I sat on the end of the bench, so he collared me and he shook me, much as a dog shakes a rat.

"Git out o' here, you!" he hissed.

My companions were on their feet instantly, guns in hand, muzzles trained on the militant churchman.

"Now, look-a-hyeah, suh," drawled one of the men, "we-all's hyeah t' see this hyeah show, en' we-all's a-goin' t' stay till it's aout."

The churchman felt persuaded to let us stay.

After coming into civilisation, I had also occasionally attended divine service.

Once I followed a well-dressed procession into a church and became deeply interested in the doings of

228

I Meet the Salvation Army

several young people who were cooped up in a small pen back of the minister.

A little fellow arose with a stick in his hand and struck at a young lady. She began to scream.

He threatened a man with the stick and he hollered.

The small dapper young fellow then flourished his stick as though he meant to tackle the whole bunch, and they all hollered at him.

Those young people reminded me of bull-whackers I had heard on the plains, when urging the cattle to do their best work. What they were hollering sounded very like "whoa-haw-back! gee-e, buck!"

Not having educated ears, I was unable to detect the music they were supposed to be making.

When I started to leave the church, a man at the door asked me pleasantly to remain a while longer.

"Naw, I've had enough. What do yeh call it, anyway?" I asked.

"Why! church, of course," he replied.

He eyed me curiously, as he went on.

"Church, my dear sir, is the place where the best people in the world go. Of course—ah—there are others—ah—who—well—ah——"

He stopped hitching along, and started in again.

"This morning when the others go out, the good people are going to stay in, and they are going to have a good time. I would be pleased," he finished smoothly, "to have you remain."

I stayed.

The bad people went out.

Tahan

The good stayed in. They gathered up near the front of the church and sang something about sin, death, the grave, and hell.

Then a nice-looking old lady arose and told the others how mean she was. When she had cried a little, she sat down.

They sang again. That song reminded me of an Indian death-song.

After it an old gentleman with side-whiskers got up. He had the look of one who had just committed a crime. He declared he was a worm, and tremblingly finished by confessing that he was about the worst man that any of them had ever laid eyes on.

I took my hat and started out.

I had been among some bad people in my time. But this was the worst crowd I had ever struck.

I was greatly puzzled by what I had seen and heard. I was bad enough, but I felt pretty sure it would get out on me, without my telling any one about it.

In the Salvation Army meeting I noticed that the singing was different. It had a victorious ring.

Men and women stood up and looked at me with eyes that had been half put out by sin. But they exultantly declared that God had taken the badness out of them; that once they had been blind, but He had made them see; that once they were in the miry clay, but now He had placed their feet upon a solid rock. And they shouted out their gladness.

230

I Meet the Salvation Army

I told myself that was what I wanted—that brand of religion, instead of the kind they have in church.

One night I sat in the meeting with leaden heart. I was tired, hungry, discouraged and bitter—ready for anything, no matter what the end might be. Who cared?

I know what physical pain is. I know the pain of heart-hunger. But the anguish that comes with the thought that "no one cares" I have found greater by far than any other suffering.

That night as I sat in torment, a little girl—a prattling child—came to me and timidly told me in a whisper of Him who is the friend of sinners. To me that child's whisper was a shout in a silence. It was a feast in a famine. Kneeling at my side she prayed for me. Often have I thought since then that The-Above-Ones must have hushed their music to listen to that child's prayer for the good-for-nothing, outcast nobody.

That night the world turned over, and people turned right side out.

CHAPTER XXXVIII

THE next day I got a job at breaking stone. It was on the turnpike out in the country, and I found a boarding-place with a farmer. The contractor who hired me stood sponsor for my board.

When I was shown to my room in the farmer's house, I stepped for the first time into a bedroom.

I turned snail-like about me to get the meaning of the neatly arranged furniture; of the pictures on the walls.

My gaze came to rest on the snowy pillows and equally snowy sheets neatly turned down.

I looked long at the bed before I neared it. I touched it cautiously. The thing under my hand shrank down and seemed to flinch, as though hurt by the contact. I stepped quickly back.

A thing like that was not made for me to sleep in.

The thought enraged me. I walked up and struck the thing with both my clenched fists, throwing all my weight into the blow. My arms sank to the elbow.

It was a feather bed.

I wondered how a person could sleep with a thing like that shrinking and squirming about him every time he moved.

232

I Find Work and a Good Home

I took off my dilapidated coat, looked at my dirty shirt, then at the snowy sheets. Ashamed, I put on my coat again. I glanced up to the wall. My eyes rested on a picture of a child praying at its mother's knee.

How long I stood there looking at that picture, I do not know. There seemed to be something familiar about it—the faintest shadow of memory—or perhaps the picture was simply to me an expression of a yearning which I had never realised.

I took off my shoes, stole softly out into the night and crawled into the strawstack.

I could never be induced to enter that room again.

At the farmer's house I got three square meals regularly every day. And neither the hard-working farmer nor his gentle, sweet-faced wife ever asked me any questions about myself. They seemed to understand.

When I got my first pay for my work, the queen on the silver pieces sang me a song of kingship as I jingled them in my blistered hands. Here was real money that I had worked for as other men work for it. I would get more. I would henceforth be like other men. I would take my place with the best of them, in time.

That night when I went to my boarding-house I noticed that the grey-haired woman was tired.

I looked around for something to do for her. There was no kindling-wood under the stove. I went out to the wood-pile, split a big armful of good pine and carefully put it in its place. The good woman gave me a smile and a "thank you."

As I went out around the corner of the kitchen I heard her say to her husband,

"My! but ain't that a fine young fellow! He's going to be somebody some day if he keeps right on going."

I nestled up against the stone chimney and hugged myself. Praise was a rare thing to me. Always I saw to it that there was plenty of kindling-wood under the kitchen-stove.

Came a rainy day and I couldn't work.

I wandered restlessly about, eager for the hour when the good housewife would sit down to her knitting.

I liked to listen to her talk and to watch her nimble fingers ply the needles.

She unconsciously taught me many a lesson when she talked.

The knitting hour came, and as we sat together I led her to talk of her younger years—of her courtship and marriage.

She began with a blush and a little laugh.

"When John came a-courting, I fooled him. I fooled him into believing I was the dearest and sweetest girl he ever knew."

She broke off with a blush and a bit of a laugh that she hugged to herself.

"I fooled him again," she went on, "into believing I was a good housekeeper."

234

I Find Work and a Good Home

This time the memory made her laugh across at me.

"It was all easy enough to do before marriage," she sighed, "afterward it meant work, if I meant to keep him fooled."

She laid the knitting in her lap and looked through the window. What she saw did not lie outside.

"I buckled to the work with a will," she said. "Often and often I was so tired, I had hard work to smile. But when John came in from the field tired from work, or from something gone wrong, I always met him with the best of all my smiles. And how he would brighten up and brag on me!" she murmured dreamily.

She came to herself with another blush and a laugh, and took up her knitting again.

"So, I've been smiling my prettiest and working my best for forty years, and John has been bragging on me all the time. He hasn't found out yet," she finished with a chuckle, "that I fooled him forty years ago."

From all the good old lady said I summed up this: If we would help people to better their lives, if we would inspire them to do better work, there is no better way than to express to them our appreciation of what they try to be and do.

CHAPTER XXXIX

MY stone-breaking job did not keep me from the Salvation Army meetings. They were a great delight to me, for I found there fellowship as well as encouragement.

We always gathered at the barracks previous to our regular evening parade.

One night the captain of the corps called for a volunteer to beat the drum during the march on the streets. At the same time he stated that the drummer would surely be imprisoned, for the city authorities had made a law prohibiting Army noises on the street.

"I'm your man, Cap," I shouted. "I want to do something for Him."

I got the drum and the drum never got a harder beating.

I headed the procession of more than a hundred enthusiastic Salvationists while we sang:

"We beat our drums for Jesus because we love Him so."

A policeman confronted us with the order to disperse.

"Where do you get your orders?" demanded our captain.

"In the name of the Queen, I command you," he replied.

236

JOSEPH K. GRIFFIS (TAHAN), ON THE EXTREME RIGHT, AND TWO SALVATION
ARMY COMRADES, FROM A PHOTOGRAPH TAKEN AFTER THEIR RELEASE
FROM THE LONDON, ONTARIO, JAIL

New Ambitions

"We get our orders from the King of Kings," retorted our doughty leader. "Get out of the way or we'll march over you."

At this the policeman arrested us and ordered us to follow him to the station-house.

He faced about with a flourish of his club and headed the procession. We all kept step to my drumming while we sang:

"See the mighty host advancing, Satan leading on."

As I was the real offender, the judge sentenced me to a term in jail.

At this time I must have been not far from thirty years of age, and I didn't know A from Z. But I learned the alphabet while in prison. My teacher was an old Irishman awaiting trial for murder.

One day an old man came tottering feebly into my cell. His body was bent and twisted like the oak on the rock-ribbed hillside, when the season is far spent. His head was white, not with the frosts of the years, rather with blossoms from the tree of life. He opened a book and marked a place for me to read.

I told him I couldn't read, and why.

The aged man prayed for me while I knelt at his feet. His tears rolled down his furrowed face and fell in benediction upon my head.

"Young man," he said, "you could not be in a better school—in jail for Jesus' sake."

He grasped my hand in kindly farewell, and left me. He never came again.

Tahan

My prison sentence ended, I took my place in the Salvation Army as a soldier, and tried to tell of my redemption.

It was very difficult for me to express myself in the English language, and people often laughed at my attempts. But this made me all the more determined.

When alone I practised pronouncing the words which my tongue refused to manage properly.

I soon became conscious of a new ambition—to put letters of the alphabet together in such relationships to each other that they would stand for the objects I saw around me.

How to get started, that was the question.

The farmer's wife would help me!

I had gone back to her home the day after leaving jail, for my old job of stone-breaking was mine again.

My first lesson, however, was from a little boy. He, with other children, passed me every morning on their way to school. He had his books under his arm, so I stopped him.

"How does your book say 'boy'?" I asked.

The roguish urchin stood and grinned at me a moment, then darted away and ran.

I threw down my stone hammer and went after him.

When I caught the runaway, I threatened him.

"Now make your book say 'boy,'" I thundered.

The little fellow began to whimper and to try to jerk away from me.

I found force wouldn't work, so I coaxed. This

238

New Ambitions

way won him over. He opened his book and showed me the word I wanted to see. It was printed under the picture of a bare-headed boy.

I went back exultant to my stone pile, the letters forming the word clearly before my mind's eye. That day, as the stones crumbled under the blows of my hammer, I must have spelled the word audibly hundreds of times.

At night I hunted through a newspaper until I found the word.

"B-o-y, boy!" I almost shouted when my eyes fell upon it.

Before I went to my bed in the hayloft, the farmer's wife helped me spell out several other short words.

I was now on fire to acquire the art of reading, and talked with the farmer at breakfast about it. The man's education was very limited. He advised me to get a dictionary, explaining that it contained every word in the language.

When I went home from the Army meeting the next night I was the proud possessor of a huge old "Webster's Unabridged." I bought it on credit, for one dollar and fifty cents. But alas! I soon discovered that my big book would not talk to me.

Finally a schoolboy, a Salvationist, started me in a primer. After that my progress was much easier.

My enthusiasm was boundless when I had learned to form the a, b, c's with a pen, and was able to set down my ideas on paper.

Tahan

The farmer's good wife let me have a lamp in the kitchen, and sometimes the roosters would be crowing for daylight before I quit my lessons.

So far as learning to speak the English language better was concerned, the Salvation Army meetings proved a good school for me.

I found it difficult to pronounce some of the letters, particularly the letter "r." It took me more than a year of arduous practice before I could articulate it correctly.

CHAPTER XL

AN EVENT AND SOME INCIDENTS

WITHIN a year I became an officer in the Salvation Army, and was stationed at the Richmond Street barracks in Toronto.

The meetings began suddenly to take on an added note of interest.

It was a note of merriment, and was furnished by a young woman who came regularly and always sat in the same seat.

It didn't take me long to discover that she came to the services solely to see me. This sounds like conceit. It isn't.

She thought I was the funniest thing she ever saw or heard. She came to laugh at my queer, broken speech and my comic make-up.

The Army uniform I wore—also my hair. It was long and black and glossy. I was proud of it.

When I found what I stood for in the young woman's mind, I——

Well—I thought of Buckskin.

To most people who sized me up, my make-up was like my old bronck's—one big laugh in itself.

When he showed what he could do, the laugh turned into respect.

Tahan

I would show this young woman what I could do.

I made her acquaintance. I went to her house. I met other young men there. I entered the race.

I became a frequent visitor at her home—too frequent, according to her step-mother's notions.

The old lady herself met me at the door one day.

I braced myself and spoke as pleasantly as I knew how.

"Is Miss Rebecca in?"

"Miss Rebecca Rooney," came the reply in her rich Irish brogue, "will *never* be in again—to you!"

She slammed the door in my face.

I stood there, shook my fist at the door and registered a vow.

"Rebecca *will* be at home to me, not some day, but every day—at *my* home!"

I kept my vow.

I was in the running about two years.

But, like Buckskin, I won.

We were married in Orangeville, Ontario, and ever since Rebecca has been at *my* home.

It is a good home, for she has made it that, as she has made a good wife and a good mother to the five children born to us.

While with the Salvation Army, part of my time was given to special work.

When a corps was in need of money I was sent out to some place where I could collect a crowd. I did it by telling of my life as a savage and as a denizen of the underworld.

"WE WERE MARRIED IN ORANGEVILLE, ONTARIO, AND EVER SINCE
REBECCA HAS BEEN AT MY HOME." (MRS. JOSEPH K. GRIFFIS TODAY)

An Event and Some Incidents

I often raised considerable sums this way.

It was this special work that led me to feel I might do some good as an evangelist.

So I left the Army and started work in the rescue missions. I found it interesting, illuminating and sometimes amusing.

In the Jerry McCauley Mission, New York City, where the wrecks wash in, I once got my hands onto a well-soaked piece of driftwood. Two weeks afterward when the new life within him had in a degree pushed off the old, tattered garments and some of the marks of dissipation, he spoke in the meeting. He said but little, but it, with his glowing countenance, was convincing.

"Boys," he wound up, "I'm not what I was two weeks ago to-night. Then I didn't give a d—n whether I went to hell or not."

He said it with perfect sincerity, unconscious of the language he used. The old habits of speech still clung to him as broken shackles to an escaped convict.

That man eventually became a successful pastor in a western town.

It was in St. Bartholomew's Mission, New York, that I again got my hands on one of the lowest of bums. He was among the men who came to the meeting for a cup of coffee and a sandwich. He was also looking for a lodging ticket.

I singled him out as I used to single out a buffalo from the herd, and I soon had him down on his knees at the seekers' bench.

Tahan

The superintendent, Colonel Hadley, was a kind-hearted, but gruff-speaking man. In his usual harsh way, he came out with:

"What do you want here?"

"I want t' git saved," whined the bum.

"Pray then!" thundered Hadley.

"I don't know how, sir," whimpered the penitent.

"Ever ask your mother for a piece of bread and butter? That's how to ask God for what you want. Now, ask him!" commanded the militant colonel.

The bum prayed:

"God!—but I want som'thin'. Give it here."

He did his best there on his knees, the colonel standing over him. When the poor old outcast was about to give up in despair, the mentor again thundered,

"Pray more earnestly!"

The penitent pounded the bench with his fists and cried out:

"Oh, God save me! Why th' h—l don't ye save me?"

And He did. That man became an effective worker in the mission.

During my mission work I kept up my studying. I worked alone in my school of hard knocks, until I made myself fit to be ordained.

I became associate pastor of the First Free Baptist Church, of Buffalo, N. Y., and afterwards acting pastor of the Second Free Baptist Church. After that I went to Woonsocket, R. I., where with the Reverend William Sheafe Chase, now Canon Chase, we estab-

An Event and Some Incidents

lished a Rescue Mission. Later I returned to Buffalo, N. Y., where, after a rigid examination, I became a Presbyterian minister.

My first pastorate was in Akron, N. Y. While there I was also missionary to the Tonawanda reservation of Seneca Indians.

From Akron I was called to the South Presbyterian Church of Buffalo.

CHAPTER XLI

IN Buffalo I became a member of the Ministers'
Meeting. In it was represented nearly every
school and shade of theological thought. In it were
clergymen, living in the religious beliefs of hundreds
of years gone; standing with their faces over their
shoulders, their eyes on the road of the past, which
leads to dead issues.

Some were so dense that it was difficult for them
to see a hole through a sieve with daylight on the
other side of it. Some were of the broadest minds
and highest culture, while others of them belonged in
the cornfield rather than the pulpit. Some were
womanish and very ladylike in their manners; some,
manly, full-blooded men.

One was so small in personality I always wanted
to look at him through a microscope to make sure he
was a man.

One was sun-like, and with him I felt a need of
smoked glass to keep me from being blinded by his
brilliance.

Still another was moonlike, a world burnt out by
bitterness. A telescope was needed with which to view
his lonely caverns and bleak mountains. This man
was a destroyer of struggling life.

246

I Surprise the Clergy

Most of them were in a rut—which is a grave with both ends kicked out.

Nearly all of these men were charitably disposed, but one brother of my own denomination did his best to send me to jail because he felt sure I was a criminal.

Another, the Stated Clerk of Buffalo Presbytery, had my name dropped from the roll of ministers of the Presbyterian Church on the plea that my place of residence was unknown, although he had in his possession at the time a letter—which he afterwards acknowledged—giving my address; moreover, several of the brethren knew where I lived. Accidentally discovering that I had been unjustly deposed from the ministry, I appeared at a meeting of Presbytery, when my name was restored to the roll.

But, taken as a whole, the members of the Ministers' Meeting were the finest men with whom I have ever been privileged to associate. Those of high intellectual attainment and character were of inestimable benefit to me. Indeed, to such as I, they made the club a university.

But among all the wonderful things I learned, the most surprising was to hear the ministers lament over having to unlearn so much they had learned while students in the theological seminaries.

The meetings were held on Monday afternoons and lasted two hours. At each meeting some member in his turn would read an essay or preach a sermon, which became the subject for discussion and criticism. A dinner followed each session.

While I always received help from contact with these men, I am sure that at times the spirit of my old life expressed itself in a way that grated upon their refined sensibilities. For it takes time and effort to adjust oneself to the demands of a new environment.

One of my unexpected doings happened after my visit to the Gun Club one Monday. Sportsmen were there from every part of the country, and they were trying out their guns preparatory to the regular tournament. At the moment they were making up a "pot" to pay for the clay pigeons which they were to use. The money remaining after they were paid for, was to go to the man who would break the greatest number.

Judging from my clothes that I was a minister, and expecting to have some fun at my expense, one of the men winked at his fellows and said: "Let's ask the preacher in on this."

His tone was facetious but was tinged with contempt.

"Yes; come on in, preacher," indulgently invited the man collecting the money for the "pot."

"I am not familiar with a shot gun. I have been used to the rifle," I demurred.

"Oh! come on in, preacher. Be a sport," laughingly challenged the sportsmen in chorus.

Now, I never liked to be called a preacher, and the apparent contempt with which these men viewed my

I Surprise the Clergy

calling, made my blood tingle, and it decided me. In my pocket was a dollar in small change. I put it into the "pot" and took one of the proffered guns. I used several during the day, and fired until my shoulder was so sore from the recoil I could hardly raise my arm.

The sun was low in the west when I remembered I was due at the Ministers' Meeting for dinner. Thither I hastened and piled my winnings on one of the tables. I was thirty-nine dollars to the good, after paying for my share of the clay pigeons and the ammunition.

With no little pride I told how I had earned the money. My story was greeted with roars of laughter from most of the brethren. Then followed discussions of the ethics of shooting for money. A majority decided, though somewhat jokingly, that I had upheld the dignity of my calling, and, finally, one of the oldest ministers carried the day by showing conclusively that it was not gambling, but skill, through which the money became mine.

As for myself, I was content, for I enjoyed the satisfaction of having won over the crack marksmen. But the next day the same minister who had championed my cause, induced me to accompany him to an Indian reservation. Lest I be tempted again, I surmised.

During my five and a half years' pastorate of the South Church in Buffalo, I started two missions under its care. One of these—The Faxon Avenue—had its

249

beginning out-of-doors on a street corner, and my pulpit was an old wagon which I had borrowed from a saloon-keeper. Both missions have since grown into churches.

In all these years of my Christian ministry a menacing cloud hung over me. It was the memory of my old military offence. I had never spoken of it to any one, and I brooded over the thought that I, a clergyman, was at the same time an escaped convict. The thought with its sting grew as time passed.

Surely, no man ever occupied a position so peculiar.

I finally decided I had made a mistake at the outset of my Christian life in not making a clean breast of my secret, and applying for a pardon. But I did not know how to go about it, so I dreaded the consequences which might follow a confession. Suddenly came the crisis which forced me to take action in the matter. It came shortly after I had visited the Kiowa and other tribes in Oklahoma.

JOSEPH K. GRIFFIS AS PASTOR OF THE SOUTH PRESBYTERIAN
CHURCH OF BUFFALO, N. Y.

CHAPTER XLII

THE VISIT AND WHAT CAME OF IT

THIS visit was a risky thing to make, but I longed to mingle again with the warriors in whose fortunes I had shared on warpath and in camp. Many years had passed since I had left them, and I trusted to the long time to keep my identity a secret. For, there were certain occurrences of the old wild days I knew some of them would remember.

A strange experience—that visit! Often I was on the point of revealing myself, long believed dead, but caution held me back. My friends, I knew, would welcome me, but—so would my enemies, for an entirely different reason.

One day, at a council of the Kiowas, Comanches and Apaches there were signs that led me to fear a certain few had recognised me, and these few were—*not* my friends.

Convinced that it would be well for me to leave camp and get away as speedily as possible, I mounted my horse and headed for Fort Sill. But I felt I was followed by several of my foes.

On Medicine Creek, above the post, I found accommodation in an old block house with bullet-pierced logs—a relic of frontier days, turned into a kind of hotel.

Tahan

When I retired to my room that night, memory of the long-ago days, together with the danger I was in, kept me awake.

About one o'clock in the morning I heard the tramping of horses' feet. Peering through the little window, I saw a company of horsemen. That they were after me I had no doubt. The Indians had set the officers of the law on my trail! Behind the door was a gun and a belt of cartridges. At sight of them the old spirit took possession of me. I felt a wild joy at the prospect as I took up the Winchester, threw in a cartridge, and sat down on the bed to await developments.

Presently there was a knock on the front door. I was sure it was made with the butt of a sixshooter. The door of the front room opened to bring to my straining ears a whispered conversation and approaching footsteps.

I took one brief glimpse of myself as a civilised man and a minister of the gospel. Then I dropped back into the old life of a savage at bay, ready to die like a man.

Came a knock at my door. I cocked the gun, my finger on the trigger to keep it from clicking, as I stepped to an advantageous position so as to get the first shot.

"What do you want?" I demanded.

The answer came in a woman's voice—the landlady's. She explained that several cowboys had just arrived with one of their fellows who was very sick,

The Visit and What Came of It

and asked that he might occupy the other bed in my room.

I mentally debated the matter. It might be a ruse to gain admittance. I peeped at the visitors through a crack in the door. Even in the dim lamplight I could see that my suspicions were unfounded. Setting my gun in its corner, I invited them to enter.

The next day I lost no time in getting away from the place. On my way I stopped at Fort Reno, and as I stood at a distance and watched the sentry at the guardhouse pacing his beat, I was filled with fear. I didn't stay long, for I knew again the feeling I had experienced when escaping from the place many years before.

Again in Buffalo, I went to the Reverend Doctor Henry Ward and unburdened myself of my tormenting secret. He introduced me to a law firm, one of whose members was a Senator, one a schoolmate of the President, Grover Cleveland, and another the man in whose house President McKinley afterwards died. They at once took the matter in hand, and one day, about two weeks later, while attending a missionary meeting in Calvary Presbyterian Church, Doctor Ward handed me my pardon from the highest authority of the United States.

CHAPTER XLIII

ALWAYS homesick for the scenes of my childhood, the call of the prairie became so insistently strong that I gave up my pastorate of the South Church, and returned, a missionary, to Oklahoma.

On the old Chisholm trail, in the city of Pond Creek, I built a church. I began without a dollar, and the missionary board gave me no aid towards its erection.

But the townspeople were with me, and a generous contribution came in from the outside. My friend, Rev. W. J. McKittrick, pastor of the First Presbyterian Church of St. Louis, Missouri, gave me five hundred dollars.

The church was paid for before its dedication, and was pronounced the prettiest, if not the most artistic, church in Oklahoma.

Those of all creeds and no creed had lent a helping hand, and when it came to the building of the manse, it was the Roman Catholic priest who gave me the ablest assistance in planning it.

It was here I was elected Moderator of the Presbytery of the Cimarron. As this Presbytery was named for the river on which I was captured by the soldiers

I Become a Missionary

after my desertion from the company of scouts, I considered the circumstance no small honour.

I now had the opportunity of making inquiry among the tribes for my son Tapahyeete. More than twenty-five years had passed since I had left him in the arms of the good Cheyenne woman, the night his mother lost her life in the treacherous quick-sands.

My search was long and diligent, but I found no trace of him.

One day I reached home to find sitting on the ground before my door a tall, long-haired, buckskin-clad Indian. I was told he had been there without moving for hours. I spoke to him.

Came the revelation that he was my son Tapahyeete. He had heard of my long hunt and wanted to see me. I could not induce him to enter the house. He had come with a band of Utes from Colorado, and in a few days he went away with them and never returned.

I was now located in the neighbourhood of tribes I had known in the days of my boyhood. I had answered the call of the long-ago time only to follow with heavy heart the changes that had come to my prairies and to my people.

Where the shaggy buffalo and the quick-footed antelope had fed, were waving fields of grain. Instead of the tepee camp, were towns and cities. Iron pathways ribboned the plains where now were left only dim and broken pieces of the trails made by unshod hoofs in the days long gone. And the Indians themselves—the once proud possessors of the boundless prairies!——

Their standard of morality broken down; their religion a mixture of fragments—the white man's and their own; their old occupations gone, and their hands feebly grasping the tools of civilisation without knowing how to use them; hindered on all sides by the grafter, they were trying, with breaking hearts, to set their feet on the white man's road, and were prisoners on a spot of land called an Indian Reservation.

Years ago I learned that an island is a body of land surrounded entirely by water. Since then I have discovered that an Indian Reservation is a body of land surrounded by thieves—thieves who steal not only material property but manhood and womanhood as well; that within the reservation reigns a monarch called an Indian agent, with greater power than the king of any nation of the world. He can lease the land to whom he pleases. He can withhold the annuities of the Indians. He can refuse to issue food to the hungry men, women and children. These things and many more of their kind can this mighty person do to the enrichment of himself.

There have been and are good Indian agents, but the evils of the system are only too apparent.

CHAPTER XLIV

IN his dealings with the savage Indian, the civilised white man has been ignorant, apparently, of the fact that the Red Man's mind works differently from his own. And it also seems that he has not taken sufficiently into account the radical difference in ideals.

The supreme aim of the average business and professional white man, is to win place and power and property for himself. The chief ambition of the savage Indian was to succeed for his tribesmen's sake. In the trophies of the chase and of war, all of his people shared.

The civilised man gets to keep. The savage gets to give.

So, the difference in mind is neither constitutional nor fundamental. It is traditional and social.

According to the natural laws of the world, every life which becomes larger does so by orderly process. Yet the Great Father at Washington would put the tools of civilisation into the hands of the adult untutored Indian and expect him at once to become a civilised man—to take up the responsibilities of citizenship as quickly as does the immigrant—the product of the oldest civilisation in the world—and at the same time remain in an uncivilised environment.

257

Tahan

The Indian needs the opportunity to develop himself according to the laws of evolution; he needs the chance to fit into the trend of modern progress; but he cannot have this opportunity while confined in a prison called a reservation.

The American Indian has occupied a unique position in the life of this nation. He has been regarded as a sovereign, yet treated as a ward. He has been independent in his tribal relations, yet dependent upon the Government surrounding him. Again, he has been restrained in his tribal relations and expected to conform to the ways of civilised life. He has been a part of the Government, yet not a member of it. He has been subject to the laws of the land, yet often without protection under them and without the right to participate in their enactment. And the only man in the world who cannot sue the United States Government without special act of Congress is the reservation Indian.

To the end that he may obtain his rights the Society of American Indians has come into existence. It is of, by, and for them, and its formation is pronounced by thinking men to be the greatest epoch-making event in the history of the race.

It recognises the inevitable—the assimilation of the Red Man with the conquering Caucasian race, and its purpose is to break down every barrier in his progress toward civilisation.

One of the biggest obstacles is the lack of definition of his legal status. About one-half of the 266,000 In-

The Red Man and the White

dians are citizens with all the rights and privileges which the term implies. But much confusion exists concerning the other half.

In Oklahoma there are educated red men who are citizens. In New York those of like culture are not. In North Carolina Indians are citizens of the State but not of the United States. Nebraska gives citizenship to those holding allotments of land. Wyoming does not. In many instances in the same State allottees are voters while others are deprived of that privilege. Indeed, in some places, university graduates even are not allowed the franchise. But the most ignorant negro, the most illiterate immigrant, may enjoy it, and this in the Red Man's own country!

Here is but one of the several wrong conditions which I, as an officer of the Society, hope to see righted.

For I, with my brothers, bow to the inevitable. I know the Red Man must become merged into the life of this nation if he is to exist at all. I know that he must cut loose from his old ways or perish.

But for the brave, virile people of the plains among whom I grew to manhood, my admiration has increased with the years. They were patriots who were deceived by the windy legends of the crookedest thing in the world—the white man's tongue; their life was spoiled by the blackest thing in the world—the white man's heart; they have felt most heavily the strongest thing in the world—the white man's hand; they were trampled beneath the heaviest thing in the world—

the white man's foot; and they fought even after hope was gone, fought to the last for their own, and without self-pity went down in defeat.

And those who are left? They do not want to fight. They wait and they listen to the voice that is calling from the far-away time. It is the voice of the Mystery Man which reminds them:

"When the buffalo disappears, the Indian shall cease to be."

Because of health conditions I went to Wisconsin. While pastor of the Presbyterian Church in Neillsville, I visited Chicago, Illinois, where a couple of highwaymen attempted to hold me up on the street one night. I fought them off. One of the robbers was wounded in the scrimmage, and I took his six-shooter from him. During the scrimmage I got a bullet through my coat. A Chicago paper published a vivid account of the affair, also the Neillsville Times, of October 4th, 1904.

After serving the Ripley, N. Y., Presbyterian Church a short time I became engaged entirely in lecturing, booked by a Lyceum Bureau.

TAHAN IN THE INDIAN WARRIOR COSTUME HE
WEARS ON THE LECTURE PLATFORM TODAY

CHAPTER XLV

A S I look back along the trail I have travelled from the campfire of the savage to the pulpit of the Christian and the wider field of the lecture platform, I realise that the way was winding, uphill, thorny and long. I realise, also, that whatever progress or achievement has been mine, it had its starting-point in the lovingkindness of a little child. For it was her whispered words in the Salvation Army meeting which revived the spirit that was all but dead within me.

Then, what served to keep my face toward the East, was the knowledge that good women and good men believed in me. In undying gratitude my memory holds them all—especially the Reverend Doctor Henry Ward—the friend of the under dog.

Yet, while I recognise the fact that it was God Himself that gave life to my stupefied soul, my belief was, and always has been, that anything anybody could do for me was nothing as compared with what I could do for myself; that, indeed, what I could do for myself was the most important help of all. The acorn does not wait for some one to break its shell in order to grow. It works its own way out and up into its

Tahan

height and girth. So must it be with men, and men have the advantage of a choice of environment, and environment is greater than heredity.

Having fought my way from below the bottom of human society up into respectability, I am certain that no one is so low that he cannot get up and out into the purifying sunlight where every human being belongs. Not a soul is so black that it cannot become white. One of the whitest living things in this world is the pond lily. But it has its beginning in the blackest mud at the bottom of the pond, where the spotted frog leaps and the mud turtle crawls.

And a thought which to me has been a water-spring under a shady tree in the desert when the sun above was a coal of fire and the earth beneath an ash-heap, is this: I am more than anything that can happen.

From the darkness of the past I have brought with me many memories to which I shall ever cling. So am I one with my people of the long-ago time. For, according to one of our oldest legends, these people were not satisfied with the world in which they found themselves. So they dug their way up through the roof into another world which was better than the first, but they became discontented with that one. They again tunnelled upward, to find a world still better. But their discontent became greater than ever. Again by hard work they emerged into a higher and better world, and again and again. But always their dissatisfaction increased, and their yearning for some-

The Trail of the Years

thing better grew. Yet, back in every one of the worlds they had left there were things they loved.

So with me.

Some of the shadows of the past held for me not a sun-fleck, but there is one in which I want to remain forever. It lengthens with the westering sun. It is the shadow of the old rawhide tepee. For within it I first became conscious of the human heart-throbs answering to my own, and it was there I learned the principles of true manhood. And within its shadow shines the hope of seeing the mother who in the door-way of our prairie cabin gave her life for me; of knowing again the company of my long-ago brothers of the prairie; of looking into the face of that other one who gave up her life in my behalf.

For I cannot believe that heart-hunger grows only for the famine, but that the Master of life will some day stoop down and kiss into life and beauty those whom we've loved and lost awhile; and that together we shall rejoice where the hills are glad of the morning and there shall be no more night.

THE END

ANDELE,

OR

The Mexican-Kiowa Captive.

✳

A Story of Real Life Among the Indians,

BY

REV. J. J. METHVIN,

Superintendent of Methvin Institute,
Anadarko, O. T.

✳

1899:
Pentecostal Herald Press,
Louisville, Ky.

PREFACE.

This is a volume of simple narrative without any effort at literary skill. It is not fiction, but truth; and truth is stranger than fiction. In connection with this story of the life of "Andele" among the Kiowas, much of the habits, customs, and superstitions of the Indians is given; and, indeed, no incident is related that does not set forth some phase of Indian life in its real light. When historical events are given there may be some discrepancy as to exact dates, but the actual events themselves are as related. The condition of things, as exhibited in this little volume, is fast passing away; indeed, many changes have already taken place, and the Indians are taking on gradually, but surely, a real and permanent civilization. Years of association with the Indian has increased my hopefulness for him. His salvation and his development into a permanent and substantial civilization are as bright as the promises of God. This is being demonstrated all the while, as the work of the church and the government goes on with them.

To start with, there never was a people, perhaps, in whom there was so little upon which to base a hope of building a civilization. No homes or home life, no enterprise, no written language; but wild, nomadic, barbarous, savage, their glory the glory of war and plunder, their religion that of bloody revenge; the conscience and moral instinct dead. But among the wild tribes, as well as the civilized, the gospel proves the power of God unto salvation to every one that believeth. There is a wonderful chapter to be written in this respect, but what God has wrought among them will be told in a separate volume later on.

The author sends forth this true story of Andele's life with the hope that the young people of the church to whom it is affectionately dedicated may find both pleasure and profit in reading it.   J. J. M.

CONTENTS.

CHAPTER I.

THE MARTINEZ FAMILY.

Jaun Martinez was born in June, 1807. He was of pure Castilian blood. In 1773 his father, when yet quite a boy, had come with his parents from Old Mexico and settled in the United States, near Las Vegas, in New Mexico. At the age of thirty-four he fell in love with a beautiful young lady, a Bastago, herself also of pure Castilian blood, Senorita Paulita Padillo, and married her in 1841. It was a happy union, and, from the first, prosperity smiled upon them.

They settled soon after at Los Alemos, but after a few years removed to near San Geronimo, twelve miles west of Las Vegas, a place lying between Geronimo and Hot Springs, in a vicinity where, as yet, no one else had settled. Here were born to them four sons: Victorino, Dionicio, Regordio, and Andres, and three daughters, Francisca, Sabina, and Marcilina. With this interesting household of seven children the Martinez family became one of influence and power as population increased and the country developed.

Andres was the youngest son, and perhaps, physically, the weakest in the household, but of quick wit and acute mental perception. Living on the frontier, exposed to the frequent marauding, plundering expeditions of the various tribes of wild Indians wandering over the country, they grew up inured to dangers and equipped for emergencies. People by necessity become quick witted and skilled in the midst of the trying emergencies that come up in a frontier life. Many a latent power and sleeping faculty have been stirred to life and called into action in the face of a great danger or extreme emergency, that, in luxury and ease, would have slept on forever undeveloped. Trials, conflicts, emergencies, are necessary to arouse and develop the latent faculties of our being, hence we should count it all joy when they come.

Often had the Martinez family to guard themselves against the stealthy attacks of the wild Mescaleros and other marauding tribes, and at the time this history begins (1866), there were rumors that the Apaches were prowling about in the vicinity, but as such rumors had been constantly circulated during the past month, the community had grown careless and no watch kept up. Evil be the day when a man ceases to watch.

CHAPTER II.

THE MESCALEROS CAPTURE ANDRES.

It was a bright, beautiful morning, October 6, 1866. The Martinez family were astir early, for wheat threshing was on hand for the day, and everyone who could be of service must be called into requisition.

"Andres," called Jaun Martinez, "my little boy, you must herd the cows to-day, for I shall need Regordio to aid in the wheat threshing. Drive the cows out to the range and keep good watch over them, and about noon I will come to you and bring you some dinner. Be a good boy. *Adios.*" Just at this moment little Pedro, Sabina's son, set up a plea to go with Andres, but, being refused, he watched his opportunity, ran away, and joined him on the way.

Poor little fellow! he little dreamed what this act of disobedience would bring him. He little thought that he was turning his back on his home forever; that the music of mother's voice and the light of her loving smiles would never more gladden his little heart; that his own life would be put out as a candle by cruel hands, and his own little body, pierced and

11

bleeding, would be left out on the broad prairie alone among the sage weeds and grass to feed the coyotes and the wolves.

'Tis so often thus, in the prospect of present enjoyment, the happy youth loses sight of disobedience's dire results, till destruction comes and despair like night settles down forever.

"We will drive the cows into yonder little *vega*, Pedro," said Andres, "for there the grazing is good, there is no timber to hide them, and we can watch them better as we play there in the edge of the timber."

"All right," said Pedro, and they turned the cows in that direction. Soon the herd was comfortably grazing with heads toward the southwest, and the boys, as they watched, were playing in a cluster of low oaks at the edge of the valley.

The morning fast passed. One hour had gone and then another. "Look," said Andres, "the cows seem to be uneasy and are heading for home. Let us run around them and turn them back." With some difficulty having accomplished this, they resumed their play in the oak thicket, gathering together and arranging in groups to represent herds, the white stones that lay scattered here and there upon the ground, and naming individual stones for the familiar old milk cows in the herd they were watching. Suddenly the sound of voices arrested their attention.

"Father is coming," said Andres, "for he said he would come out about noon to see me and bring me some dinner. It is rather early, but I am getting hungry anyhow, and"—but looking up, the little boys were filled with dismay to discover, about fifty paces away, coming directly toward them, a band of wild Mescalero Apaches, with painted faces, and shields, and bows and arrows. Some of them were riding burros belonging to Andres' father, which they had doubtless stolen from the farm the night before.

But their attention, before discovering the boys, who had now crouched down amid the bushes, was directed to a Mexican man, who was traveling the road which passed through the edge of the little valley towards San Geronimo. The Mexican had two burros, loaded with flour, which he was driving along before him.

"Lie down, Pedro," said Andres, "keep still, they see the Mexican yonder and are started in pursuit, and when they are fully passed, if they do not discover us, we will run for yonder timber and make our escape for home. Keep still, Pedro,"

continued Andres, "keep still, your life depends upon
it. If you make a noise, they will find us out and we
are lost. It may be they will not see us. Keep still."

As the savage band passed on, their interest fully
set on the Mexican, and the boys were just in the act
of slipping down through the low bushes that lined
the valley to the timber beyond, they were discovered
by two Apaches, who, for some reason, had wandered
from the main band, and who now ran upon the boys
with a wild shout of delight. Rejoicing at the prospect of becoming chiefs, each singled out his boy, ran
upon him, struck him with his spear and then claimed
him as a captive. This is a custom among the Indians, that whosoever first strikes a captive, or kills
and scalps an enemy, becomes a hero, and great honor
is done him on his return home, and he is ever after
considered a great chief. His word commands attention, his wishes must be respected. It matters not
whether he kills a man or captures a babe, he secures
a title to chiefhood.

It may be stated here that it is not often that
Indians kill little children, if they can carry them
off, and it is a marvelous fact that, notwithstanding their fearful savage natures, they often show
the tenderest affection for children. But it seems

that the Mescaleros are among the most abandoned and cruel, and the two who had captured the boys hurried them along, calling out in mock tenderness, "Come on, come on, little boys, we will take you to see your mother, you must go to see your mother, she is crying for you now," until they reached the band who had gathered around the Mexican and his burros. They had cut the flour sacks open and scattered the flour to the prairie winds, and stripped the Mexican of every rag of clothing, till he stood there naked and trembling, his yellow skin glistening in the sunlight of that October morning, a pitiable sight.

The two boys and the naked Mexican were placed in the circle of howling Apaches and hurried along on foot, followed by a part of the band on foot, while some rode the burros and made sport as they pierced them with the points of their spears and shouted in triumph their victory over the three Mexicans.

Arriving, after a half mile travel, upon the banks of a little stream, lined on either side with a dark, heavy growth of timber, the band halted. A short consultation was held, but the captives understood not what was to befall them, when directly a tall, erect Indian, the lines of whose face indicated some degree of compassion, stepped forward with spear in hand, advanced slowly towards the naked Mexican and then hesitated. He seemed to be unsettled. He soliloquized: "In that man's veins flows the same blood that courses in mine. My father was a Mexican. I can not kill him."

He turned and handed the spear to another Indian, upon whose face savage hate and cruel bloodthirstiness had plowed its furrows deep and lasting. With devilish delight gleaming in his eye he stepped forward, eyed the Mexican with eager pleasure for a moment, then suddenly springing upon him he thrust the spear entirely through his body. As the spear was withdrawn, and the blood spurted forth, the Mexican sprang forward, forced his way through the band of howling Apaches and leaped like a deer down the bluff to the creek, but ere he reached the water's edge his quivering body was filled with arrows. With a wild wail of despair he lifted his hands toward heaven and fell full length at the water's edge. Holquin was dead. This was an awful scene to Andres and Pedro, and haunted them in the visions of the night. They knew not how soon theirs would be the like fate.

STUMBLING BEAR.
A KIOWA CHIEF.

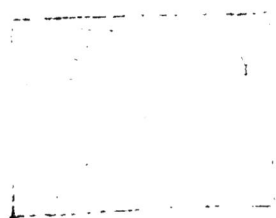

CHAPTER III.

A Vain Pursuit.

ıt was now noon. The force of wheat threshers
had ceased work and were at dinner.

"I must go now," said Don Jaun Martinez, "to
see the little boys and carry them some dinner. Pedro
deserves to go hungry for his disobedience, but I sup-
pose he is hungry enough by this time to eat in spite
of a guilty conscience. I shall hurry back, but let
the threshing go on in the meantime. It is only two
miles over there and I shall be back directly. I may
have some difficulty in finding them, however, for I
know not the exact grazing grounds to-day."

Martinez hurried on and soon came to the little
valley. He discovered the cows standing under the
shade of a large oak at the far end of the valley a half
mile away, and of course expecting to find the boys
near there, he rode in that direction. Disappointed in
his search, he began to call, but no answer came.

"It must be," he said, "that they have gone for
water to that spring yonder." He waited awhile,
then started in search. As he rode across the valley,

17

to his surprise and horror, he discovered the tracks of moccasined feet. He shouted out, calling in wild despair. He followed the tracks out to the road, where he found the flour scattered from the sacks of the Mexican.

"The Indians have stolen my poor little boys," he exclaimed, as the truth dawned upon him fully. "Curses on them," and putting spurs to his horse he sped home, to gather sufficient force and follow the Indians in hot pursuit.

There was consternation in the Martinez family, and in the whole community, when the news of the little boys' disappearance was received, and soon preparations were made to follow the marauding band of Apaches. Some delay was occasioned, however, and by the time the force was fully organized and equipped night was settling down, and it was thought not advisable to start in pursuit till morning, lest they be caught in ambush by the wily Apaches.

No sleep closed the eyelids of Jaun Martinez and the family that night. It was a night of heart sorrowing and weeping; a night that seemed never to end. But morning dawned at last, and the party was out and on the trail of the Apaches. They found the tracks of the little boys at the spot where the savages ran upon them. Following on they came to the scene of the capture of the Mexican and his burros. From here they found a plain trail, and soon came upon the mangled body of the murdered Mexican lying full length at the brink of the little creek where he had been so horribly pierced with spear and arrows the evening before.

Following the trail on in the direction of Las Vegas, they came to a stream, but after crossing it, the savages had so adroitly covered their track that no trace of them could be found, and thenceforth all must depend upon conjecture as to the direction the Indians had gone. The party, however, continued pushing forward in the direction of Ft. Sumner, till they arrived at that place, hoping that, while they had lost the trail of the savages, they might still hear from the lost boys through the occasional bands of friendly Indians that visited that point. They waited here for several days, but hearing nothing and giving up hope, Jaun Martinez, with tired body and broken heart, turned his face toward home. He never recovered from this awful shock, but after three years of anxious search for the little boys through all the savage tribes of the Southwest, with broken hear the died.

CHAPTER IV.

The Flight. Little Pedro's Death.

Let us return to the little captives. Leaving the dead Mexican at the creek, in too much haste to scalp him, the Apaches hurried on a few miles towards Las Vegas and hid among the rocks in the hills near Hot Springs. The boys dared not make a noise, and they could only sob in silence.

Poor Pedro! how his heart smote him when he thought of having run away from home that morning. How he yearned once more to hear his mother's tender voice, look into her loving face, receive her forgiving kiss, and feel the presence of her loving arms about him again; but he was destined to see her no more till they should meet before the Father's face up yonder. Andres tried to comfort him, but the hope held out to him was too vague; it brought no comfort. Night settled down, and the Indians came out from their hiding place among the rocks and underbrush of the mountain side, and stealthily made their way towards Las Vegas, crossed the river near by and found a hiding place in a thicket, not far from the sleeping town.

Here they held a consultation, and leaving four men with the boys, the whole band scattered out in different directions. This is their plan when they go out to steal horses, but when they go out to kill, they stay together, if they have any idea their foes are gathered at any point in numbers.

It was a long night with the little boys. It seemed that the light would never come again. They were confined each between two savages, who threatened them with cruel torture every time the least audible sob or cry was heard from them.

"Shall I ever see home again?" thought Andres, "When the morning dawns, will father come for us? Will the morning ever dawn again? Oh, I want to go home, I want to see mother. Surely I can go back home to see my mother." And all the long, dark night the boys sorrowed as no one can describe.

In the first early dawn, the Apaches began to return from different directions as they had departed, but all mounted on good horses, and leading four extra horses intended for the four men who had been left with the boys. Here they waited but for a moment, for they knew they would be pursued as soon as the light of day revealed their maraudings. The four Indians sprang upon the backs of the extra horses brought for

them, and the two who were the boys' captors seized
them with rough hands, pulled them upon their horses
behind them, passed a rawhide rope around their
bodies, and tied them securely to their own bodies to
prevent either falling off or any possible escape in the
thick jungles through which they must pass in their
flight.

Passing out through the thick undergrowth down
to the river, they recrossed, and to deceive any who
might follow as to their real purpose and destination,
with rapid movement they bent their course eastward,
and by daylight were out on a broad prairie.

After a few miles the band, turning their course to
the southwest, in sweeping gallop, went thundering
along, never daring to stop, lest the people, aroused
and in hot pursuit, should overtake them upon the
open prairie, where they would be no match for the
white man or Mexican. It is only in the brush or
among the rocks that the Indian becomes a match for
other people. He will not fight in open prairie, if he
can avoid it, and out on open prairie, one man behind
his horse, or other object, can keep many Indians at a
distance. In the brush or rocks, however, he is the
superior of all others.

At sunrise, the band went like a whirlwind, thundering down into a beautiful little vega, or meadow, where several thousand sheep were grazing. Spying the poor shepherd, who, on account of the elevation of land to the westward over which the Indians were coming, was not apprised of their approach till they were between him and the little rock fortress just on the opposite side of the meadow, they let fly at him a perfect shower of arrows, many of which fastened themselves into the poor man's quivering flesh. With a cry of despair he fell forward upon his face in apparent painful death.

Just at this moment a report was heard, a whizzing missile, sent from the rifle of a man in the little rock fortress, stayed the purpose of an Indian, who was just in the act of scalping the dead man as he lay there upon his face. But the Indian, behind whom Andres rode, coming up, and seeing the body of the poor shepherd lying there filled with arrows, sticking out like the spines of a porcupine, shot one more into it, then resolved upon recovering some of them. Urging his horse up near the bleeding body, he reached down, took hold of an arrow and pulled; but the steel point, with reverse barbs, was too securely imbedded and fastened in the man's body to be easily extracted. He pulled again, but with no better success, this time lifting the body from the ground as he tugged at the arrow. The next effort was to make his horse stand with his forefeet upon the body to hold it down while he again pulled at the arrows, but this too was ineffectual, and the Indian, seeing that he was being left far behind his fleeing band, gave up the effort and hastened on.

Continuing eastward for a few miles, the Apaches suddenly turned to the southwest. All day long they continued at a rapid rate. Night coming on, they slackened their speed, but did not stop. They had been in too many marauding, murdering expeditions to be caught sleeping. The night travel only would measure the distance between them and whoever should pursue them, if only their pursuers could once get their trail correctly.

The poor little boys were tired and worn, and from sheer exhaustion their heads would droop in sleep, to be awakened in an instant by the abrupt, irregular gait of the horses.

"Andres! Andres!" cried little Pedro, as in the flight they came close to each other, "Andres, I want to go home, I want to see mother, will I ever see mother again! Oh, Andres, I am so tired. I am—"

"Hush, Pedro," said Andres, "I can not help you

now, and your cry only hurts me the more. Don't call me again.''

And here the Indians, in mock tenderness, called out, ''We are taking you to see your mother, we know she is crying for you now.'' And the whole band laughed at the grim, tantalizing joke.

The weary night passed away at last, and the second day dawned; but its rich and mellow light brought no joy to the little boys, for the Indians again increased their speed, being fully persuaded that they would be followed in hot pursuit, and as yet they had not traveled through country where they could well cover their trail. All day long they continued their southwest course. Knowing the country, they kept out of sight of all habitations, lest being attacked and engaged in fight they should be delayed, and then overtaken by their supposed pursuers.

The day passed, night again settled down, but still no halt was called. The long night wore away in travel, and the morning of the third day came, clear and bright, but doomed to be a day of darkness and sorrow to the boys.

Pedro was completely exhausted, and could not sit up. He was crying piteously. He and Andres both, rubbed by the saddles in front, cut by the ropes around their bleeding bodies, and bruised and sore by the constant jogging and irregular gait of the horses, were suffering untold agonies.   They had eaten nothing since the morning they left home to herd the cattle in the little *vega*.

Pedro could go no further.   He fainted away in his agony, but revived again and continued to cry piteously.   The Indians stopped suddenly.   A hurried and earnest consultation was held, when the Indian behind whom Pedro rode sprang from his horse carrying the little boy with him.   The little fellow could with the greatest effort only stand upon his feet, strained in every limb, heartbroken, dying.   Taking a spear from his belt, the Indian, standing behind Pedro, with a murderous grunt, thrust it through the body of the little sufferer.

Andres, seeing this horrible performance, and forgetting his own sufferings, with a quick jerk at the rope around his body, freed himself from the Indian to whom he was fastened, sprang with surprising adroitness from the horse and caught his little nephew just as he was falling pale and lifeless to the ground. An Indian at this moment urged his horse forward, struck Andres in the forehead with the end of his spear, inflicting a wound which leaves its scar till this day, caught him by the hair of his head and threw him to his place again on the horse. Quick work this was, and the Indians resumed their journey in a gallop.

Poor little Pedro's body was left alone upon the broad prairie, far away from home, to be eaten by the wolves by night or dried into a mummy by the winds and sun by day. No ghostly marble pointing to the pale and pitying stars shall mark his resting place. The resurrection morn alone shall find him. He sleeps alone till then.

The purpose of the Indians was to reach a timbered and hill country, where they felt sure that pursuit would either be impossible or easily evaded. Yonder to the south, among the rocks and the low, stunted growth, they felt sure that they would be secure for awhile at least. So they pressed their way in that direction eagerly, till reaching the summit of a hill they halted. Here they scanned the country around in every direction to see if there was an enemy in sight. Being assured there was none, they prepared to tarry here till their horses were rested, and they themselves were refreshed. The horses being too much jaded to run off, were set free to graze upon the rich prairie grass growing in profusion everywhere.

But one of the horses must be slain to appease the

hunger of the starving Indians themselves. A pony, looking less able to endure the hardships of further travel, was selected, when two Apaches dropped to their knees, drew their bows, and with sure aim sent their arrows to the horse's heart. In a moment the starving Indians gathered around the dying pony, and with butcherknife and dirk, cut off the quivering flesh in great hunks, threw the pieces upon the fire, and scorching them a little began eating with an eager relish, which only a savage appetite could know.

"Little boy, who wants to see his mother, come here. Eat. Good," said Andres' captor, as he handed him a piece of the scorched, but still bleeding horseflesh. "No," said Andres, as he staggered back in disgust. But the Indian struck him a blow with his girt that nearly prostrated him, for already he was weak and bleeding from cuts and bruises received the past few days along the way. Great pieces of skin and flesh hung down from various parts of his body.

"Eat," repeated the Indian, as he raised his girt for another blow. Andres took the piece offered him, bit it reluctantly at first, but in a moment his appetite was awakened, the gnawing of his stomach responded, and he began to eat with as much apparent relish as his savage captors.

When Indians suspect that an enemy is upon their trail, they never halt in lowlands or open prairie, but always seek some high point, commanding a view of the surrounding country. At such a place they can rest and watch at the same time. At this time they were so guarded, and here they remained till their horses were rested and they had about consumed the one they had killed. When they again took up their journey, feeling that danger of pursuit was about over, they traveled more leisurely. Reaching the Pecos River they found a great herd of cattle, deserted upon their approach by the herders, grazing along its banks, a large number of which they collected together and drove away for beef as soon as they should reach their camp, only a few days journey now to the west.

CHAPTER V.

ANDRES' SUFFERINGS. RESOLVES TO DIE. EN-
GAGES IN A DEADLY CONFLICT WITH THE
APACHE BOYS. IS RESCUED BY THE KIOWAS.

Twenty days had now elapsed since the capture of
the little boys near Las Vegas. They had been days
of horrible scenes and fearful sufferings to Andres.
Hardly a spot upon his body that was not bruised and
bleeding. Great pieces of skin hung from his arms
and shoulders. He wished for death. He envied
Pedro his sleep back upon the prairie. He longed for
a spear through his own heart to end his sufferings.
Then the memory of home and home associations
came like a flood tide upon heart and soul. Mother's
sweet face and loving voice, father's prudent reproof
and kindly advice, and even Dionicio and Regordio's
occasional jokes, all crowded the heart and memory
almost to bursting.

"Shall I never see them again?" thought Andres.
His heart was breaking, and he resolved to die. He
determined to do something to make the miserable

Mescaleros murder him. Here was the Pecos River. This would be a good place. They were about to cross it again. This would be his opportunity — but just at this instant there was heard the strange, weird mingling of female voices in the distance up the river. The noise died upon the breeze, but in a moment it came again, louder and yet more near.

The band of Apaches listened a moment, then raising the triumphant war-whoop dashed forward with all possible speed, for they recognized in the wild song coming to them on the air, the voices of wives and mothers and sisters, who, being notified by a messenger sent ahead several days before, had come a day's journey to meet the triumphant warriors returning with scalps and captives. Instead of greeting first their returning husbands and brothers, the squaws ran upon Andres, four of them striking him each a blow across his bruised head and bleeding shoulders. There is a peculiar honor and privilege accorded to the squaw who first strikes a captive, and a little less honor to the next, and on to the fourth, after which there is no special inducement to strike a captive but wanton cruelty, which is often indulged in by the squaws, to which, as we shall soon see, Andres could testify. After the assault upon him and abuse, they turned to

pay their respects to husbands and brothers in the
returning band.

Soon they were moving forward again, carrying
before them the herd of cattle stolen the day before.
Again crossing the Pecos, they push their way along
its banks, till yonder in the distance, close at the
mountain's base, could be seen an Indian settlement.
Their camping place was in sight. It was home to
them. Indians have no definite abiding place, except
as civilization closing in around them forces them to
a local habitation. Their wigwams or tepees are only
temporary structures, made of skins or ducking, that
can be taken up and moved on short notice. When
left free to wander, as in the days of these events, they
camped only a short time at a place, never more than
a few months, often less than a week. But this camp
had been established two months before by this band
of warriors for the benefit of their women and children, when they started out on their marauding expedition into New Mexico. They were instructed to
remain here until their return, as it was a secluded
place and secure against an enemy's approach unde-
tected.

The camp was in a stir as they saw the returning
band approaching. A wild, savage shout from both the

A WIGWAM, OR TEPEE.

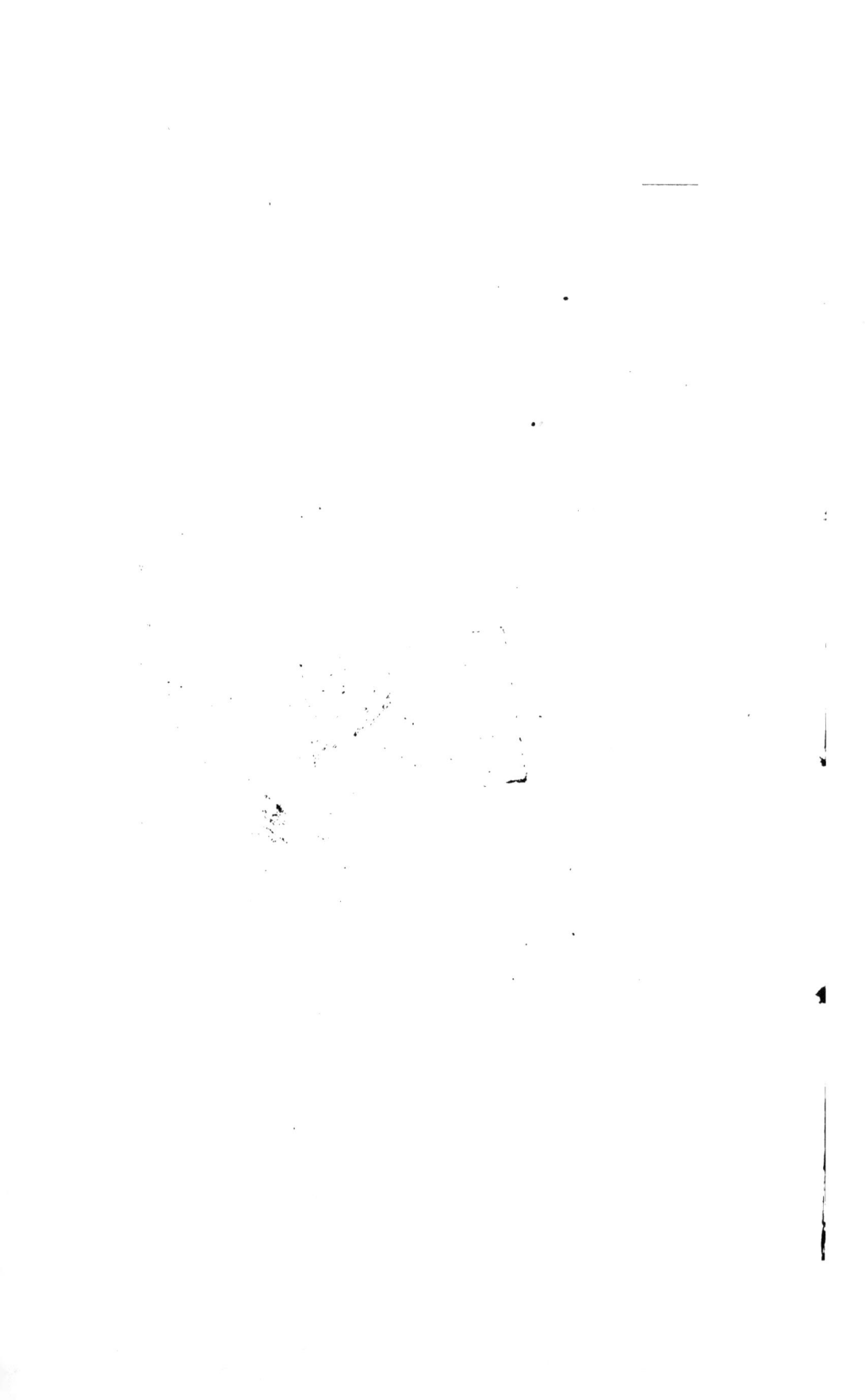

warriors and the campers made the surroundings hideous, and Andres' heart sank in despair as he thought of his possible destiny. But this time they paid but little attention to him. The squaws took the horses, staked them out by the long hair ropes, or rawhide lariats, led their husbands away to their tepees for rest, while the young men surrounded the cattle and began to kill them, till more than a hundred lay prostrate upon the ground. The squaws came out, and with shouts of joy and songs of triumph dressed the beeves. Fires were built and soon the feast began.

The names of the captors were on all lips, and a discordant song in their honor was made for the occasion, while each Indian of the marauding band was bragging about his own achievements. Andres was placed in the center of the circle and ridiculed and used as sport for the wild, exultant savages. After cruel jest and wanton sport, for the howling crowd continued till night, Andres was given over to his captor's wife, a little lame woman, who seemed to have some little spark of human sympathy left in her heart. It is often the case that only suffering will bring one into sympathy with other sufferers, and now the little lame woman was the only one in all that crowd who showed any feeling for the little captive. She took

the exhausted boy by the arm and led him along with
such kindness that his bleeding heart was to some
extent encouraged and refreshed.   He was placed into
a little cowhide tepee and fell exhausted upon a bed
of straw and longed to die.   He fell asleep, however,
and awakened, not till the bright light of the morning
peeped in upon him.   He was alone.   How strange
the surroundings!   He lay there and gazed at the
shelter over him.   He had dreamed of home and
mother.   He could not realize where he was; but
as full consciousness returned, he remembered all the
fearful experiences of the past three weeks, and became fully aware again of his surroundings.   He
had never slept in a tepee before.   It was made of two
cowhides stretched over the mature stems growing
from the center of the yucca plant.   Sometimes three
hides are used in this way.   The wealthier Indians
use three or more hides.   These hides, either buffalo
or beef, are dressed on both sides, and are made as
pliable as ordinary tanned leather.

Andres was not allowed to remain undisturbed
long.   He was soon called out and given the refused
beef, after others had eaten their fill.   He soon began
a life of servitude, carrying wood and water, and tending
the horses on the range; but he was closely watched,

and not allowed to be long alone. It was an almost hourly occurrence for the Apache boys to gather around him and hoot and jeer and throw stones at him, till his body was covered with bruises and festering sores. This made life unbearable, and he again resolved to die. He made up his mind to go into a desperate conflict with the Apaches and thus die fighting them. He resolved to do this the next time he was sent for water to the spring at the foot of the hill, for it was when he went to the spring that the Apache boys tormented him so.

At the tepee the little lame woman protected him, for she, among them all, seemed to be the only one who had any spark of love or human kindness left in her soul.

At this time Andres' captor put him to digging a hole in the ground. After digging it about two feet deep, and about the same in diameter, the Indian took a cow skin and lined the hole with it, so that it would hold water. He then filled it with water and mixed into it a considerable quantity of pounded mesquite beans, covered it closely, built some protectection around and then left it alone. Andres became interested in the performance, and watched to see what could be the object. He forgot his sufferings for awhile, and for several days the Apache boys for some reason did not trouble him, except by jeering him as he passed along.

One day, about a week after this, there came to the camp some visiting Apaches from another settlement up the river. The little lame woman was sent out to the hole dug in the ground the week before, and she came in with a vessel filled with mesquite beer, a liquor upon which the Apaches often got beastly drunk. After having drunken freely of this intoxicant, Andres was, as he thought, traded to the visiting Apache for a quantity of liquor. The little lame woman pleaded for the privilege of keeping him, but to no avail, and Andres was forced to take his place in another camp under new hands.

But he did not remain in his new quarters long before he was again traded or given to another cruel Mescalero, and here his sufferings began anew. Night and day he was tormented by his persecutors who took the greatest delight in seeing him suffer. One night the chief of this new camp stood out in the dim light of the camp fires, and in a wild, weird voice began to call. Andres could not understand what he was saying, but as he saw the people coming together he imagined that they were devising some new method

for torturing him, and his heart sank within him.
But as he anxiously· watched, he discovered that the
Indians, painted in most fantastic style, were gathering
around a tepee down near the creek.   Before the
tepee a few paces, was a large cedar branch standing
stuck in the ground.   The Apaches, keeping time to
the tom-tom beating within, circled around the tepee
three times, then bowing toward the rising sun stooped
and entered.

The tom-tom, the rattle gourd, and the discordant
song began in earnest, and the Indians were indulging
in a Mescal revelry.   While they were thus engaged,
Andres had a night of rest, for all night long the
tump, tump, tump of the tom-tom, and the noise of
the rattle gourd and the singing continued, and when
the sun came up and their revelry was ended, they lay
down in stupor and slept.   When they awoke orders
were given to break camp, and in half an hour they
were on the march to find a new camp at some more
propitious place.

Two months had now elapsed since reaching the
Apaches settlement at the foot of the mountain. They
were in a land of other marauding tribes, and scouts
were kept constantly in advance.   One day the scouts
in turning a bend in a little valley were suddenly

confronted by a band of marauding, warlike Kiowas, their old enemies. They were too close to make any effort to escape, so they proposed terms of peace, and offered to conduct the Kiowas back to the Apache camp, for the full band of Apaches had not that day taken up the march. The Kiowas, well knowing the treachery of the Mescalero Apaches, prudently declined to be led into any trap that might be laid for them, and so to secure safety for themselves they took two of the Apache scouts, placed them under guard, and sent two of their own warriors with the remaining scouts to the Apache camp to have the terms of peace agreed upon and confirmed.

The sudden and unexpected appearance of the Kiowas so deterred the Apaches that it was not long before the matter of peace was confirmed and the scouts had returned answer to the Kiowas.

"The Kiowas are coming," said an Indian to Andres, "and they will get you."

"Anything in preference to what I am now enduring," thought Andres; and in spite of his surroundings a faint smile came upon his face, the first perhaps since his capture. Soon the Kiowas came in sight, and although terms of peace had been agreed upon, they went through the Apache camp with some degree of insolence, and seemed to be intent either in provoking them to war or in showing them their superiority; but the Apaches were too prudent to resent it, and endeavored to take everything in perfect good humor.

After the excitement had somewhat worn off, and the Indians of both tribes had nearly all gone to their respective camps (for all had camped close around), Andres was sent to the creek for water. He fell in again with his tormentors, the Apache boys, and one of them striking him, there began a desperate fight between him, single handed, and half a dozen Apache boys. He struck one of them a blow upon his head which felled him to the ground, and springing upon him, he was in the act of dealing a deadly blow with a stone he held in his hand, when a missile sent from the hand of an enraged Apache struck him a severe blow on the arm. His hold on the struggling Indian beneath somewhat relaxed, and the weapon fell from his other hand, when suddenly, he was hurled by a quick movement of his writhing antagonist to the ground himself. The howling Apache boys rushed forward, and Andres thought now the end is come, when to his surprise, they began suddenly to scatter and run, and in a moment all had disappeared down the steep bluff near by.

Looking up Andres discovered two Kiowas stand-ing near, who had come upon the scene just in time to save him from the cruel torture of the Apaches. "Tagnoe akonte" (Apaches no good), said one of the Indians, as they stood there with spears in their hands.

This was a strange tongue to Andres, and he wondered what new trouble had come to him now, as he watched them in their feathers and paint and wild paraphernalia. But one of the men spoke to Andres in Spanish, seeing that he was a Mexican. He himself was a Mexican, captured long years ago, when but a boy, and raised among them, and in ways and habits and dress was scarcely distinguishable from the real Indian.

"Little boy," said Santiago, for this was the sup-posed Indian's name, "why are you here, and where did you come from?"

"The Apaches stole me from my home about two months ago," said Andres.

"Is this the way they treat you?"

"Yes; they have nearly killed me several times, and this time I thought I would fight till they killed me and so end my sufferings, for I had rather die than be tormented every day as I am."

"You were giving them a good fight," said Heap

O' Bears, who caught what Andres was saying, although he understood but little Spanish, "and we are sorry that you could not have scalped the crowd, and could we have got our hands upon them we would have scalped them for you. You are brave and now I want to take you from these Apaches and give you to my daughter to be her son in place of her own little boy who died not long ago. You see yonder tepee? To-night, after everybody is asleep, you slip out and come there and I will conceal you. The cowardly Apaches dare not undertake to go into my tepee, and after a few days I will take you across the Pecos River and you will be safe. My daughter will love you and you will be happy with her. Go, now, and when night comes and sleep closes the eyes of the Apaches, you come." All this was spoken in a mixture of broken Spanish and Kiowa, but Andres was so intensely concerned that with a little assistance from Santiago, he understood all that Heap O' Bears had intended.

"Sabe?" said Heap O' Bears as he was turning to go. "Si Senor," answered Andres quickly, for hope of better times sprang up in his heart, and he was ready for any emergency to bring about this end.

Heap O' Bears and Santiago disappeared down the

bluff over which the Apache boys had gone so pre-
cipitately a few minutes before, while Andres, with
much apprehension, went back to the Apache camp.
News of his encounter with the Apache boys and the
interference of the Kiowas having reached the camp
ahead of him, he received another horrible beating,
but he endured it more patiently, for he felt sure that
he would soon make his escape from their cruel hands,
and he longed for the night to come.   But the Apaches
had been watching, and suspected that their enemies,
the Kiowas, would seek to steal him, and when the
time for sleeping came they placed him close behind
an old Indian who was to guard him.   He lay very
quiet for some time, but at last, feigning sleep, he
rolled away from the old Indian, who, with a savage
grunt, reached over, struck him and pulled him back.

For a long while Andres did not move again, till
the deep breathing of the Indian assured him that he
was asleep, and this time he rolled away from him an
inch at a time till he had gotten back against the tepee
wall.   Fearing he could not step over the Indian
without waking some one, he reached his hand out
under the tepee covering, and pulling up a stake that
held it down, he lifted it, making a sufficient opening
through which he could roll.   In a moment he found

himself lying out in the darkness of the night, prone
upon his back, looking up at the pale and pitying
stars. But he had no time to indulge the memories
of home and mother and loved ones as they came
crowding him and choking him as he endeavored to
suppress them. Without even rising to his feet he
slipped along upon his hands for some distance.
When he was at a sufficient distance, as he thought, to
be secure, he arose to run, when he was, to his astonishment, suddenly confronted by an Indian, who rose
up before him from behind a large stone lying beside
the narrow trail.

"Bueno muchachito, mucho bueno," (Good little
boy, very good). And to Andres' great relief he
found it was Santiago, who had been watching for
him to come, and together they hurried away to Heap
O' Bears' tepee.

After partaking gratefully of jerked buffalo meat,
prepared for him by Hon-zip-fa, Heap O' Bears' wife,
Heap O' Bears said:

"Little Mexican boy—"

"Wait," said Andres, "my name is Andres."

"Umph! Andele," said Heap O' Bears, for he could
not frame his Kiowa tongue to say Andres. And
Andres, the Mexican, now becomes *Andele, the Kiowa.*

"Andele," he continued, "I have decided to buy you of the Apaches to-morrow, and if they will not sell you, we are determined to fight for you and take you any-how. You go back to-night, and to-morrow if a fight begins, you may know the trouble, and you watch your opportunity and come to us. We have no love for the Apaches anyway, and if we take their scalps it will be good. Be quiet and patient and we will get you, if not by trading for you peaceably, we will get you anyhow."

With full instructions, Andres with anxious heart went back to the Apache camp, lifted the hide cover-ing of the tepee and rolled back into his place behind the old Indian just as he was beginning to wake, and so close was Andres lying, that the old Indian never suspected that he had been out at all.

CHAPTER VI.

Sold to the Kiowas. Becomes the Adopted Grandson of the Chief, Heap O' Bears.

Andres had, by the night's experience related in the preceding chapter, become so excited that he lay awake till late thinking of the coming morrow, when he hoped deliverance would come to him. He at last fell asleep, to be awakened abruptly by some one jerking him from the pallet upon which he lay. It was in the broad light of the morning, and he waited with anxious heart for the Kiowas' proposed trade.

At last, Heap O' Bears, having arranged everything for whatever emergency might arise, approached the Apache camp. Santiago was with him, and when Andres saw them approaching he could hardly conceal his emotion.

"Heap O' Bears has come," said Santiago, "to ask you to sell him that little boy you have there," pointing at Andres as he addressed the Apache chief.

"How much?" said the Apache.

In answer Santiago led forth a little black mule,

and down in front of him he threw two buffalo robes
and upon them a bright, new, red blanket.

" He will give you these for the boy," said Santiago.

The bright, red blanket caught the eye of the
Apache, who had never before beheld a thing so
attractive to him.

"May be so me swap," said the Apache, speaking
in broken English.

" Boy, you catch 'em. You give me mule, buffalo,
blanket, good." So saying, he turned to his squaw
and directed her to take the mule and robes to their
proper places, while he drew, with much delight, the
red blanket over his shoulders. The squaw objected
to the trade, but to no avail, and with a scowl of dis-
approval she thrust him from them with a force that
Andres never forgot. This was the woman who first
struck him when he was carried captive towards the
camp at the foot of the mountain. She saluted him
with a blow then, she bade him adieu with a blow
now.

With a glad heart leaving the Apaches, Andres
was soon established in the affections of the Kiowas.
Hon-zip-fa took him to her heart at once, kind and
loving as a real mother. She prepared him a dish of
jerked beef and raw liver.

"Andele," she said, "your head is sore."

"The Mescaleros beat me and made my head sore, and my body is sore, too. But now I will get all right. You are good to me," replied Andres.

"Ta-quoe a-kon-te" (Apaches no good), said Honzip-fa, as she drew Andres down upon her lap.

Taking a butcherknife, and scraping it back and forth over a stone to sharpen it, she proceeded to cut Andres' hair. She carefully worked at it until she had trimmed it close to the scalp, matted as it was with the sores. Having finished this, she dug up the root of a yucca plant, or soap weed, which grew near by and proceeded to make a wash for his head, and soon she had it well cleansed. Hurriedly making him a suit of buckskin, after the Indian fashion, she dressed Andres up, and he felt like a new creature.

Such a change from oppression and cruelty, to one of comfort and kindness, made Andres very grateful and took his mind at last from thoughts of home. In a few days his head was well and the great sores on his body had healed up, and Andres was happy and contented with his new friends. As soon as he was cared for and dressed in the regular Indian paraphernalia, the Kiowas broke camp and started on to continue their marauding expedition with the purpose of so shaping their course as to reach their home, away to the northeast on the Washita, in early spring.

Heap O' Bears was riding a white mule, and taking his new son behind him led the van. He gave Andres a good bow and quiver filled with arrows, and very carefully and assiduously taught him how to use them. After the first day's travel, coming upon a herd of horses and mules, Heap O' Bears captured a beautiful Spanish mule, quick and sprightly, which he gave to Andres. Hon-zip-fa took a cow hide and shaped it upon a crude saddletree that she had made, and thus constructed a saddle for him. He was now equipped for traveling in as grand style as his adopted grandfather.

The Kiowas went on to the southwest, between the Pecos and RioGrande rivers. Turning across the high land of that region, they soon reached a section that was for many miles destitute of water, and for three days they suffered agonies from a burning thirst. Reaching a rough and rugged section, they came upon a herd of wild cattle, but being so thirsty no one felt disposed to disturb them; but seeing the cattle gave assurance of water near.

The way being so rough it was difficult to ride over it, Kankea got down from his horse and started afoot in search of the water that he knew must be near at hand.

CHAT-TLE-KON-KEA.
A KIOWA CHIEF.

In spite of their suffering, a wild shout of merriment went up from the band when they saw Andres leap from his little Spanish mule and start out, keeping abreast with Kankea, and sometimes ahead of him.

"Ziddlebe, Andele, ziddlebe, kataike,"* they shouted.

Reaching the summit of a little hill, the two discovered, lying in a little valley below, a most beautiful lake of water, reflecting from its clear and placid bosom the blended hue of verdant earth and azure sky. Never was a sight more welcome—nor more beautiful. Never was there a more intense physical agony than that of a burning thirst; never was there a more grateful sight than a fountain of living water to slake that thirst. So in the spiritual world. The agonizing wants of the soul are met by that fountain of living water springing up unto eternal life.

With a wild shout of delight, and a wave of the hand to the deployed band, Kankea and Andres rush down the slope to the edge of the lake, fall prostrate and drink till they could hold no more. Then sitting up, Andres fell over deathly sick, while the water ran from his mouth and nose and eyes. Soon recovering, he drank again, and at last felt quite relieved. In a

---

*Brave, heroic Andres, good, very good.

moment, the whole band, horses and men, were at the water's brink and in the lake, and soon all were revived.

After reconnoitering the vicinity, it was decided to camp for awhile somewhere near the lake, and go out on a horse stealing and plundering expedition. Andres, two men, and Hon-zip-fa were left in charge of the horses and the camp, while the others took lariats, bows, and quivers well filled with arrows, and started out on foot in search of horses. When Indians go out in search of scalps they ride their fleetest horses, but on a horse stealing expedition, they ride their slowest, laziest horses, and if they hope to find them near, they often go afoot.

Andres and those left behind made their camp about four miles from the lake, lest other marauding bands, coming for water and discovering them, should fall upon them. But one of the band, from a hidden place, kept watch each day over the lake to see who came there and to give warning of any approach in their direction. After night settled down they would drive their stock to the lake and take the pack mules with the water jugs each day.

Their water jugs were made of the beef or buffalo paunch. When a jug is needed, a beef or buffalo is killed, the paunch is taken out and cut open, the rough inner lining is removed, the paunch is dried, and the edges are pinned together with smooth, wooden pins, which bring it together, looking, when filled with water, very much like a large, short-neck gourd. Two of these are filled with water and placed across a pack saddle and carried sometimes long distances.

After a week the Kiowas began to return, but without any horses, looking defeated and forlorn. Their "medicine" had failed them. There was something wrong. They waited in silence for the return of the rest of the band. Several days more passed, and yet Heap O' Bears, Big Bow, Napawat, and Santiago had not returned.

The band grew uneasy, but continued to wait. Two more days passed away with increasing anxiety, when, just as the sun was dropping out of sight and the Indians were preparing to "make medicine" to ascertain the fate of their comrades, they hear in the distance the wild, weird song of coming victors. It was the song of triumph, discordant and wild as the howling of demons from the lost world. An answering shout went up from the camp, and strange as it may seem, the missing four came in from different

directions, each bringing in a considerable herd of
horses. Instead of a night of mournful worship, as
had been intended, the night was passed in wild feasting and savage joke.

CHAPTER VII.

KIOWAS REACH HOME. THE BIG MEDICINE DANCE.

After a day's rest, the band broke camp and started
for home. It had now been more than eight moons
since they started on this expedition, and it would
take not less than two moons more to reach their home,
away to the northeast on the Washita. Bending their
way as expeditiously as possible, they came, after
several days, to Rock River. A big snow had fallen
and it would be slow traveling for a time. A consultation was called one morning, and it was decided, as
they were now out of probable danger from pursuit
or attack from an enemy, and there was none
between them and home, that those who could travel
faster should go on in order that their people,
who must by this time be getting quite uneasy, might
know that all was well. Heap O' Bears, Stumbling
Bear and To-hor-sin, the three chiefs, with the larger
portion of the band, therefore hurried on, but left
sufficient force to bring on the stolen stock. Andres
and Somtottleti were put in charge of Heap O' Bears'
horses, and, both being Mexican captives, soon

became fast friends and remained so ever after.   Pai-ti drove Big Bow's horses.

After traveling slowly along for several days, one day, reaching the summit of a rise in the prairie, they were confronted by a vast herd of buffalo. Stretching northward as far as the eye could reach, the whole prairie was black with them. They had not been hunted enough to be wild, and the Kiowas drove unnoticed right into their midst. For days they traveled surrounded by the buffalo. They killed several every day before halting for the night, and cut out choice pieces of the flesh for cooking, but always consuming the liver and kidneys raw, with a portion of the paunch and entrails before leaving the carcass. These were always considered choice and delicate bits.

It was the custom among these Indians from early spring till July, to kill buffalo to get their hides for tepee covers. The hair was too short for robes, but later in the season, when the hair was long and nappy, they killed them for the purpose of making robes of the hides and storing away the meat, while it was fat, for the winter. For a small tepee, about eight buffalo hides were used. For the ordinary size, twelve were used, but sometimes the head chief used as many as twenty, thus making a very large tepee, or wigwam, twenty-five or thirty feet in diameter. These hides intended for the wigwam are dressed on both sides by the squaws. They scrape off the hair on the outside, and the inner, fleshy lining on the inside by a tedious process with bone instruments manufactured from the larger bones of the buffalo or beef. Later, when they could get iron, these instruments were made of iron. It took much labor and a long while to dress the hides in this way, but when done, they were as pliant as any leather manufactured after our most improved process. The hides intended for robes are of course dressed only on the inner side, but they are made very pliant and comfortable.

When a boy or girl grows up to sufficient size and age, a Pa-lo-tle-ton is set apart for his or her exclusive use. This is a buffalo robe, neatly dressed, made of a full skin, with the head fastened by the lips to the head of their lounge-like, willow beds. The young people, the boys especially, enjoy special privileges and attentions when they are fifteen or sixteen years of age. They have their own way and they control the household. The on-ta-koi is the ordinary robe for the bed. It is only a half robe, and cut off also at the neck. The hide for the pa-lo-tle-ton is carefully taken off, with all the skill of the taxidermist, so as to preserve the full covering of the head, with even the horns and eyes and ears and lips, and also the legs down to the hoofs, and sometimes even the hoofs are retained.

After many days' travel through the buffalo, the band had secured enough hides to supply the fullest demand for wigwams or tepees, for every pack mule or · horse was loaded down and could carry no more.

Nearly three months had now elapsed since the Kiowas had started on their homeward march, and they had reached Red River, which they crossed where now is located Quannah, Texas. They had encountered, during all this time, no one, save a band of friendly Quojale Comanches. After crossing Red River, they pushed on more rapidly than before, and soon reached the Washita, where their people were camped. The squaws seeing them approaching, rushed out to meet them and raised the war cry, as was their custom when a band of warriors was returning home. All was strange and wild to Andres, but he felt perfectly at home, as the Kiowas had been very kind to him and given him all the rights that belonged to one of their own number.

There were a great many tepees in this camp, and Andres was anxious to see on the inside, as he had

never yet been in one intended for a whole family.
But first he started to unsaddle his little mule, but a
squaw pushed him aside and unsaddled the mule herself. Andres looked at her in astonishment, and was
about to resent it, when he discovered that the squaws
were attending to all the stock, both unpacking and
hobbling them out upon the prairie. This was the
Indian custom, but not according to the polite Spanish manners taught him by his mother. He submit-
ted, however, and turned to enter a tepee, when
another squaw pulled him abruptly back. This time
he felt offended and made some resistance, but the
squaw was too much for him and he had to give up.
He went, however, to Santiago to know why he was
not allowed to go into the tepee.

"Pull off your quiver and other war implements,"
said Santiago, laughing. "No warrior is allowed to
enter a peaceful home with accoutrements of war and
plunder on, and you look too warlike."

This speech made Andres feel very much larger,
but he soon divested himself of his quiver and warlike bow, and, together with Santiago, entered a tepee.
The bows and quivers and buffalo skins were all
turned over to the squaws, whose business it was to
keep everything at hand ready for use.

Andres watched everything with profound interest, and he took on the Kiowa ways very rapidly. Opportunity was soon given for becoming a convert to their superstitious worship, and engaging in their dissipating amusements, for they had been in camp only a few days when, suddenly, he discovered the whole camp in a stir and commotion. The tepees were all taken down, and, together with the blankets and buffalo robes, were rolled up and placed upon the pack horses, while the tepee poles were tied at one end, half a dozen on a side, to a rope around the neck of a pack horse, while the rear end dragged upon the ground. In a remarkably short time the whole camp was deserted, and the whole band was on the march. The time of the annual dance had come and they were getting ready for it, and since the return of all the warrior-bands without hurt, they must worship and make sacrifice to their idol gods, lest they be angry and give them no further success.

Grand preparations were going on. Heap O' Bears had made a circuit of the tepees of the whole Kiowa tribe, for it was to be a grand occasion. It was the custom for the chief "medicine man," when the time of this annual worship drew near, to hang his "medicine" or idol around his neck, tie a representation of it to his saddle, and circle every tepee whose occupants he wished at the dance, and all those who were thus cir- cled were bound by every sacred obligation to go, under threat of heavy penalty; for if they refused to attend, some great disaster would be visited upon them by the idol during the year. If any tepees are left out by the medicine man in his rounds, either by accident or with intention, the inmates were sure to suffer great evils during the year.

The medicine chief, before starting out on this cir- cuit, always paints himself white from head to foot, and the only garment he wears is a buffalo robe thrown over his shoulders. He neither eats nor drinks till he has circled all the tepees, unless it takes more than four days, in which case he is at liberty at the end of four days to stop on his way and build a "sweat house" and worship, and then partake of food and drink, after which, being refreshed, he goes on his journey till he has circled every tepee of his tribe.

It may be interesting here to tell what a "sweat house" is. It is built of slender poles, usually wil- low, about two inches in diameter, which are stuck into the ground in a circle about six feet across, and then bent together at the top and tied, thus form- ing a dome-shaped structure, which is covered with

buffalo robes and blankets, making it as near air-tight
as possible.   This makes a tepee, or medicine house,
about four or five feet high.   The ground on the inside
of this booth is covered with a thick coating of prairie
sage gathered around here and there on the prairie.
This plant the Indians have special reverence for as
having special and mysterious powers, and it figures
very largely in all their superstitious worship.   In the
center of this medicine, or sweat house, a hole about
six inches deep and a foot in diameter is dug.   The
"medicine man" takes into this place his idol, or
medicine charm, a bucket of water, and an eagle
feather fan.   The eagle feathers are also held in special
reverence and are supposed to have peculiar power in
sickness and in war.   Hence they use a bunch of eagle
feathers over the sick in their superstitious rites, and
their war bonnets are made of eagle feathers.

Rocks are heated in a fire built near the sweat house,
and then taken and placed in the hole in the center.
The chief medicine man with all the worshipers goes
in, the robes are tucked down securely, so that no heat
can escape, and but little air can get in.   The bucket
of water is then poured upon the hot rocks, and the
worshipers lie down or sit around in a cramped position.   The steam arising from the seething rocks soon

causes the perspiration to pour off the worshipers in great profusion, when their weird incantations begin. No one is allowed to use a fan till the chief medicine man has gone through the first act of worship, calling all the while upon his grandfather, ''kon-kea, kon-kea, kon-kea,'' in continued repetition, accompanying his voice. with the well-timed motion of the eagle feather fan. It would be a sacrilege to use any other kind of feathers. After this first act by the chief, all the others may begin chanting and fanning and calling upon their idols and their dead ancestors. After this sweating, worshiping process is through, the worshipers make whatever offering is required, and the worship is ended.

The sweat house is used also in case of sickness without the worship. The sick person is placed in the booth, the water poured on the hot rocks, and when the pores of the skin are expanded, and the perspiration is pouring from every heated opening, he rushes out of the sweat house and plunges into the river. This either kills or cures. In some cases it cures, in many it kills.

The ''medicine'' of which mention is so often made, is the idol or image that the Indian worships. This consists of a little rock image with its face painted with a solid coat of yellow, and on this yellow

background are alternate stripes of red and black
drawn down in zigzag course, radiating from eyes and
mouth. This image, when the Indians are not on the
march, is hung up on the back of the tepee in a sack of
buckskin made for the purpose. On the inside is another
similar sack, hung on the west side of the tepee, containing scalps, paints, rattles, medicine charms of
various kinds, which superstition has led them to
gather from time to time

After the medicine man has made the circuit of all
the tepees and has returned to his own, the Indians
break camp, and, gathering from all directions, come
together at one place. This was the grand move that
first attracted Andres' attention after reaching his
adopted home.

On this first move, Etonbo, Heap O' Bears' daughter, who afterward married Zilka, took Andres to her
home and bosom to be her son. He lived with her
till the death of Heap O' Bears, and she was ever
kind and affectionate as a mother to Andres.

After the tribe had all come together and settled
down, the four chief medicine men got together, made
an offering of some kind and then selected a tree, straight
and sleek, which was to be cut for the post around
which to dance, and to which they were to tie the

buffalo. The order was as follows: They select a good level place near the timber and water. The medicine men then return and send out messengers to announce that the place has been selected, and all things are ready. But if no place has been selected, it is so announced, and another effort is made by the medicine men going through the same form of worship as before. But before the medicine men make this second effort, the whole camp must move to another place designated by them. At last, when a place has been decided upon and so announced, the dog soldiers get together, paint their faces and bodies, shout out the signal, beat their tom-toms, and make the surroundings a perfect pandemonium. On the next day, the crowd, ready and excited by this time, begin their approach towards the consecrated spot selected for their worship. The chief medicine man leads; his wife, carrying the chief idol, following close by his side. The captive Mexicans come next and then the twelve chosen medicine men follow with signs and symbols of superstitious worship, and at the last the great multitude, with the dog soldiers on either side as out riders. They go a certain distance, then halt and worship. This is repeated four times, and at the last halt an old Indian, noted for his age and wisdom, steps forth and announces to the crowd, expectant and eager, that when the word is given, the first one who reaches and knocks down yonder pole upon the consecrated ground, nearly a mile away, shall be endowed with special privileges and honors, and peculiar blessings shall come to his band of dog soldiers during the year. As soon as this announcement is ended, and the signal is given, a wild, mad, tumultuous rush is made in reckless abandon as to personal safety, or the safety of anyone else.

There are four honors, the first one reaching the pole taking the chief one, and the others in the order in which they come. After this rush is over, the circle is formed. Within the circle at the west side is located the "medicine tepee," into which the idol image is carried, and in which the "medicine man" remains the four days of the dance. Early next morning a captive Mexican woman, accompanied by the dog soldiers, is sent out to cut the tree that has been selected. They approach the tree, halting and worshiping four times before reaching it; then the Mexican woman strikes one blow with the axe and stops, when she and the soldiers again sing and pray; then another stroke followed by worship, and on till the tree is cut down. The dog soldiers then rope the tree,

SUN DANCE.

and by the four-fold method of approach and worship carry it to the grounds and put it into its place in the center of the circle. While this is going on, the great crowds are gathering together poles and limbs of trees, and, with much enthusiasm, completing the arbor for the dance.

It takes about four days to complete the whole arrangement. When everything is ready, those who dance go outside the circle, strip themselves of all clothing except the breech clout, paint their bodies white, dress in a buffalo skin, and finally go in, making the noise of the wild buffalo bull. They circle around the medicine man's tepee four times, then go back to the entrance of the large circle, then to the entrance to the arbor around the center pole, circling this arbor four times, each time motioning to enter, but not entering till the fourth time.

They then take their places in the dance circle. The medicine man steps forth from his lodge, circles around four times, as did the dancers, and entering, hangs the idol upon the pole, and takes his place in the lodge behind the idol. The musicians go through the same performance, and take their place near the entrance, just inside the lodge. The musicians begin their monotonous music with tom-tom and rattle-gourd, when the medicine man steps forth, perfectly nude except his buckskin breech clout, the ends of which are drawn up before and behind through a panther skin belt around his waist, and, hanging down between his painted legs, keep time in resultant motion with the movements of the medicine man and the wild freaks of the prairie winds. His body, instead of being painted white, as the common dancers, is painted yellow, while his feet are painted black. Bunches of prairie sage are tied to his wrists and ankles, and he wears upon his head a jack rabbit bonnet. In one hand he carries a bunch, or fan, of crow feathers, called the '*Tsine-ke-ah-lah*, and in the other, a whistle made of an eagle bone.

He goes up to the image, takes into his mouth, as he worships, a bit of root of some wild plant, grinding it in his teeth, turns to the circle of dancers and goes round spitting and blowing it out upon them. He next takes his eagle-bone whistle and runs around the circle blowing it with all his might. He goes through this performance four times before the way is open for the common dancers. The eager crowd then begin their wild performance, singing, leaping, yelling, praying, till out of breath. They then rest awhile, but soon begin again. They stare at the image, hooting and howling in the wildest manner, then at the sun, in a wild, foolish, fixed, idiotic stare, and cry out, "Yes! yes! now our enemy is blind. He can do us no hurt. We will take his scalp and steal his horses, and we will be secure."

The medicine man, taking the 'tsine-ke-ah-lah, or crow fan, calls the attention of the dancers, runs around the circle several times himself, then in wild gyrations whirls the 'tsine-ke-ah-lah around and around, while the dancers, fixing their gaze upon it, try to keep eyes and heads in harmonious movement with the motion of the 'tsine-ke-ah-lah, till dizzy and exhausted many of them fall prostrate upon the ground in apparent unconsciousness, hypnotized.

Thus they lie for a long time, and often profess to see visions that indicate their future destiny in life. If an Indian, during the year, vows that he will dance before the idol, and don't do it, some sure calamity will befall him. An Indian arose one day in a camp-meeting being held by the Methodist missionaries and began wailing. After a little while he stopped suddenly and began to talk. "I vowed," said he, "that I would come here and cry before your God, for I believe he is strong and can help me, and now I want to keep my promise and fulfill my vow;

for I have had much sickness and the Indian medicine
(or idol) has failed me. I want to turn to the white
man's God, for he is strong.'' And then he continued
wailing, thinking that was the correct way to get the
ear of the white man's God. He was endeavoring to
carry out the ways of superstition in the worship of
the true God. He wanted to pay his vow. He was
afraid not to do it. He was taught the way of God
more perfectly, and soon after professed faith in Jesus
and joined the church.

While all these things were going on, Andele was
looking on in astonishment, learning rapidly the Indian
ways and absorbing fast the Indian superstitions. He
watched Heap O' Bears, and wondered how it was
possible for him to do so many wonderful things. He
listened to the crowd of howling dancers and watched
them as they leaped around in their nakedness before
the idol. It was all wild and weird to him.

CHAPTER VIII.

The Quo-dle-quoit. Andele has a Fight. The Scalp Dance.

The big dance was at last over, and the Indians broke up and scattered abroad. But before breaking up, on the last night of the dance, all those who expected to go out on the warpath, or stealing and plundering expeditions during the year, gathered around a buffalo rawhide, took hold of it with one hand, and with small sticks in the other beat upon it, while they called upon their idol to help them and bless them, thus:

"O, Kon-kea-ko-on-to, O, Grandfather, blind our enemies while we creep upon them, keep them asleep while we plunder them, help us to get many scalps and captives, and steal good horses, and don't let us get hurt."

And thus they went on beating the rawhide, singing and marching and praying, till satisfied with the performance, they broke up to start out in small bands to the various fields of plunder and murder. The men who did not intend to go out on these raids during the

year were not allowed to go through this performance, for it amounted to a pledge to join in some
marauding expedition.

The Quo-dle-quoit constitute a privileged class
among the Kiowas. It is an honor or privilege that
is transmissible, and no one can be Quo-dle-quoit
longer than four years, when a successor must be
selected. Each Quo-dle-quoit selects his own successor, who must of necessity accept the honor and
submit to be painted after the manner of the Quo-dle-
quoit, which is as follows: Around the forehead,
at the edge of the hair, are parallel streaks of black,
and these are continued around the face and drawn
down under the chin. On each cheek bone is the
picture of the moon very far advanced in crescent.
On the center of the chest is the picture of the sun,
and on each side of the chest, a little lower down, is
again the crescent, painted in dark green, shading out
into a very light green toward the open side of the
crescent which is turned upward. The sun on the
chest is also a light green, but the whole body has a
coat of solid yellow as a back ground to all these
other ornate colors.

The Quo-dle-quoit wears a jack-rabbit bonnet,
ornamented with the ears of a jack rabbit and with

eagle feathers. Instead of *painting* the sun and moon on the chest, they are often *cut* into the flesh, leaving for all time to come great sun- and moon-shaped scars. When one is selected as a Quo-dle-quoit, and, according to custom, is painted up and ornamented, he must pay his predecessor well for it, and each year as his predecessor paints and ornaments him, he is obliged to pay an additional installment of ponies, blankets, robes, etc., for four years, when his Quo-dle-quoit ceases. He must then in turn transfer it to some friend and receive remuneration from him in like manner as he had to give to his predecessor.

This works oppressively sometimes, but no one dare refuse to become a Quo-dle-quoit when once selected. The Quo-dle-quoit never looks into a mirror of any kind. He dare not see himself. He is denied the privilege of eating dog, or polecat, or of being around the fire where cooking is done, or enter a tepee where a dog is. There are many other things denied him, but he enjoys security in war. No weapon of war can hurt him; he is secure.

The morning after this first big dance the men all scattered abroad in various directions. Andres was left with the women. They had all learned to like him. At the first he was kindly received. His adopted mother had made some clothes for him, even before he had reached the Kiowa settlement. Santiago's wife, who was Heap O' Bears' sister-in-law, carried him first to her camp. He felt free and did as he pleased. He was the adopted grandson of the chief, and he had been instructed to resent any attacks made upon him by the Indian boys.

During Heap O' Bears' first absence, he suffered somewhat from the boys who had become jealous of him on account of the favor shown him, a captive, but he soon had an opportunity of showing them that he was able and ready to take care of himself. It was during a scalp dance after Heap O' Bears' return. He had been gone about two months when he returned with two scalps, that of a negro and a Ute Indian.

The scalp dance is a grim performance and generally lasts about three weeks, and they dance night and day. No man is allowed to dance who was not in the fight when the scalps were taken. But all the women are privileged to dance. If no scalps are taken, or one of the band is killed, no dance is held; but when they return with scalps a grand jubilee is held. When a successful band is approaching home, they slip up stealthily until near by, when suddenly they raise the war-whoop and charge upon their own home, which

QUO-DLE-QUOIT.

creates a panic till they are discovered to be friends instead of enemies, and instantly a responsive war-whoop is given by the wives and mothers, and preparations begin at once for the dance.

They hang the scalps upon a pole, while they go dancing in a circle around it, singing and beating the tom-tom, and all the while calling in tantalizing jeer to each of the dead men: "Poor fellow, he tried to save his life, but look at his scalp! He cried aloud, but we only laughed. We shot him through the heart. He fought hard, but we overcame, and his scalp looks beautiful hanging there. Our medicine made him blind while we killed him."

While going through this performance they constantly shout out the praises of the men who took the scalps. They are the heroes of the occasion. In all this wild, weird performance the squaws show the greater fierceness and devilish joy.

After the dance is over they offer the scalps to the sun, or sometimes to some particular idol to which they had made promise before going out to war. When they make the offering to the sun (or some idol), they pray: "O, Sun, give us power to get other scalps. Give us long life and make us brave chiefs. Keep our enemies blind and deaf so they will not detect our

stealthy approach." Often they keep the scalps to tie
to their medicine charms and to grace their belts.

At these scalp dances the boys are allowed the fullest liberty, and encouraged to take part in, and enjoy,
the hideous performance. It was at this scalp dance,
upon the return of Heap O' Bears, that Andres gave
evidence of his purpose to defend himself. While
the dancing was going on one night, he and other
boys, dressed in buffalo robes, were running through
the circle and jumping over the fire in the center and
bellowing like a mad buffalo, when suddenly he and
Pakea collided as they met in the center. They both,
with bruised heads, fell backward. After they had
recovered from the shock, and were on the outside of
the circle, Pakea, while Andres was not aware of his
intention, or even of his being angry, struck him a
blow that nearly felled him to the ground.

He arose with all the fire of his Spanish blood
stirred to the utmost, and began a fight that must
decide his standing among the Indians in the future.
If he was overcome by Pakea, then he would be
the butt of ridicule and contempt and imposition.
But if he overcame, he would stand as a respected
chief among the boys, and be an object of admiration
among the old people. Indians have great respect for

the one who wins in a fight, whether the winner be of
their own race, their friend or foe, and so this fight
meant much to Andres. He was determined to win,
and so he put his whole heart and muscle into it, and
in the very first onset he struck Pakea such a blow as
caused a wail from him that indicated the result at
once, and when the Indian dancers, who had suspended
dancing for a moment to look on, saw what the result
was, they cried out, "Ziddlebe Andele," that is,
"brave and dangerous Andele." Some touched him
on the breast and on the back muttering out some
exclamations of approval and admiration. It was a
victory that became an epoch in his Indian life. From
henceforth he had no more trouble.

If an Indian band who has been out on a marauding expedition returns without scalps, there is no
dance. If one of the number has been killed, there
is wailing and lamentation, and very soon the chief
who was leading the band must go in search of the
tribe or people who did the killing and get a scalp.
If he fails, he must very soon go again, and again,
till he succeeds. He goes to the spot where his comrade was killed and begins his search. He paints his
face a shining black, something like a stove polish
color. He throws away his mourning apparel, and

goes forth, not as a mourner, but as a proud warrior. In carrying .out this principle of retaliation one can readily see why the Indian tribes were in constant or continuous war with each other.

On a certain occasion, Andres, with a considerable band of Indians, obtained permission from the government agent at Anadarko to hunt upon some of the unoccupied lands of West Texas. While they were there hunting a company of Texas Rangers came upon them, killed one of their number, scalped him, cut his finger off and left him. The Indians hurried back to their own reservation, stated to the Indian United States Agent what had occurred, and demanded of the agent that they be permitted to go again to Texas and kill a Texas man in revenge. Whether the agent through fear for his own scalp gave his consent, it is not known, but the Indians did go and in a little while returned with the scalp of a hated Texan, held a big scalp dance and were satisfied. After an Indian has been killed, the daily mourning is kept up till scalps of the enemy are secured, and then the mourning ceases.

CHAPTER IX.

Heap O' Bears is Killed by the Utes, and is Scalped. Somtotleti dies with him.

Three years had now elapsed since Andres had been stolen near Las Vegas. It was the spring of 1869. Andele had become a veritable Indian with but little trace of civilized life left in him. He had learned many things of the Indian life, and had accepted them all. The annual sun dance had been held, when Heap O' Bears, with his band of Kiowa dog soldiers and allied bands of Comanches, Arapahoes and Cheyennes, started westward on an expedition against the Utes, against whom Heap O' Bears, on account of past offenses, had a "bad spirit." He hoped, with the aid of his allies, to give them a blow from which they would never recover.

Passing on westward after three days' travel, and coming to a mountain pass through which ran a small mountain stream, a fierce bear, with swift gait and seeming fright, came towards them from the windward, and circling around them passed out of sight down a mountain gorge. In a moment every Indian drew rein and sat in silent awe. For sometime no one spoke—all seemed to apprehend that a dread calamity was before them. Finally Heap O' Bears broke the silence:

"Now, we started out under 'strong medicine,' surely we are not to be forsaken by our god, but what means that Tsaitim (Bear) crossing our path to the windward, and lifting himself as if in warning of future doom if we go forward? But it can not be, for the medicine was good, the signs were right. The medicine said, 'go, kill Utes.' We will go forward."

"Hold," said the Comanche leader, "your 'medicine' is broken. For some reason the wind blows you down and it sends the Tsaitim here from the windward to warn you, and whatever be the 'medicine' you trust, the matter has been given over to to other hands, and you dare not go forward. If the bear had passed on the other side of us, and had not raised those warning feet of his, you would, with us all, have been safe. But you know what it means when a bear crosses a warrior's path to the windward."

"Umph! Umph!" sanctioned the respective leaders of the Arapahoe and Cheyenne bands.

"I dare not go back," said Heap O' Bears, "lest I disobey and insult the 'medicine' that assures me aid in all my wars, and thus suffer punishment at his hands. I will defy this new, and doubtless evil omen, and go on any how, but if you people are afraid, I will let you return, and I will go alone to scalp the Utes. The squaws will doubtless entertain you upon your return, and help you to dance around the scalp of a jack-rabbit instead of a Ute.''

Heap O' Bears spoke this with much earnestness and sarcasm, but at the same time betrayed some apprehension on account of the dilemma he was in. The Comanche leader straightening himself full in his saddle, and while his eagle eyes in proud gaze stared upon Heap O'Bears, made answer:

''We are here, Heap O' Bears, as you well know from conflicts with us in the past, behind no one in courage and in readiness to scalp the Utes, but the tsaitim indicates that your medicine is broken and your doom sealed should you go on, and we do not wish to see your scalp taken nor to feel ours jerked from our heads by the howling Utes. We can do nothing when the power of the medicine under which we go is destroyed.''

Heap O' Bears sat awhile in deep thought and finally spoke, ''As leader of this expedition, I feel the weight of responsibility. I would not see you murdered through my mistake at the hands of the Utes. Let us camp here till another sun comes up, perhaps new light will come with it. This night I will go alone out upon the mountain yonder, and consult the medicine and pray for direction, and what I receive shall be for our guidance."

"Umph! Umph!" and approval came from the allies.

So the whole band moved down upon the little creek to camp for the night and wait developments. As night came on Heap O' Bears painted himself white, having washed off the black war paint, gave instruction that no one come near him during the night, went out upon the mountain side and there remained alone all night till the early sun began to peep over the eastern hills, when he came in with a revelation from his medicine. All listened with deep silence as he spoke.

"I must go back home," said he, "and start again after a short rest and a sacrifice to the medicine. Let the whole band await me here. Seven suns will see me back again."

"But we must all return," said an Arapahoe.

"No, no!" said Heap O' Bears, "for I find the sign was for me and affects my people alone, and it is only necessary for me to return."

He was reluctantly allowed to go alone. The band waited patiently till the evening of the seventh day and as they saw the sun rapidly sinking in the west, they began to grow anxious. Their fears were soon relieved, however, for just as the last lingering beams of the sinking sun were kissing a departure to hilltop and boughs, Heap O' Bears from a mountain pass came suddenly in sight of the place of encampment.

"Heap O' Bears comes ready for the Utes this time," said he, as he neared the camp and alighted from his horse. The allied bands all received him with gladness and on the next day they broke camp and moved on weswtard. After a hurried and continued march of three days, they descried a band of Utes on a hill some distance away watching them, and while they were consulting what to do, to their surprise there came from another direction a band of Utes sounding the warwhoop and eager for the fray. Before the allies could recover from their surprise, the Utes were full upon them. The allies whirled into line, confronting the Utes, when suddenly both sides halted, and sat upon their horses, gazing into each others faces, neither side speaking a word nor otherwise breaking the silence for some while; when at last a young Kiowa raised his spear and struck a Ute full in the face, and cried out as he did so:

"If by striking the first blow upon a hated Ute I become chief, then am I chief now, for the deed is done."

This was the signal for a general engagement, and in a moment a dozen lifeless forms, pierced by arrow and spear, lay full upon the ground. Desperate was the fight. The Utes seemed to know no fear. They were upon their own territory, and their homes were at stake. They closed in upon the Kiowas. The Comanches were panic stricken and fled. The Arapahoes and Cheyennes who were farther to the left, seeing the courage and desperate fighting of the Utes, did not venture to the help of the Kiowas, but kept at safe distance. Heap O' Bears, becoming separated from his band, was surrounded and pressed upon every hand.

"I shall die here," he said. "I can fight, but I can not run and here will I pay the penalty of my foolish distrust in my medicine by turning back when I should have gone on. Let my braves leave me to my fate and save themselves."

The band was rapidly retreating, when Somtotleti learned of Heap O' Bears danger. He rushed back, and declaring his purpose to die with his friend and chief, he forced his way through the band of Utes and stood beside Heap O' Bears, who was already bleeding from several wounds. He shot one Ute from his horse, and then another, and still another, and the Utes were about to give away, when they discovered that Heap O' Bears and Somtotleṭi had no more arrows. They rushed upon the two helpless comrades with renewed fierceness and hate, filled their bodies with arrows and scalped them while they were yet gasping. When this was done the Utes looked to find the allied bands, but they had retreated to a safe distance, and were fast making their way towards the rising sun again. Thus this war was ended.

CHAPTER X.

MOURNING FOR HEAP O' BEARS. HORRIBLE SIGHT.

Ten days had passed since the battle with the Utes
and Heap O' Bears' death. Night had come on, and
the fierce prairie winds, with renewed force, were
howling mournfully as they swept through the village
of tepees, or wigwams, at the foot of the bluff near
the Washita, located there till the braves should
return from the Ute war. In much merriment, Andele
and the Indian boys had been going through with a
mimic performance of "medicine making," and he
had at last lain down upon his bed in the west side of
the tepee.

All was quiet. He was not yet asleep. He was,
perhaps, indulging a faint thought of the home from
which he had been stolen, of the mother upon whose
loving bosom he had so often been pillowed to
sleep, of the scenes that he had encountered since
he had last seen her, of little Pedro's cruel death;
then of the Indians' wild dance, of the discordant
songs to which he had listened, and wondering, still
wondering, he had dropped into a half-conscious sleep.

HON-ZIP-FA.

His memory had taken up the whole chain of events, and was passing them before his mind like a panorama in vivid colors, tracing in rapid succession from this to that, when a thousand painted faces, hideous and wild, stood before him, and suddenly a wild wail, mingling with the mournings of the western winds as they swept over the far-stretching prairie, came like lamentations from some lost soul wandering from the regions of the dead. He sprang up in horror, and trembling from head to foot, stood speechless.

After a little while, recovering himself, he concluded that it was only a bad dream, and that it was but the night wind howling around the wigwam. He was just in the act of lying down again, when once more he heard the strange, wild wail, this time coming nearer and nearer and more distinct. Heap O' Bears' wife awoke, listened a moment, and then throwing up her hands, began howling in accord with the noise of the seeming demoniacs approaching in the darkness of the night. Andele was nearly dead with fright, but he soon found out that it was the band of warriors who had gone to fight the Utes under Heap O' Bears. They were returning without their chief, who was left lying back upon the prairie, scalped by the Utes.

In a moment Heap O' Bears' wife gathered up a

whetstone and a butcherknife lying near, stripped herself perfectly nude down to the waist, raked the knife back and forth over the stone, and then began cutting herself. She cut her arms from the shoulders down to her wrists, and gashed most horribly her breasts, and then smeared upon her face the blood that gushed forth from every wound.

Andele was horrified as he gazed upon her there in the dim light of the cotton wood fire. Heap O' Bears' wife, not content with cutting her arms and breasts and smearing the blood upon her face, placed one of her fingers upon a rock and asked a friend to chop it off. And there she stood, bleeding and howling, accompanied with the howling of all the camp in such discord as can be portrayed only by emblems drawn from the world of fiends. All night the howling went on, and next morning as the sun came up, a great fire was made of all Heap O' Bears' personal property and a number of ponies were killed for his use in the happy hunting ground. He was a chief and great honor must be done to his memory; and besides, he must have a chief's full equipage for the hunting grounds beyond.

CHAPTER XI.

According to Indian custom, Sunboy, who was
Heap O' Bears eldest brother, in a short while married
Hon-zip-fa, Heap O' Bears' widow, and Andele went
to live with Napawat, Heap O' Bears' successor.
Here he found it very disagreeable, for Napawat had
two wives and they were frequently in quarrels, and
Andele suffered from their contentions, as he under-
took to serve both.

Mourning for Heap O' Bears was kept up all year,
at sunrise and at sunset of each day, till the next
spring, 1870. When Indians are mourning they go
out some distance from the tepee and stand with faces
toward the sun as it rises or sets and howl most
pitifully.

At this time Napawat, with a large band of Kiowas,
was camped near the borders of the Cheyenne reservation, and just across the line the Cheyennes had
scalped a white woman, and were holding a wild scalp
dance, while Andele, with other Kiowas, was still

mourning for Heap O' Bears. One morning, about
three o'clock, the whole surroundings rang out with
the crack of rifles in rapid succession. The soldiers
from Ft. Reno had stealthily surrounded the Cheyennes
for the purpose of capturing them, but when they saw
that they were holding a scalp dance around the scalp
of the white woman, it so enraged them that at once
they began killing them. Andres, with Afpoodlete,
rushed out and caught the horses hobbled out on the
prairie, the squaws packed up and they started down
the Washita River as rapidly as possible. Andele and
Afpoodlete were ordered to go with the squaws, but as
soon as they had started them well on the way, they
slipped back and went with the band to the scene of
conflict.

When day dawned the soldiers had disappeared,
but the battle field, or rather the slaughter pen, was a
scene of horror, that gave Andele no good opinion of
the white man or his God. Here were Cheyenne men,
women and children, slaughtered and lying promis-
cuously in the snow stained with their own life blood.
A woman with her lips burned off, stiff and cold, was
propped up against a tree, a horrible, grinning spectacle. Men and women perfectly nude were placed in
such positions as would not be proper to describe here.

This was done by the civilized soldiers of a Christian land, to mock the barbarous savages of heathen tribes. Which is worse, — the civilized (?) soldier, or the brutal savage?

This sight enraged the Indians and a yell of revenge went up from them as they looked on. The Kiowas and Comanches from every quarter began to gather to aid their friends, the Cheyennes. They were preparing for the attack next day, but the soldiers, who were in camp a few miles away, hearing of the proposed attack of the allied tribes, took up the line of march back to Ft. Reno. The Indians followed, however, and in the attack cut off a considerable troop of soldiers from their command and killed them nearly all.

Andres, being yet but a boy, was compelled to go back with the squaws to a place of safety down the Washita. As they went, an old squaw discovered near the trail they were traveling a little hollow stone image with both legs and one arm broken off. She snatched up the image, called the hurrying crowd to a halt, held the image out in her extended hand, and began praying, "O good image, O grandfather, give us long life. Never let us grow old. Give immunity in war and success in battle. Make our enemies blind

that we may kill them. Give us long life, give us
long life, and in it all, youthful strength and beauty.''

She then passed the image to the next one in the
circle, for by this time a large circle had been formed,
with instruction to pray as she had done, especially
for long-continued youth and beauty. Each one
prayed thus as they worshiped the image till it came
Andele's turn. While he believed in Indian superstitions with all his heart, yet as he gazed at that broken
image he could see no possible good to come by worshiping it, so, in the spirit of humor and ridicule, he
took the image in his hand, extended his arm and
began, "O good medicine, O grandfather, I pray to
you, I never want to be older and uglier than I am
now. I want to be always young and beautiful and
never old and ugly like the old squaw that started
this worship.''

He did not get any further with his prayer, for the
old squaw in her wrath and the crowd in their merriment broke up the worship in much confusion, and
soon all were again on their way.

The soldiers were driven into the fort, but in a few
days they started with reinforcements again in pursuit
of the marauding Indians. They came upon a band
of warriors near the Washita and after a sharp engage-

ment, they captured Lone Wolf, Big Tree and Tsain-
tanta. Under a flag of truce they called a council
with the Indians at which they told them if they
would bring in all the warrior chiefs with those on
the warpath, that the three captured chiefs would be
released, but if not, they would be shot. This was a
bitter pill for the Indians to swallow, but there was
no alternative, and they were compelled to submit.
At this council, therefore, peace was made and the
chiefs released.

CHAPTER XII.

SCALPING THE UTES. A GRIM JOKE.

It was now fully spring and Napawat sent an old man out to announce that he was going to start out on a certain day to avenge upon the Utes the death of Heap O' Bears, and that all who wished to go under his leadership must be ready by that time.

The dance was held, the band gathered around the rawhide, worshiped in the usual way, and at the appointed time, started westward in search of the Utes. They reached the Ute country about forty miles north of where Heap O'Bears was killed. Napawat had ridden apart from his band some little distance, watching carefully as he went, when suddenly he spied a Ute watching a deer. He raised his bow and with unerring aim sent the arrow through the heart of the unsuspecting Ute. As he fell lifeless another Ute, before unseen, sprang up from the weeds close by and was in the act of shooting when Napawat thrust him with a spear as he ran upon him, and he also fell.

By this time Napawat's band of warriors came up, but too late to aid in the killing. Napawat scalped both the Utes, but the second one was not killed, but was left wounded and scalped to suffer and slowly die.

Napawat was now satisfied. He ceased mourning and felt jubilant. He started with his band for home at once. Big Bow was somewhere not far away with his band, for they had separated the day before, to come in on the Utes in different directions, but Napawat did not take time to hunt him up and notify him that Heap O' Bears' death had been avenged. He reached home in triumph and the scalp dance began at once. The dance had been going on nearly a day, when Big Bow came in with a Ute war bonnet, quiver and bow, which he had obtained in the following manner: When Napawat killed the first Ute, the Ute's horse, standing near, got away and ran off. Not long after Napawat had scalped the Utes, and with his band of warriors had started in triumph for home, Big Bow, ignorant of Napawat's whereabouts or doings, arrived with another band at or near the same place, captured the Ute's runaway horse, and was moving along slowly and cautiously, when he came upon a Mexican.

"Show me to the Utes, and I will spare your life, and give you this horse," as he pointed to the captured animal.

"Bueno," said the Mexican, as he mounted the

horse.   Leading the band of Kiowas along, he pointed
out the wigwan of the Ute who had been scalped, but
was still alive.

"Umph!" said Big Bow in satisfaction as he pushed
on in the direction of the tepee, while the Mexican,
taking advantage of this movement, disappeared down
a bluff on the new horse he had so easily obtained.
But that horse was destined to give him trouble as we
shall soon see.

The Ute who had been scalped was carried as
soon as discovered to his tepee.   He was a chief,
and when his friends saw the Kiowas under Big
Bow approaching, they put on him his war bonnet,
put a bow and arrows in his hands, and propped
him up in a dignified posture, that he might deceive
his enemies, and die like a chief, and then, to save
themselves, left him, and disappeared down the steep
bluff close by.   When Big Bow come up, seeing him
with war bonnet on and bow and arrows in hand, he
supposed he was ready for fight, but quickly found
him an easy prey.   He stabbed him two or three times,
jerked off his war bonnet to scalp him when, to the
consternation of his superstitious soul, the scalp was
gone!   He rushed back, mounted his horse, called to
his band, and started in full sweep for home, the

thought all the time arising, "where is that Ute's scalp?" He had killed the man, he knew that. He saw him die, but the scalp—unless he could carry back the scalp to grace his triumph and make merry over, what good was it to kill a man? "Where was that scalp, anyhow?" he continued to enquire as he hastened onward.

He reached home just in the midst of Napawat's scalp dance, and after some hesitation told of his venture—how he had killed a Ute, but when he jerked off his war bonnet, and went to scalp him, the man's scalp was gone.

Napawat raised a yell of fiendish merriment that astonished the crowd. He then related how he had scalped the Ute while he was still alive and that he was now dancing around the scalp of the man that Big Bow had so courageously (?) killed. Big Bow, downcast and ashamed, left the dance. Napawat danced on, while he indulged in grim jokes about the man alive with no scalp, and about the brave (?) chief who killed him.

Napawat became a great chief. He took the idol that had been kept by Heap O' Bears for his own. But before he could be secure in its protection, he must undergo the torture, which was as follows: He went

to the mountain, into some lonely place where no one
would disturb him, painted himself white, put on a
buffalo robe with the hair side out, took a pipe, and
mixing together tobacco and certain medicine leaves,
began smoking and praying to the sun, and making
offering to the sun of his own blood as he cut himself
in nearly every spot.   He neither ate nor drank for
four days and in the feverish condition induced by this
torture he dropped off to sleep and dreamed.

Before sleeping he smoked to the sun and prayed
that he might understand whatever revelation the sun
might give him through the dream, whether he was
to be a war chief or a medicine chief and what was to
be his life mission.   The vision of successful war and
bloodshed and plunder came before his feverish brain,
and when he awoke he stepped forth with proud and
elastic tread in spite of his emaciated condition, strong
in the conviction that a great war chief was he.

The Mexican to whom Big Bow gave the Ute's
horse, not long after was riding the horse along the
streets of Trinidad.   The news of the killing of the
Ute chief had already reached Trinidad where he was
well known, but it was not understood that he was
killed in war with the Kiowas.   Bands of Utes often
visited Trinidad, and had made friends with many of

the Mexicans and mixed breeds and whites who lived there. That was their trading post at that time.

A band of them were standing near the entrance of a grocery store when they saw the Mexican riding by, and they at once recognized their chief's horse. Had they found him out on the prairie they would have killed him at once, but as it was, they could only make known the matter to their friends in Trinidad. As soon as it was known, the Mexican was promptly arrested and placed in jail. He lingered there a long while and when placed on trial the circumstantial evidence against him was overwhelming, but through some technicality in the law he was finally released.

CHAPTER XIII.

Foot Fight. The Indian Worship. The Sweat
Booth. Buffalo Medicine Song.

The Indians during these years wandered from
Kansas to Texas, and westward and southwestward
to the Rocky Mountains and Mexico, plundering
wherever they went, the numerous tribes as often in
war with one another as with the hated whites. They
never stopped more than ten days in one place, their
wanderings depending much upon the movements of
the buffalo, upon which they chiefly subsisted. Sometimes in their wanderings, the different bands would
get separated, and for more than a year never see each
other, but when they got together again, there was
general rejoicing and the occasion was usually cele-
brated by a foot fight.

This is a pugilistic exercise, only the feet are used
instead of the boxing glove. The two sides, consisting of from one to a half dozen on a side, stand apart
a dozen or more paces, and at the signal given, run
toward each other, and, just before meeting, whirl,
jump as high as they can, and kick backward with

full force.   Often one antagonist plants his moccasined foot right into the chest or abdomen of the other and kicks him senseless for awhile.   It is often as dangerous and brutal as a pugilistic encounter between Corbett and Sullivan.

Andele became completely Indianized.   He took up his time in studying the Indian ways, for he had now come to believe all their superstitions, and engage in their worships.   He had caught the spirit of their aspirations, and he hoped to be a great war chief.   He thought the Indian idol, or "medicine," would pity him and help him, and so he cried to it, and often at night he would get up, go to the medicine man, worship, and offer a blanket or bit of property he possessed.

At the medicine man's tepee the idol is tied to a pole which is leaned against the back of the tepee, and over this pole is a rope of buffalo hair, tied near the idol and drawn entirely around the tepee.   When a worshiper comes to make an offering, he stands outside crying thus, "*Kon e-ko-on-ta*, Grandfather, help me.   I want to kill my enemies.   I want to be a great chief.   Let me live long, and when I die, let me die the death of a brave man in war."

After he has kept this up for some time, the wife of the medicine man comes out, loosens the rope and lets the idol down. It is enclosed in a crescent-shaped buffalo-skin sack. She takes it and places it on a tripod a few feet just back of the tepee, and then the worshiper goes to it and prays to it directly, after which he ties to the stand or tripod upon which the idol is placed a blanket or other article which he gives as an offering. That offering remains there till next day, when the woman takes it into the tepee and places it beside the "medicine," and after a few days it is put to the use intended. If the offering is a pony, a stick about six inches long is tied to the crescent-shaped sack containing the idol, while the pony is hitched somewhere near by. The medicine man himself goes to the pony, cuts a lock of hair from his head and tail, prays to the sun for a blessing upon the worshiper, and then buries the hair. That pony is a sacred offering, and must never be struck over the head.

Often Andele engaged in this worship as above described, and sometimes in the early morning, after a night of anxiety, he would go and gather poles and build a sweat house, that he might worship in that way. He had heard the medicine chief say, "You have to feed the idol if you get any benefit from him." And so seeking the greatest benefit, he was ready to make any sacrifice.

On one occasion he promised the sun-god to make a sweat house in his honor and worship in his name. He put a squaw to cleaning off a spot, while he himself went to a willow thicket and brought the necessary material for the medicine booth. After the preparations were all made, he went to the tepee of the chief medicine man. After the usual ceremonies he entered, circled around to the left, as is their custom, till he came to the idol, which he untied, and, retracing his steps, walked back to his newly constructed sweat house. He was soon followed by the medicine man himself, who, before entering, looked up to the sun and prayed, then called out, "All who wish to worship here now, come, come, come."

This soon brought together all those who wished to worship at this time. They assembled near the door of the sweat house and stripped themselves entirely nude before entering. Upon entering they all circled to the left, the medicine chief taking his place in the west side facing the east, with the idol lying just in front of him. The long-stemmed pipe, well filled with a mixture of ground sumac leaves and tobacco, which, according to custom, had been placed near the idol, was taken up by the medicine man prepatory to smoking, while Andele stepped out upon the prairie for a piece of dried horse ordure, which he lighted and then took it in a split stick and held it to the bowl of the pipe, while the medicine man proceeded to smoke and mutter some petition to the sun as he puffed the smoke upward. Andele put the split stick down near the fire in the center of the tepee till the smoking was ended.

Just outside, at the entrance of the tepee, was placed a buffalo head with the nose toward the entrance, and a few feet further away was a little moon-shaped furnace with a fire in it. In this worship, after the smoking is over, the split stick is taken and placed upon the summit of this moon-shaped furnace. The rocks are placed in this furnace to heat. The medicine man takes a little tobacco and prays to the sun, to the moon, to the earth, and to the idol before him in the tepee. Four times he goes through this form of smoking and praying to the heavenly bodies and to the earth and to the idol. While he offers the smoke to these idols and motions towards the four cardinal points of the compass, he also prays to his grandfather: "O, Grandfather, give me power over my enemies; make them blind that I may kill them; help me to steal good horses. Give me health and long life."

After the medicine man is through he passes

the pipe to the one at his left, who worships and smokes as the chief before him had done, and he in turn passes it to the next worshiper at his left, and so on till the extreme left is reached. The pipe is then passed back around the semi-circle to the extreme right, when the smoking and worship begins again and passes on as before to the left.

The smoking both in worship and in social life is done in this way. A semi-circle of three to ten or even twenty is formed. One of the number lights a pipe, or often a cigarette made of leaves, smokes a few whiffs, passes it to the man at his left, who likewise smokes, and passes it to the left, and on till it reaches the last one on the extreme left, when it is then handed back to the right, and it passes on as before, each one smoking a few whiffs and passing it to his left. It would be a serious breach of etiquette to pass it to the right instead of the left.

It is seldom an Indian ever smokes alone, but he shares the same cigarette or pipe with others. Often there may be only two of them sitting together smoking, but the same rule is observed whether there be two or a dozen.

In the worship, after the smoking is over, the medicine man orders the hot rocks to be brought.

The one who makes the sweat house and calls for the worship must go for the rocks. He places them at the door of the tepee, when the medicine man goes through the four-fold mode of receiving them. He worships, then motions as though he would receive them, but does this the fourth time, when he takes them and places them in the center of the sweat house in the little hole prepared for them. Then he receives the water in the same way. He begins to tap upon the bucket with a small switch, and, after motioning to do so four times, he pours the water upon the hot rocks, praying each time as he motions. The steam arising from the hot rocks and water causes the perspiration to pour forth from every pore in great profusion, while the worshipers strike themselves over shoulder and upon back and sides with buffalo tails and grass. They sing some and call upon their dead ancestors, "O, Grandfather, give me success in war, that I may get many scalps and much plunder and never be hurt myself."

If, while they worship, it gets too hot, they go through the four-fold form of worship before raising the tepee to let the cool air in. After the worship is ended they all pass out, filing to the left. If in this worship they hear the voice of a woman or a child, it is a good omen, but they dare not look at themselves in any sort of mirror, nor come near a jack-rabbit, or bear, or other wild animal.

Andele got accustomed to this form of worship. He became an expert and at last ventured one day to try to cure a wounded man whom a Texas Ranger had shot. He gathered with the crowd of medicine men around the man and began to sing the buffalo song. This song is sung only over men who have been wounded. It would be a sacrilege to sing it for mere amusement, or on other occasions than bloodshed. They shook buffalo tails over the man as they sang, and finally one of them cried out, "I feel like my gods are all over me." He slapped his sides, and shook himself, and roared in mimicry of the buffalo bull, and began to spit red paint that he had in his mouth into his hands and rub it upon Andele's face, and say to him, "There, I give you that to make you a great medicine chief." And Andele verily thought that this would endow him with greater power.

When he had, therefore, according to custom for medicine men, tied a lock of buffalo hair to his own scalp lock on top of his head, the man who gave him the paint said, "Go now and dream, and when you have dreamed, return and let me know, and that shall indicate more fully your future strength and power.''

Andele at once went away alone. His purpose was to get all that there was to be had from the idols. He had deep faith in the unseen, the supernatural, and fully felt that there was power above that could be transmitted to men, and *would* be in answer to sacrifice and prayer. And if there was anything that he could do to get this power he felt that he must do it.

Receiving instructions as to how to paint his body, he went to his hiding place in the mountains to dream. In the earnest, excited, almost fevered condition of mind he could not but dream, and so the dream god soon revealed to him that he must secure from the medicine man who gave him the paint a certain shield in which there was great virtue. So going to the tepee of the man, he took down the shield and carried it and placed it on the top of a sweat house he had previously prepared, but carried the idol to the inside.

Sankadotie, seing the purpose of Andres to get the shield, tried to dissuade him.

''Why,'' said Andres, ''do you not want me to get the shield when there is so much power in it?''

''Because,'' answered Sankadotie, ''if you get that shield it will prove a great burden to you.''

''In what way?'' asked Andele.

"Very many ways," said Sankadotie. "Let me show you, for instance; every time you cook you have to place on top of your tepee for the god of your shield a piece of the meat you are about to cook, and if you should forget to do so at first, then you are compelled to throw the whole of it away, for it becomes polluted meat and the anger of the shield's god will be against you, if you go on cooking it."

"But my purpose is to get power, that I may subdue my enemies and be successful in war, and I am willing to carry a burden if I can but secure that," said Andele, as he turned away, lest further persuasion should be used. He went on with his performance to get the shield.

"Here," said the medicine man, "are some crow feathers, deer hoofs and buffalo hair, tie that to your hair for a sure and powerful medicine."

Andele replied, "I will take this, but I want your shield with its powers transferred to me. What can I do to secure it?"

"Here," again answered the medicine man, "take this," and he handed him a long curled lock from a cow's tail painted green, "with this your powers will he increased. When you wish to paint, put this in your mouth and blow, and you will get the paint needed."

"But I want your shield," again Andele replied. He was so persistent that the medicine man seemed to be at a loss what to do, so he said, "You have not paid me enough yet."

Andele had already given him many things, but he was ready to make any sacrifice to get the shield, for he felt he must have it. He went away disappointed, but still planning how he could become the owner of the shield with its powers. Among the young, he often made a display of the powers already conferred upon him by the gift of the paint, crow feathers, and cow's tail. One night he dreamed that to get the shield he so much coveted, he would have to give a white horse, but he had none, and he was unable to get one, unless he went out on a marauding expedition and captured one.

CHAPTER XIV.

Marauding Expedition into Texas. Massacre on the Washita.

It was now the opening of 1871. Napawat while on a visit to the military post at Ft. Sill, took sick and lingered, in spite of (or on account of) the skill of the medicine men, till spring. He promised his idol that if he would make him well he would go on a marauding expedition into Texas.

In answer, as he thought, to this vow he was soon able to get out. He then took a considerable band of young warriors, went down to Greer County to hold a dance, and prepare for the warpath. Andele was quite young, but he determined to go.

"Andele," said Napawat, "you are too young for war."

"No, no," he answered, "I want to go, I know I can scalp the enemy. My medicine is strong."

"If you go," said Napawat, "you will go with me. Come, and while I do not like to take children to war, you may learn something for future conflicts. We will dance around the rawhide and get ready."

Next day after the dance, Napawat and Andele got horses and called together the band and started for Texas. Mokine, Kankea, and Quo-e-kon-kea, were also in this band, and well had they proven their skill in past conflicts in jerking scalps from the heads of dying victims. The band crossed Red River and went several days journey down into Texas, and finally reached a timbered country.

Alighting for a short rest, they hid their saddles away in the underbrush, and went on bareback for two days. About the middle of the afternoon they reached the summit of a hill from which they could survey the country for many miles around.

Two villas were in sight not many miles away. Napawat stood gazing intently toward one of them muttering something to himself, when he discovered Andele close at his side.

"Andele," said he, "you want to be a great chief, and you want to be successful in war and plunder, and now look yonder at the hated Texas man's houses. You shall have an opportunity soon of showing whether you be a man or squaw. If you be brave you shall have all my property at your command, but if you be a coward and play the squaw, you will have to go home and carry wood on your back, and water for the squaws. Very soon the sun will go down and the Texas man with his wife and children will be asleep and know not that the braves of the Kiowas are coming to take their scalps. You must not be afraid either to scalp the hated Texas man or steal his horse.''

The indignation rose in Andele as Napawat talked. To be called a squaw is about the greatest insult that can be offered an Indian, and Andele was indignant that Napawat should even intimate that there was even any probability of his being like one. He replied as the fire flashed from his eyes:

''I will never be a squaw. If you don't find me as ready in conflict as any in this band, then you can put me to carrying wood and water and nursing the papooses for the squaws, but I am sure to leave that job for some more woman-hearted warrior in your band.''

''Good,'' replied Napawat, as he looked at Andele's swelling form, for he seemed to grow larger as he made his boast. ''A trial of your courage will soon be made,'' and Napawat pointed again towards the villa at the foot of the hill.

The sun soon sank out of sight and left all in darkness and quiet, save the bustle of the people in the village below. It was cloudy but the moon came up, and, now and then through the rifted clouds shone full and bright. The band led by Napawat, with Andele close by his side, stole quietly and cautiously down the hillside and listening, waited patiently till every thing was still and all were asleep.

"Let us keep together," said Napawat, "and break in yonder"—but suddenly the violent barking of a huge dog awakened the inmates of the house to which Napawat pointed, and knowing from the violent conduct of the dog as he sprang forward to the full length of his chain, that there was something unusual, the Ranger grasped his gun and peering out at the window of his log house, discovered the Kiowas as they approached, and began firing so rapidly that the Indians concluded there were many men hidden away, who had possible learned of their presence, and were fully prepared for them. Without raising the warwhoop at all, Napawat called off his men, but as they passed around between some houses a pair of mule's ears were discovered by Andele sticking out from a stable door.

"If we are to be deprived of the expected conflict and it is to end thus," said Andele, "I will venture to take that mule as a fit trophy of this raid." Springing forward, he threw back the half broken door, cut the rope with which the mule was tied, led him out and just as he was clearing the entrance to the corral, the white man who had fired upon them, sallied forth with rifle, but for some unaccountable reason did not fire. Mokine called to Andele:

"Leave the mule and run, for the white men are gathering. Don't you hear the guns?" and gun answering to gun was heard in every direction. The white men, the Texas Rangers, who were so well organized in those days, were gathering from everywhere, and the Indians had lost their opportunity. It would be a narrow escape if they got away at all.

"I am no squaw," answered Andele, "I may not be able to get a scalp, but I will take back some fitting trophy of this shameful and cowardly retreat, to help you and the squaws carry wood and water, or I will lose my scalp in the attempt," and defying all the danger that surrounded him he pulled that mule along, till the mule, at first reluctant, became frightened at the approach of the Texas Ranger behind, and springing forward kept pace with the horse Andele now rode, for he had remounted. He soon overtook the retreating band of marauders, when he discovered that Kankea and Napawat each had secured a horse apiece.

"We must travel without rest till the sun comes up," said Napawat, "for the Texas man will be upon our trail with many men by the first light of the morning, and if we wait they will overtake us before we cross Red River back into our own country.''

All night long they pushed forward in a rapid gallop, for after leaving the immediate vicinity of the village they were on open prairie, with nothing to hinder their course. As the sun came up again they reached the skirt of the timber where they had hid their saddles several days before. They stopped for an hour's rest, when they saddled their horses and remounted. Early in the morning, after another night's travel, they reached the Brazos River at a very bad crossing, and turning up the river they concluded to recross where they had forded some days before. As they were rounding a bluff near the place of crossing, Kankea, who was at this time at the head of the band, suddenly whirled his horse around, threw his body down to one side of his saddle, and in the low gutteral tone of the Indian exclaimed, ''Soldiers!''

The whole band of Kiowas plunged into the river from the bluff and swam to the other bank, when the soldiers, who had mounted as rapidly as possible, dashed up. But seeing that the Indians had crossed, they hurried back to the regular ford and were soon in hot pursuit of them as they swept over the prairie toward the northwest. All the morning the pursuit was kept up, the Indians throwing back defiant signs as they hurried on.

About noon the soldiers halted; the Indians seeing this rode on a short distance and halted also, for their horses were well nigh exhausted. Had the soldiers known this, they could, by a rapid race, have overtaken them. They rested here for a while, keeping eyes on the soldiers, and then started on. During the night they crossed Red River and camped for a short while near the foot of Wichita Mountains. The next day, having pushed on towards the north, they had reached a place near a little creek north of the Wichita Mountains, when suddenly they were startled by the war-whoop coming from a band of warriors returning from the westward, who had captured a number of horses and taken several scalps.

The taunts and jeers of this band cast at Napawat for his failure to get scalps, raised Andele's indignation so that he did not, as he had intended, tell of their cowardly retreat from the Texas village. He knew that neither he nor any of the band would be allowed to dance or rejoice with the victorious warriors around the scalps that they had taken. He consoled himself, however, when he saw a number of the victors on foot, their horses being so jaded that they were unable to carry their owners. He knew that it was a sure sign that they, too, had been compelled to run before the hot pursuit of the hated Texas Ranger. So it was with a revived feeling of pride and condescension that they loaned the returning victors a number of good horses that they themselves had taken in Texas.

The victorious band hurried on from here and soon reached their camp, where they held their scalp dance. Napawat with his band turned his course eastward, toward the mouth of Chandler Creek, as they had learned that their squaws and children had in their absence moved the camp to that place.

In a few days many had gathered here, but the band of victorious Indians had gone on towards Anadarko and camped near the agency, where, fresh from their marauding expedition, and flushed with success, they were very insolent and soon had brought on a state of affairs that presaged a massacre. Those near the mouth of Chandler Creek had been notified by the military at Ft. Sill to come in and surrender their warriors, and while they were consulting what to do, there came news that an outbreak had been already made near Anadarko and a number killed. At once the whole camp broke up and started to join their people in the conflict.

Reaching the Washita they crossed the river a few miles below the agency and going up the river they found the agency deserted. Big Bow led his band to the store of the Indian trader, broke it open and plundered it of such things as he liked. He secured a considerable amount of money in greenbacks, from the smallest shinplasters to the larger denominations, and not knowing the value of it made cigarette paper of it for smoking the mixture of sumac and tobacco.

While this was going on, Andele was active in his efforts to so learn the arts of Indian warfare that he might become a great chief. He had been now in so many exciting scenes that he cared no longer for the shield of the medicine man, and ceased his efforts to secure it. When this outbreak at Anadarko (1872) took place, the various military posts were notified, and soon troops from Ft. Sill, Ft. Reno and Ft. Elliott started for the conflict, for it was apprehended that the outbreak would be general and would take many men and much time to subdue it. The Indians finding that the United States troops were gathering from Ft. Sill and the other posts became alarmed and started westward for the Rocky Mountains.

CHAPTER XV.

TAHAN, THE CAPTIVE TEXAN.

Once when a band of Kiowas were on a marauding expedition down in Texas, they plundered a frontier home, and murdered all the family except a boy of about five years of age. Him they carried captive away, to be given (for adoption) to a squaw who had lost her only son. The Indians not knowing nor caring for his real name called him Tahan (meaning Texas man), for the reason that he was captured in Texas.

All Indians are named from some circumstance connected with them, and this is why there are so many singular names among them. "*Stumbling Bear*" looks like a great awkward bear reared back on his haunches, hence his name. A boy was born about the time the Indians had ceased mourning in a certain camp, hence was called, *Kea-kee*, or "Quit Mourning." Another was born at a time when the mother was far away from home, hence he was called, "Born a long ways from home." If Tahan was old enough when captured to know his name, he was too young to give it correctly to the Indians, and hence he at once accepted the name given by them.

At the time of this outbreak near Anadarko, Tahan was about eighteen years old, and was as complete an Indian in habits, customs, and superstitions, as the most extreme Indian, and was as bitter and cruel in purpose of bloodshed and plunder. When the Indians started westward, and had, after a day's travel, reached a point several miles north of the Washita River, they pitched camp, hoping to rest several days before they went on. Tahan seeing what was before them, and remembering that he had left his best horse at their former camp, and that he would need him, started after him. It was about ten miles to the south, but he could go there and get back in time to go on with the band westward.

He had, on some raid, secured a good rifle, and when he reached the crossing on the Washita, on the Ft. Reno and Ft. Elliot trail, he discovered a deer. He shot and wounded it badly, but did not kill it. He sprang from his horse, hitching him hastily with the larriat to a bush, and leaving his gun hanging to the saddle, he ran after the wounded deer, which had fallen some little distance away. He butchered the deer, and returned to get his horse, but just as he took hold of the larriat, a troop of soldiers rode up from the steep banks of the river and took him prisoner. It was a squadron of cavalry going as couriers with papers from Ft. Elliott to the commanding officer at Ft. Reno. They hurried Tahan on before them, not knowing at first that he was a full blood white.

An Indian scout who had been watching the trail saw that Tahan was captured and soon communicated the news to the Kiowas. At once Napawat called the whole band of warriors to mount, and away they went in hot pursuit. In the course of a few hours they came in sight of the squad of soldiers, but just as the soldiers were meeting a large troop coming with a train of wagons from the direction of Ft. Reno.

Napawat, seeing there were too many now to attack openly, decided to try strategy. He turned and went with his warriors back towards the crossing on the Washita, near which was a deep canon through which the soldiers must pass in traveling towards Ft. Elliot. It was decided that they would conceal themselves there at the summit, and when the pale-faced soldiers were in the cut, they would attack them. Napawat and the band got to the place decided upon, dismounted, stripped themselves, and painted themselves in such a way that they were a hideous sight to behold.

They had not long to wait, for soon they beheld the head of the column coming cautiously along. As they lay in ambush, they watched anxiously for Tahan, for the only purpose they had in view was to recapture him. He was veritably an Indian. He knew not the white man's language. He loved the Indians, and they loved him. Tahan they must have, and Tahan was just as anxious to get back to them.

They soon discovered him in charge of two soldiers, one on each side. Becoming over eager, the warwhoop was raised too soon, for the soldiers had not yet reached the most disadvantageous ground, and when they heard the war-whoop, and saw the hideously painted Kiowas coming, in quick movement they whirled their wagons around into a kind of fortress, and were ready for the attack.

The Indians seeing the celerity with which this was done, and the accuracy with which the soldiers fired, were deterred, and hesitating awhile, fell back in some disorder. They soon rallied and came again, but were again repulsed. Again and again they charged upon the encampment, but the soldiers had now secured themselves by spade and shovel in throwing up breastworks. Night came on, and the fighting ceased till next day. During the night some of the Indians crawled up as close to the soldiers' encampment as they dared, and began to call, "Tahan, Tahan, ema, ema." (Tahan, Tahan, you come, you come). They continued to call him, "Run away from the soldiers and come on, your grandfather is waiting for you. He wants you to get him some buffalo meat. Come on." For three days the seige was kept up, each night the Indians calling for Tahan, who was kept under close guard by the soldiers.

Andele all this time was among the foremost in every charge, and several times he made narrow escapes. On the third night the Indians held a council and decided that if they did not accomplish something next day, they would withdraw, and go on their way westward. They had settled on plans for the next day's attack, and had all gotten quiet, when some one in subdued voice was heard calling:

"Where are you, grandfather, where are you? Are you all gone?"

"Listen," said Andele, "who is that? Somebody calls."

All listened with fear and superstitious anxiety; for while it sounded somewhat like the voice of Tahan, yet it seemed to be far away and weak. But again the voice came, clearer this time as it called out:

"My people, where are you?"

"Who is that?" called Napawat.

"I, Tahan. I come."

In a moment the whole camp was in commotion, running together and crying out, "Tahan! Tahan! he has come, he has come," and they threw their arms around him and rejoiced over him.

After sometime all was quiet again. Tahan was telling with much interest to his dusky friends how he had, by rolling out from under the blanket under which he was lying, slipped away and made his escape in the darkness, and he supposed the soldiers who were guarding him had not yet detected his absence. While thus engaged they discovered just there in the darkness, slipping stealthily along in their direction, the form of a warrior.

In a moment every man grasped his spear, for they thought it the approach of the enemy, and they were ready for the conflict. But they heard some one speak in the Kiowa tongue. Napawat called, "Who are you?"

"Umph," grunted back the voice. "Your friends have a hard time to find you, Napawat," for it was one of his own band who was left several days before at the river crossing to watch that, and who had come to warn him of danger.

"You need to be quick. If you have accomplished nothing here, it is too late now, for soldiers are coming from the way of the setting sun in great numbers. The whole earth is covered with them, and they are camped to-night not far from our squaws and papooses, and are headed right towards their camp, and to-morrow our squaws and papooses will all be murdered, as were the Cheyennes not far from here not long ago, unless something is done quick."

Napawat listened until this speech was through, then called out to his men to mount, saying, "If we be men, let us put ourselves between the squaws and papooses and danger. Let us die like brave men should die, rather than see our children murdered and our women outraged as were the Cheyennes." Every man in the whole band gave the grunt of approval, and soon all were on the march.

The soldiers knew not that the seige was raised till next morning. They ventured out cautiously and soon found that the Kiowas had all disappeared. Where, they knew not. Could they have known, there would have been no need of caution as they broke camp and continued their march. As it was, they marched slowly and with every precaution, lest the Indians should undertake another ambush attack.

When Napawat reached the camp of the women and children in the early morning, he found that the soldiers coming from Ft. Elliot had camped not far away, and that now what was done would have to be done quickly. While he was considering the matter, news of another troop of soldiers from towards Ft. Sill reached him.

He began to call the band of warriors to arms, but found that, through fear, many of them were slow to move, and others were advising against fighting, and cowardly hiding away. Napawat seeing this, called them squaws and upbraided them for their cowardice, but it had little effect. Fear had overcome the would-be braves. Napawat finally called out, saying,

"Seeing you are all so cowardly, and will not fight, I intend at once to go and give myself up to the soldiers, and get the best terms I can." And he turned at once and galloped away with a few followers towards army headquarters. After much difficulty and some risks, he finally reached Ft. Sill and gave himself up, promising to secure to the government all of those who continued on the warpath, if they did not surrender by a certain time.

But Tahan joined Za-ko-yea, who went on westward, making raids wherever he could find people to

murder, or plunder to steal.   It was difficult to catch
these marauding bands at that time, for there was such
a vast unoccupied territory over which to roam, and
plenty of wild game upon which to subsist.   But the
United States troops continued to wage war upon them
with the purpose of putting down every marauding
band.   Most of the Indian chiefs had come in and
surrendered, except Za-ko-yea, and he had committed
so many depradations that he was afraid to surrender,
lest he should be killed without mercy.   But he saw
that he would eventually be caught, and he began to
study what he should do.   If he could conceal his
identity and surrender, or if he could in some way
prevent proof of his bloodshed and plunder, or manage
to fasten it on others, he might be safe in surrendering.
He felt that so far as the testimony of the Indians
was concerned he was safe, for he was chief and they
dare not tell anything against him.   As he thought
thus he glanced at Tahan, who had been with him in
all his murder and plunder, and had aided him with a
ruthless hand.   He thought:

"Tahan is a white man.   If I go in and surrender
and Tahan with me, he will be induced to tell on me.
It is true he has shown himself in all our wars true to
the Indian, and he knows nothing of the white man's

talk and ways, but in his veins courses the white man's blood, and a like spirit that may soon spring up in friendship if he once becomes familiar with them.''

The thought of this disturbed him, and while he studied about it he decided that it would never do to let Tahan be taken by the white man. It would mean death to him. The bare thought of being betrayed by Tahan angered him, although there was not the least ground for suspicion, for Tahan hated white men as bad as any Indian, and had proven it by the many bloody deeds committed upon them.

But Za-ko-yea was in desperate mental surmisings, and the bare imagination of Tahan's betrayal haunted him. This desperate state grew more severe, till in a fit of frenzy, he whirled around and with a trembling but desperate hand drew his bow and sent an arrow whizzing through the heart of Tahan. Tahan looked with a wondering, despairing look, and without an utterance fell backwards, *dead*.

Za-ko-yea looked upon him for awhile as he lay there upon the prairie sand, and then turned away with that last look of Tahan forever riveted upon his mind. He was left lying there to be fed upon by the wolf and the vulture; but Za-ko-yea, savage as he was, carried the vision of his dying face upon his guilty conscience to the end of his days.   He would have given the world, doubtless, could he call back the deed.

This story of Tahan's end is left in some doubt, for some of the Indians say, and Za-ko-yea himself so claims, that after the fight with the soldiers near Llano, in their retreat across the prairie, in an almost barren region, Tahan was overcome with heat and thirst, could get no water, and that he fell by the way and died.

ZA-KO-YEA'S SON AND GRANDSON.

CHAPTER XVI.

INDIAN CENSUS TAKEN BY CAPT. R. H. PRATT.

Not long after Napawat surrendered, and was encamped with his band near Ft. Sill, Capt. R. H. Pratt was ordered by the government to take a census of the Indians. Day after day he went out to Napawat's camp to enroll the names of the Indians upon the census book. As each name was called, the Indian had to appear for himself, and answer such questions through the interpreter as were asked him. Finally, Andele was called, and as soon as Capt. Pratt saw him, he, with the other soldiers, gathered around him, for they saw that he was a captive Mexican. Andele became alarmed, and also very much angered, when they came around him and began to scrutinize him so closely. They were talking very earnestly about him, but he could not understand a word they were saying, and if there were any Indians present who did understand, they did not care for Andele to know, but they rather added to his aversion to the white man by telling him such things as would alarm his fears. As soon as they quit noticing him and left him alone, he drew up over his head and close around his face his buffalo robe so that he might not be seen so easily, and afterwards kept as much as possible out of sight of the soldiers.

However, sometime after this, Agent Tatum, hearing of a young Mexican captive among the Kiowas, sent for him. Mr. Tatum had already recovered fourteen white and twelve Mexican captives from the Indians, and he hoped to be able to identify this one and return him to his people. Andele was brought into Mr. Tatum's office, all the while in much dread, as Napawat was going with him to the office. To his surprise, however, the white agent got up from his seat and with a smiling, kindly face met him as he went into the office and shook hands with him. He was surprised at this, and he could not understand it; for he could not understand a word that the agent was saying, but he could see the spirit of friendship in him, and his fears largely passed away. Agent Tatum tried to find out where he was captured, and about his people, but he could get no clue to his origin. The Kiowas could only tell that they bought him from the Apaches. Andele had some recollection of home and loved ones, but he dare not tell.

Mr. Tatum, hoping still to do something for

Andele, asked Napawat to let Andele go to school. Napawat objected. The agent then asked that Andele be allowed to remain in his office, but still Napawat objected. And so he went back to camp.

Tatum, however, continued his efforts to get Andele, when, one day, Napawat said, ''Now you and I are good friends and I don't like to refuse your request, and I will let Andele decide for himself. If he wishes to come and stay in your office, or go to school, I will agree to it; but I will let him decide it.''

Mr. Tatum told Napawat that was good, and directed him to get Andele and bring him to the office. Napawat put on the air of honesty in the matter, but before taking Andele to the office, he gave him full instructions how to answer the agent, and used both honeyed words and threats lest he should answer otherwise than he directed.

Of course, therefore, when Agent Tatum made his proposition to Andele it was answered by a flat and positive refusal. And that, according to agreement, settled the matter.

CHAPTER XVII.

Startling Incidents. Rescue of Captives.

Before passing on, it will be of interest to relate a series of events in this connection which took place from 1869 to 1873. Under President Grant's peace policy, Laurie Tatum, a Friend, was appointed agent for the Kiowas, Comanches and Apaches, and on July 1, 1869, undertook the duties of that office, with agency headquarters near Ft. Sill.

At that time there was one band of Comanches, the Quo-ja-les, who wandered westward towards the Rocky Mountains, living on buffalo and other wild game, and who refused to report at the agency at all. In frequent raids they stole horses from Texas, and traded them to illicit traders in New Mexico for arms and ammunition. They ridiculed the other Indians for submission to the white man, and, continuing their marauding expeditions, they formed a nucleus for other Indians who were warlike and restless under the white man's rule. They sent Agent Tatum word that they would never come to the agency and shake hands till the soldiers came out to fight them, and then, if they were whipped, they would come.

They thus set at defiance all authority till the fall of 1872, when General McKenzie, following them on one of their raids in Texas, surprised them and took one hundred of their women and children and carried them away prisoners. Soon after, the Quo-ja-les reported at the agency, acknowledged their defeat, expressed their readiness to submit, and asked that their women and children be returned to them.

"But," said Agent Tatum, "you must first bring all the white and Mexican captives you have in your band."

Perry-o-Cum, the Quo-ja-les chief, did not expect such a demand, and stood in stolid silence for some minutes, but seeing the determined look in Tatum's face, he gave instruction to his band to bring in the captives.

In a little while they brought in Adolph Kon and Clinton Smith, two Texas boys, and two others who had forgotten their names and every word of English. They remembered some of the incidents of their capture, and taking these as a clue, Agent Tatum advertised in the Texas and Kansas papers, and at last found their parents. Their names proved to be Tem-

ple Friend and Valentine Maxie. Twelve captive
Mexicans were also thus rescued, and one case, that
of little Presleano, was of special interest.

There was the air of superiority about him. He was
bright, talkative, quick to apprehend, and sprightly
in movement. He seemed to have been a pet in the
home and heart of old Perry-o-Cum, the chief, and the
boy loved the chief. Perry-o-Cum knew that, and felt
sure that if it was left to the choice of the boy he
would not be forced to give him up. So Perry-o-Cum
spoke up thus:

"Agent Tatum, I am willing to give up all these
other prisoners. It is right that I should, and you
have a right to demand it, for they belong to your
nation. But this boy is a Mexican, captured in
Mexico, and he does not belong to your government,
and you have no special right to him. I love him as
my own son, and he loves me. I can not part from
him, and I know he wants to remain with me. If
you will not force him away, but leave it to his own
choice, I shall be satisfied.'

Tatum watched the intense anxiety of Perry-o-Cum
as he spoke, and waited a little while before he
replied. At last he said:

" Perry-o-Cum, what you say is good as to giving

the boy his choice, and if you will let him remain here till the afternoon, we will find out what is his choice." This was readily agreed to, and the chief went away, leaving the boy in the agent's office.

The agent had a good dinner prepared, of which the boy partook with much relish; and while he was feeling particularly comfortable from the surroundings, and the kindness shown him, the chief was summoned to the office again. A Mexican interpreter had been secured, and after petting the boy awhile, Tatum began talking to him about his father and mother, not knowing that they were dead, and that the little boy had no memory of any father and mother, save old Perry-o-Cum and his wife. So when he put the question, "Do you wish to remain with Perry-o-Cum, or do you want to go back to your own people," to the delight of Perry-o-Cum, he said he wanted to remain with him.

"But don't you want to see your brothers and sisters? Don't you want to go to them?"

The little boy dropped his eyes in thoughtfulness a moment. The memories of home began to dawn upon him, and when he looked up again, he said, slowly and with a serious look upon his face, "I want to go home."

"Then I will send you," said Agent Tatum, and

as he looked across the room at Perry-o-Cum, he saw the tears chasing each other down his otherwise stolid cheeks, but he was caught in his own proposition and he felt he must submit. The boy was returned to his people in Mexico, through General Auger, commander of the military post at San Antonio.

On July 10, 1870, a band of Kiowas went to the home of Gottlieb Koozer, in Texas. Mr. Koozer was not aware of the Indians' approach till he saw them in the yard, and being defenseless, he decided it was best to show a friendly spirit toward them, so he went out to meet them, and offered his hand in friendship. Two of them took hold of his hands at the same time in apparent friendship, while an other, stepping a little to one side, shot him through the heart. They scalped him, and then went into the house, destroyed what they found therein: dresses, feather beds and many other things. They took Mrs. Koozer and her five children — one a young lady, one small girl, and three boys — and also a young man by the name of Martin B. Kilgore, who was about fourteen years of age, and started back to their reservation.

As soon as news of this outrage was received at Ft. Sill, Agent Tatum determined to rescue the prisoners, and find out and punish, if possible, the depredators. He announced to the Indians what he had heard, and declared that he would never issue any more government supplies to them till they brought the prisoners in. They demanded a ransom, for, two years before, they had been paid $1,500.00 each for some captives. He sent a letter to Mrs. Koozer by the hands of a trusty Indian, on the 7th of August, 1870. On the 18th of August the Indians, giving up any idea of fighting, went to the agency with their wives and children.

Whenever Indians are not expecting a fight, they take with them their wives and children everywhere they go, but when war is expected, they send them all away together in care of the old men. When, therefore, women and children are in sight there is assurance of peace.

They had two of the Koozer family, Miss Koozer and her little sister, with them. The little one, who had not seen her mother for several days, began crying, but was forced to hush. Indians do not allow their captives to cry. The soldiers became indignant, and stepped forward to take the captives; but in an instant the Indians pointed a dagger at the heart of the girls. The soldiers did not proceed further, for it meant sure and instant death to the girls. The Indians

took them away, but seeing they could not change
Agent Tatum from his purpose to withhold all government supplies till the prisoners were delivered, by 11
o'clock the two girls and two boys were brought in
and delivered to him. A Mexican Kiowa had the
mother, and he was stubborn and insisted upon a
ransom—"a mule and a carbine."

Having delivered the above four, the Indians called
for the supplies, but were informed that all of the
prisoners must be brought in first. Very soon Mrs.
Koozer and the other boy were brought in; but they
had left young Kilgore at their camp out many miles
upon the reservation. Agent Tatum then paid the
Indians $100.00 apiece for the captives, lest in the
future they should kill all they found on their marauding expeditions instead of taking them captive. He
then issued them the usual government supplies, with
the understanding that he would issue no more till
M. B. Kilgore was delivered to him.

The Koozer family were a pitiable sight. Nobody
can describe what Mrs. Koozer and her daughter suffered, till they found some protection and relief from
an Indian woman who seemed to have more than the
usual influence of a woman among the Indians. Mrs.
Koozer was appropriated by a Mexican Kiowa as his

wife, and he was very cruel to her, trying twice to kill her, but she was each time protected by the chiefs.

Three days later Colonel Grierson sent a detachment of soldiers to conduct Mrs. Koozer and her children to Montague, Texas, from which place she reached her home in safety. After the awful scenes of the past month and a half, what a home!

These were the last captives for whom any ransom was ever paid. Soon after this, another trial was made to extort a ransom for prisoners that utterly failed. It was about the time of the arrest of old Satanta and others. Old White Horse and six other Kiowa men and one woman went to Texas, murdered Mr. Lee and his wife and took captive their three children, Susan, aged sixteen; Millie, aged nine, and John, aged six. As soon as it was known at Ft. Sill, Agent Tatum suspended all government issues to the Indians till the captives should be brought in.

This was delayed by a proposed council, in which delegates from the civilized tribes were to be present. These civilized tribes hoped by their delegates to persuade the wild tribes to quit raiding and be peaceable. The council was set for July 22, 1872, at old Ft. Cobb, but the Kiowas did not go there till ten days after.

White Horse was stubborn, and declared that he

did not want peace, but said that he and his young men would raid when and where they pleased. Lone Wolf said they would return prisoners in their posession when Satanta and Big Tree were returned from the penitentiary, all the military posts removed from the reservation, and their reservation extended from the Rio Grande to the Missouri River.

The delegates of the civilized tribes and Kicking Bird tried to pacify White Horse and Lone Wolf and other warlike Indians, but they could do but little. Agent Tatum adhered to his purpose to issue no more rations till the Lee children were brought in, and about a month later they delivered the two girls to Agent Richards at the Wichita Agency, and they were sent under care of "Caddo George," a trusty Caddo, to Agent Tatum at Ft. Sill. The boy was brought in two weeks later, and on the same day an older brother arrived from Texas and took them home.

These were the last captives the Kiowas ever took. It had become unprofitable and exceedingly dangerous, for, as Texas became more thickly settled, the people determined to put a stop to Indian raids, and they were ready to exterminate the warlike tribes, if necessary, to accomplish that end. The government, too, was proceeding by legal process to punish those who were guilty.

Reference was made above to Satanta and Big Bow's imprisonment in the penitentiary. On May 23, 1871, General Sherman called at Agent Tatum's office, and inquired if Tatum knew of any Indian band having gone to Texas recently. He said a party of Indians, about one hundred and fifty in number, had attacked a wagon train of ten wagons, seventeen miles from Ft. Richardson, killing train-master and six teamsters. Five escaped. He gave orders for McKenzie, with all the available troops at Ft. Richardson, to follow them with thirty days' rations, but as yet he had heard nothing from the pursuit.

Tatum knew nothing, but said that he thought he could find out in a few days. Four days later the Indians came to the agency for rations, and Agent Tatum invited the chiefs into his office. He told them of the tragedy reported to him by General Sherman, and asked if they knew anything about it; that he relied upon them for the truth, and was sure that they would tell him. Satanta, after a moment's silence, arose, and in the spirit of arrogance and fiendish hate, thus addressed the agent:

"Yes, I led that raid. I have been told that you have stolen a large amount of our annuity goods

and given them to the Texans. I have repeatedly
asked for arms and ammunition which have not been
furnished, and made other requests which have not
been granted. You do not listen to my talk. The
white people are preparing to build a railroad through
our country, which will not be permitted. Some
years ago we were taken by our locks and forcibly
pulled here close to Texas, where we have to fight the
Texas man. Some years ago, you remember, General
Custer ordered me arrested and placed in prison for
several days. The memory of that outrage rankles in
my soul till now, and will till the last white man goes
down and rots into the dust again. Understand this,
that no more Kiowas are ever to be arrested. On
account of these grievances, a short time ago, I took
about one hundred .of my young warriors, whom
I wished to train to fight, to Texas, with the chiefs,
Satank, Eagle Heart, Big Tree, Big Bow and Fast
Bear. We found a mule train which we captured.
We killed seven of the men, and three of my men
were killed, but I am willing to call it even, and
it is not necessary to say anything further about it,
except to say that we do not expect to do any more
raiding this summer, but I want you to understand
that I led that Texas raid, and if anyone else claims

the honor of it, he will be lying, for I am the man.''

He sat down, and Satank, Big Tree and Eagle Heart, who were present, confirmed the statement. As soon as Agent Tatum could get away, he left his office, hurried to the fort and requested Col. Grierson to arrest the six chiefs who had been participants in that raid.

Scarcely had the order been given, when Satanta took the fort interpreter and proceeded to Col. Grierson's office. He had heard that a big Washington chief (General Sherman) was there, and he wanted to see how he measured up with him. He was promptly arrested. Col. Grierson sent for Satank and Eagle Heart. Satank reached the office, and was also arrested, and Big Tree was found just outside, and while he was being arrested Eagle Heart took the alarm and fled. Kicking Bird, who had for a long time been friendly and peaceable, plead for the release of the prisoners; but here was the opportunity of impressing a great lesson upon the Indians, and they must learn it.

A few days after these arrests, Col. McKenzie arrived from Ft. Richardson. Heavy rains had obliterated the tracks of the raiders so they could not be followed, so he had pressed on to Ft. Sill, believing that the marauding band came from the Kiowa tribe.

The prisoners were placed in his charge, and in a few days he started with them to Texas for trial. Satank was so refractory that he was put into a wagon with two soldiers, and Satanta and Big Tree into another. They were all heavily manacled. George Washington, a Caddo Indian, rode on horseback along by the wagon. This was May 28, 1871.

"My friend," said Satank to George, "I wish to send by you a little message to my people. Tell them that I am dead, I died the first day out, and my bones will be lying on the roadside. I wish my people to gather them up and take them home."

Satanta also sent a message: "Tell my people to take forty-one mules that we stole from Texas to the agent, as he and Col. Grierson requires. Don't commit any more depradations around Ft. Sill or in Texas."

In a little while Satank began to sing his death song. He was still in sight of the post—scarcely a mile away. With his back to the guards, he slipped the shackles from his wrists by taking the skin with them. He seized a butcherknife that in some myste-ious way had been concealed upon his person, and started for the guards in the front part of the wagon. He struck at one of them, but missing his body made a slight wound in his leg. Both of the guards jumped from the wagon leaving their guns. Fortunately the guns were not loaded.

Satank seized one and began loading, declaring it would be sweet to die, if only he could kill one more "pale face." But, as he was pushing in the cartridge to its place, several shots from the other guards put an end to Satank's efforts. He fell from the wagon, and in about twenty minutes died in great agony, gritting his teeth in defiance to the end. By order of Col. Grierson his body was buried at Ft. Sill; but he gave the Indians the privilege of taking it up and burying it elsewhere if they chose; but they never moved it.

Satanta and Big Tree were taken on to Jacksboro, Texas, and tried for murder. Satanta was found guilty and sentenced to be hung, but his sentence was commuted to life imprisonment. He entered the Texas penitentiary, November 2, 1871. Upon recommendation of President Grant, Governor Davis, of Texas, let Satanta out, August 9, 1873, upon parole, conditioned upon good behavior. He violated his parole and was re-arrested by General Sheridan and sent back to the penitentiary, November 8, 1873. After five years of a reticent, stoical life in the penitentiary, he committed suicide, Oct. 11, 1878, by jumping out of the second story window of the prison hospital.

CHAPTER XVIII.

ANDELE IS DISGUSTED WITH INDIAN MEDICINE.

The events related in the last few chapters made a profound impression upon Andele, and had a tendency to change the whole current of his thoughts and purposes. Could he have understood the white man's tongue and known the effort that the agent had made to get him out of the clutches of the Indians and the Indian ways, his life for the next few years following would have been quite different. As it was, for sometime he kept as much as possible out of sight of the agent and the soldiers, lest he should be taken by force from the Indians and carried, he knew not where. The Indians had so impressed him that he feared the whites, and he thought it was safe to stay away from them.

These scenes of sickening carnage and defeat had knocked the "buffalo medicine" out of his purpose entirely, and he determined to follow more peaceful pursuits. He began to turn his attention more particularly to the course of Indian medicine for the sick, but he was doomed very soon to disappointment and

146

disgust in this also, for, in the early part of 1873, Napawat fell sick, and, in spite of all the superstitious performances of the medicine men, died. Onkoite, his brother, succeeded him and took up Napawat's "medicine."

By permission of the government, he made two big dances in their superstitious worship, but he also fell sick. Andele did all he could himself, but felt that he was too young in the cause to trust his own skill in exorcising the evil spirits of disease, or applying whatever real remedies that Indians had any knowledge of. Indians have some real remedies, but the difficulty with them is, that if they hit upon some remedy that is good in one disease, they conclude that it is good in all diseases, and apply it accordingly. The reason of this is, that they believe there is a spirit in the medicine, and if that spirit is friendly to them in one case, it will be in all cases. And this is also the reason they sing and worship and go through a wild, weird performance while applying any real medicine. Whether they apply a real remedy, or merely go through with a performance, they call it all "making medicine." Sometimes they "make medicine" to bring rain or bring about some other desired thing.

Andele was anxious to get Onkoite cured. So he

went for the best medicine men in the nation. He
first got To-no-kup, a tall eagle-eyed old Indian, who
was famed among his people as a physician.   There
are certain things that the medicine-man demands for
his services and that must be given in order to make
the medicine effective.   In addition to these things,
other things are to be given at the discretion of the
patient's family or friends.   In this case To-no-kup
demanded a horse and some eagle feathers.   Andele
promised these things in behalf of Onkoite, and then
also promised four other things of value.

After everything was complete, the medicine-man
approached the sick man's tepee, and after some incantations at the door, he entered.   He sat down, lit his
pipe, and smoked, offering the smoke as he puffed it
from his mouth in prayer to the sun.   He then began
to apply suction with his mouth to the throat and
chest of the patient and spitting out before all the
accumulations gathered in his mouth.

Finally, with much affectation, he spat out a small
fish with a vessel of water.   He declared that now the
patient would be all right, for the cause of his suffering was now taken out.   He took his pony, eagle
feathers, and other things and went away.

Onkoite continued to grow worse.   Andele went

for Pho-do-dle, who came, after assurance of ample remuneration, and going through the usual ceremony of smoking and worship to the sun, he applied suction to the throat, chest and abdomen of the sufferer, and finally spat out upon the floor of the tepee a small but living snake. He looked on with affected horror, then killed the snake and buried it near the center of the tepee. The case is surely cured now, so declared the medicine-man, and so thought Andele. Pho-do-dle took his fee and left.

But to Andele's surprise, Onkoite still grew worse, and next he went for Zon-ko, or Ee-e-pan, a man of much note, whose medicine was supposed to be good. Zon-ko came, demanding the same assurance from Andele of a good fee, and after a similar worship with the others he also applied suction in the name of his special god, to the man's throat and chest and abdomen, and at last spat out a small turtle.

"These other doctors," said Zon-ko, "were lying, and their medicine was no good, but Onkoite will now get well quick; for how could a man get well with such a creature as that in him?"

Andele was sure now that the disease was cured, and very soon Onkoite would get up, and he wished as he looked at Zon-ko, that he had his skill for healing the sick. He hoped to have some day. So he paid Zon-ko, and the old man marched away as really self-deluded as he had deluded others. While he knew he had put the young turtle into his mouth himself, yet he felt that he had fallen upon the very expedient that his god could use.

But Onkoite grew worse now very fast. Andele hurried out across the prairie to old Womte's tepee.

"Womte," said he, after he had smoked a little while, "you must come quick, Onkoite is about to die. I have had three doctors to see him, and I thought in each case he was cured, but since the last one left him he has grown worse very fast. Come quick, Womte, and I will give you whatever you ask. I want you to make your medicine strong."

"My medicine is good," said Womte, "and I will cure him; I'll come soon."

Andele left Womte and returned to Onkoite. He was failing fast. Womte came with usual ceremony and went through the form of worship, and as the others had done, he also applied suction, and at last, with a grunt of apparent satisfaction, but only to call notice, he spat out upon the ground a lizzard.

He killed the reptile and buried it in the center of the tepee, then declaring the medicine good, and the patient out of further danger, he arose, took his fee, and walked away. In a few minutes Onkoite fell back upon his buffalo robe and breathed no more. Womte heard the howling of the squaws and knew that his medicine was a fraud, but little did he care as long as his practice brought him ponies and eagle feathers and robes.

Andele looked on in blank astonishment, but said not a word. A complete revolution had taken place in just a few minutes in his convictions as to the Indian "Medicine Chiefs." He had forever lost confidence in them, and as soon as he met one of them he declared with spirit, "I have no confidence in your medicine; I'll never make another offering, nor pay another thing to one of you. I did want your shield and to learn your ways, but I want it no longer. Four of you waited on Onkoite, and you see he is dead. Each one of you declared he was cured, but you see he is *dead*. I have no more faith in my dreams nor in your medicine."

As he closed this speech he turned away. It would have been a dangerous speech that would have brought down the maledictions of the whole tribe had not Onkoite's case been fresh in their minds. As it was, the convictions of the crowd who were listening were with him. This event had much to do with preparing Andele for seeking a better way.

CHAPTER XIX.

ANDELE MARRIES — HAS TROUBLE.

There are three ways of obtaining a wife among the Indians. First, a young man often steals his wife. He will get his own sister to talk to the girl for him, and let her know his heart, and if she reciprocates, a clandestine meeting is arranged, and the two go off together, and sometimes can not be found for a long while. As soon as the parents of the girl find out who has their daughter, they go to the home of the young man's father and proceed to take everything they can find belonging to the family: robes, blankets, provisions, and even the tepee itself. This becomes a frolic enjoyed by every one, except the family being robbed. Nobody interferes or objects to the robbing, unless the daughter who has eloped was of doubtful character. In that case, no price is expected for her, and none is allowed. Stumbling Bear came to the writer's house once, deposited a lot of goods and left them a long time. One day when he was in, thinking he had forgotten about them, his attention was called to them, when he said in his good-humored way, "Me savey. Me no take 'em now. May be so pretty soon me boy catch 'em squaw. Indian all come me camp, heap steal 'em. Stay here, no find 'em. Me come catch em," and like a prudent man he foresaw the evil and provided against it.

The second way of getting a wife is more civil. A young man falls in love with a young woman. Often he will take his flute, and in stilly eve go somewhere near her father's tepee, and pour forth his heart yearnings in music, consisting of about two notes. It is a monotonous sound, but often it is the sweetest music to the girl as she listens. To woo or be wooed is fascinating, and often a response to this particular method results in a clandestine meeting and elopement as above described in the first case.

The third way is a straight out trade. The man sees a woman whom he would like to make his wife. He goes to the girl's parents and proposes a trade— so many ponies or blankets or buffalo robes for the girl. If it is agreeable, the trade is made, and the girl is given over to the man as soon as the property is delivered. The girl, in most cases, has no choice in the matter, and is not consulted. Sometimes, ten or twelve year old girls are thus traded off to an old man who perhaps has several wives already.

Andele had now grown up and become a mature young man, and companionship naturally became the wish of his heart. He had been with eager eyes, watching the movements of Tonko, old Keabi's daughter, and felt somewhat the movings of the heart that perhaps Samson felt when he looked upon the daughter of the Philistine, and she was destined to prove somewhat of a Delilah to him, as we shall soon see. Without speaking to her about the matter at all, he went one day to old Keabi and proposed a trade for his daughter.

"What will you give me?" said Keabi.

"Whatever you ask," replied Andele.

"Give me one good pony and two buffalo robes," said Keabi. The trade was closed, and Tonko went to be Andele's wife.

But the arrangement was not a happy one, and very soon signs of unfaithfulness were seen in Tonko, and one day while Andele was gone, Tonko eloped with Ton-kea-mo-tle. Andele did not care,—was rather glad to get rid of her so easily. She did not suit him, and she was dissatisfied with him. He did not even go to ask her to come back, and thus the matter would have ended; but Af-poo-dle, his Indian brother, thought this was so out of the Indian way, that he upbraided Andele with cowardice in not demanding satisfaction of Ton-kea-mo-tle, as was his right.

"Af-poo-dle, since you brand me as a coward, you get ready for trouble, for you know, in a case of this kind, a brother must stand with a brother, and if I have war with Ton-kea-mo-tle, it becomes your war as well. You may get ready, for I will call Ton-kea-mo-tle to account, and we shall have trouble."

"All right," replied Af-poo-dle. "I am not afraid. I will stand by you. My sleep would not be sweet, if I deserted you in the time of war."

At once Andele mounted his pony and went galloping across the prairie toward a cluster of tepees nestling close in the edge of a little skirt of mesquite saplings about five miles in the distance. Reaching the encampment he asked for Ton-kea-mo-tle.

"He is gone away to Ft. Sill, and will come at the setting of the sun," said an old squaw, who sat near the entrance of the tepee. Andele rode away disappointed, but next morning he went again to Ton-kea-mo-tle's tepee, but was told that he had gone to another village in the distance. He rode away again, and returned again, and again Ton-kea-mo-tle had gone away.

"I'll make him see me," said Andele to himself, as he rode out upon the prairie towards a herd of ponies belonging to Ton-kea-mo-tle. In the herd was a very fine pony, Ton-kea-mo-tle's pet and best rider. He raised his six shooter and with steady aim fired. The horse fell dead, pierced through the heart. He then killed two others and rode away. "Af-poo-dle, my brother," he said, as he reached his camp again and dismounted, "you may get ready, for I could not get Ton-kea-mo-tle to meet me, and three of his best horses are lying out upon the prairie yonder, ready for the coyotes or his squaws."

"Umph?" grunted Af-poo-dle in approval, but at the same time he looked as if he had rather there was some other way of settling difficulties than this Indian way. He prepared for trouble, however; for he knew a deadly conflict was brewing, and he knew not where it would end.

In a few days there was a large gathering of Indians on Cache Creek. The brothers of Ton-kea-mo-tle urged him to take advantage of that occasion to surprise Andele and kill him without warning, but Andele knew the Indian character too well to be off guard, so he and Af-poo-dle watched closely every movement of Ton-kea-mo-tle and his friends. It was near the middle of the day, when some one warned Af-poo-dle of Ton-kea-mo-tle's movements and purpose. He had arranged to go off across the prairie, as though leaving for his camp some miles away, but to return from another direction and come upon Andele unexpectedly from a little canon near by. Learning this, Andele and Af-poo-dle slipped unnoticed into the entrance of the canon, so that they would have a commanding view of its full length.

They had but a short while to wait, for they heard voices not far away, and upon nearer approach, Andele heard Ton-kea-mo-tle saying, "We will kill him; he is nothing but a Mexican, a captive, and yet he tries to act as if he were a Kiowa, and had the rights and privileges of a Kiowa."

Andele grasped his rifle more firmly, for in some way the whole crowd had on some marauding expedition secured rifles and ammunition.

"Be ready and firm and brave now, Af-poo-dle, for the time is come, and we must prove ourselves worthy of a good wife. As for myself, I am ready to die, but I will die like a man, and I will get Ton-kea-mo-tle before I go. Ready, quick," said Andele.

Just at that moment, Ton-kea-mo-tle reached the edge of the canon, and was in the act of descending the slope, when he discovered Andele, and Af-poo-dle close beside him. He raised his rifle, but before he could get it to his shoulders, Andele fired. It was so quick and unexpected that Ton-kea-mo-tle and his comrades rolled over an embankment and disappeared. Nobody was hurt, for Andele had missed his mark, but his enemy was so panic stricken at his narrow escape that he did not return to the conflict.

The whole encampment, however, rushed out to see what was the trouble, and demand an explanation, but when it was learned that Andele had been wronged by Ton-kea-mo-tle decoying his wife away from him, he was fully exonerated for shooting at Ton-kea-mo-tle and also for killing his horses.

This settled the difficulty for that day, but it created a breach that could not be healed so soon. Three years after this occurrence, Andele was riding along one day alone, out of sight of all habitations, and entering a narrow passage way around the mountain side, he discovered his old enemy, Ton-kea-mo-tle, approaching.

" Now our trouble will be settled, for here one of us will die. There is no way to avoid meeting, and this means a deadly conflict," said Andele to himself, and he felt for his arms, but discovered to his consternation that he had failed to arm himself when leaving his camp.

He dared not turn his back upon his enemy; he was too proud for that, and besides there was more danger in running in this instance than going boldly forward. He resorted to strategy. He placed his hands as in position for grasping a six shooter, quickened his pace forward, and watched with intense gaze his enemy's movements. He was prepared for the worst, but as Ton-kea-mo-tle approached, he called out:

"Andele, my friend, we have been enemies a long time and I am tired of it. If you are willing, let us drop our difficulty and be friends."

"Ka-tai-ke" (good), replied Andele, but too glad of the opportunity to settle the matter. From the first he had not cared to have any difficulty, but according to Indian custom he could not do otherwise and be respected by the people. The pressure of public sentiment forces to many a foolish act, even among the civilized.

He had now vindicated his claim to courage and exonerated himself from the charge of cowardice, and he did not care to push the matter further. And hence he made friends with Ton-kea-mo-tle, and did not mete out any punishment to his wicked wife. When he was first brought home by the Kiowas years ago, he saw old Big Bow cut off his wife's nose and tie it around a boy's neck.

This was the punishment usually inflicted upon a wife for infidelity to her husband, and often several fingers were also cut off, and sometimes the woman was killed. Asha, an old Comanche chief, had a wife to elope with a young man who was nearer her own age. Asha, with a few friends, sought for her many moons, but in vain, till one day, taking a special friend, he started westward to visit the Navajoes. After many days he reached a Navajo settlement, and riding up to a tepee, to his surprise and gratification, he found the young Comanche who had eloped with his wife.

"Where is my wife?" he asked. Without speaking a word, the young man pointed to the tepee. Asha entered.

For somewhile neither spoke, but at last, in words of mock affection, Asha gave vent to the fiendish feelings in his soul. Without meting out any vengeance upon the young man, he took, as is often done in such cases, such property belonging to him as he could utilize. Taking his wife, he and his friend started for home at once; for he was anxious to get where he would feel free to vent his vengeance upon

ANDELE AND HIS WIFE,
TI-I-TI, OR "WHITE SAGE."

the woman who had been so untrue to him. One evening, as the sun went down, the three crossed the Red River into the Comanche country. They had traveled many days and were worn with fatigue. But now they were on their own territory and felt rested. They camped for the night. Next morning, after the woman had prepared the breakfast of jerked buffalo and fat, and the two men had eaten and smoked their cigarettes, made of dried sumac leaves, and the woman had caught the horses and packed everything ready for travel, old Asha called the woman before him. He began:

"You are a bad squaw, fit only for the coyotes. We are now back in our own country. I will give you the choice between two things: Have your nose cut off, or be killed."

The woman stood there in the yellow sunlight of that October morning, a pitiable object, but showing not the least sign of emotion. She waited for sometime, but at last with steady voice spoke:

"If I go back among my people with my nose cut off, and my face disfigured, I shall always be the object of scorn and ridicule. I can never expect anything but cruelty at the hands of him who bought me of my father for a dozen ponies and a few buffalo hides, and although old enough to be my grandfather, forced me, contrary to my cries, to be his wife. Besides, my heart is back yonder with the young man in the Navajoe camp, and I would prefer death without him, to life with you. You can kill me. Let it be quick.''

So brave and true was this speech, that Asha hesitated, but as he had given her the choice, he was, according to Indian custom, bound to comply. He turned to his friend and requested him to shoot her.

''No,'' said the friend, ''she is your wife. I have no grievance against her. Shoot her yourself.''

Asha turned to his wife. Somehow, in this extreme hour, she had grown confident, and something of the light of her girlhood had returned to her face, and she stood there, her searching eyes looking large upon Asha. He again hesitated, for her mute gaze spoke louder than she could speak in words. But he had given her her choice. She chose death, and it could not be reversed, unless she asked it. She would not ask it.

''Quit looking at me,'' said Asha, ''I can not shoot you while your eyes are upon me; turn your back.''

What an influence to deter, or to encourage, there is in the human gaze at times. She promptly turned her back, and in an instant the bow string tightened and relaxed, and the arrow went whizzing through the woman's heart. The men hurriedly mounted their horses and rode away, leaving the body to be eaten by coyotes. Such is the Indian custom.

As among all heathen people, marriage among the Kiowas is held very loosely. Andele, in a short time, married another woman, but in a little while put her away, having found no congeniality on account of disparity in age, she being rather an old woman.

It is often the case that the chiefs take the younger and better-looking women and leave none for the young men except old squaws, and thus it is not infrequent that a young man may be seen leading around a woman old enough for his mother.

About one year after this, he fell in love with a pretty young Indian woman, Ti-i-ti, or '' White Sage.'' She was tender in her attention to him, and faithful in her affections, and they lived happily together till her death.

One of the singular customs of the Indians is that a son-in-law and mother-in-law are not allowed to speak directly to each other, but must communicate with each other through the wife and daughter. If it becomes absolutely necessary to ask a question, and

the wife is not present, the son-in-law can turn away
his head, and looking in another direction, ask the
question. The mother-in-law can answer in the way.
A sister-in-law must be dealt with in the same way.
A son-in-law may, by special favors to his father-in-
law, claim the next younger daughter, and by continued favors, still the next, and on till he has every
daughter in the family. Even a boy receiving special
favors from a man may, to show his gratitude, give
away his sister, and the family will feel bound by the
arrangement. Often a man will pet a boy, bestow
presents upon him, gain his favor, and then ask him
for his sister.

At this date there is a twelve-year old boy, Ernest
Kickingbird, in Methvin Institute, who has a young
sister. Recently an old Indian visited the school,
petted Ernest, and asked him for his sister. Ernest
agreed to it, but when the man went to Kickingbird
himself, and claimed the girl, he was flatly refused.
Kickingbird had learned too much of a better way
himself to allow his daughter to be sacrificed at the
mere whim or choice of her brother.

CHAPTER XX.

Dog Soldiers.

It will be of interest here to give an account of the Kiowa Indian soldiery.

Every child, both male and female, is born a Pho-li-yo-ye, or rabbit. From the very beginning they are taken into "the circle" and initiated; and as soon as they first begin to totter on their little feet they are taught to dance in the circle of "rabbits." An old man is put in charge of the "rabbits," and when a big feast and dance is to be held, the old man goes throughout the camps calling out: "Rabbits, rabbits, get ready; paint your faces; be prompt; come to the dance; plenty to eat—grand time!"

And very soon, from every direction, they come together at the place designated, boys and girls of all sizes and ages, from the least to those just blooming into manhood and womanhood. They dance, or rather jump around in a circle, mimicing, as much as possible, the motion of a rabbit, and keeping time with the two forefingers of each hand, lifted like rabbits' feet in running, and at the same time, making a slight noise like the rabbit. The only music accompanying the performance is the tom-tom. Thus the young people are brought up and kept organized for the more trying life of a soldier; for every boy, as soon as old enough, becomes a soldier, and of course, every girl must needs become a soldier's wife.

There are five orders of soldiers. The Ti-e-pa-ko, the Tsai-e-ton-mo, the Ton-kon-ko, the Ah-tle-to-yo-ye, and the Ko-e-Tsain-ko. The five orders make up the whole army of "Dog Soldiers." The last-mentioned band is composed exclusively of those who have distinguished themselves in war. Any number of the other orders may become a Ko-e-Tsain-ko who has achieved some notable deed. They are distinguished in dress by a red sash made of painted skins, and they use only the deer hoof rattle in all their religious performances, instead of the usual rattle-gourd.

These different orders of soldiers are constantly watching the "rabbits" as they grow up, and as soon as one of them is old enough to catch for the army, it is a race between the different orders to catch him and add him to their ranks. By this means the ranks of the Dog Soldiers are kept filled by captives from the "rabbits."

When a "rabbit" is captured by one of the orders he is sent to capture another "rabbit," who is to be his file man and close companion in the army. The Ah-tle-to-yo-ye captured Gno-ah-tone.

"Now go," said the chief, "and select another 'rabbit' to be your comrade in the order."

Gno-ah-tone went at once while it was not yet light in search of Andele. He found him lying asleep in his wigwam. Gno-ah-tone sat down beside him and awoke him.

"Andele, you and I have grown to manhood now, and can no longer remain among the 'rabbits.' The time has come for us to join the ranks of the braves, who go to war for scalps and plunder. The Ah-tle-to-yo-ye have put their hands upon me and sent me to select another 'rabbit' for companion in their ranks. I come in the early morning to claim you for that service and make you my friend and companion forever."

While he was talking he was at the same time preparing the deer bone pipe for use, and lighting it, he drew a few whiffs and puffed the smoke upward to the sun, praying as he did so. Turning then to Andele he gave him the pipe, who did as Gno-ah-tone had done, and thus he became an Ah-tle-to-yo-ye, as boon companion to Gno-ah-tone, henceforth ready to sacrifice their lives one for the other.

It is a curious use the Indian makes of the pipe. Usually when smoking for pleasure, they use only the cigarette made of a mixture of sumac leaves and tobacco, enclosed in a green leaf covering, plucked from a shrub or tree near by. But they use pipes in worship, or when a pledge is to be taken or given. A man who wants to go on the warpath to avenge the blood of a friend or relative, calls his friends together, or whomsoever he wishes to join him, and after making known his business he lights his pipe, smokes a few whiffs, and prays as he puffs the smoke towards the sun, and then passes it to the next, and on to the next, till all have had an opportunity to smoke. One may decline to smoke without any insult, and will be exempt from going on the warpath, but if he smokes he dare not fail or refuse to go lest some great evil befall him. Thus by smoking the pipe, he pledges himself to whatever is proposed on that occasion.

CHAPTER XXI.

LIGHT DAWNING.

Andele had for years lived a veritable Indian. Yet, as the years rolled by, he saw the wretchedness of the Indian life and became disgusted with it. Nevertheless some of the Indian ways had become his fixed habit, and any effort to change them by others offended him.

But light was beginning to dawn upon him. He could see as far as he had been brought into contact with them, the strength and thrift of the white men, and he had gone at one time with an Indian wagon train two hundred miles away to Caddo, and had seen there a railroad train. It set him to thinking that there must be something better for him than wandering in blanket and wild robe over the prairies like the wild buffalo. The buffalo were fast being killed out by the restless, aggressive white man, and it was probable that the Indian would go likewise, unless there was a change; for the white man seemed as glad to kill an Indian as a buffalo.

One day he heard the United States agent, George

Hunt, talking to the Indians through an interpreter. He said:

"The Great Father at Washington wants all your young men to learn how to work, so that they may make money and have homes and be peaceable."

"I'll do it," said Andres to himself. "I will go at once and ask the agent for work. I'll change my life now."

That same day he took an interpreter to the agent and explained what he wanted, and asked for work. He was put into the government blacksmith shop to learn that trade. He was a wild looking spectacle, and awkward enough in a blacksmith shop with all his Indian paraphernalia on, full rigged and ornamented. But he was honest and earnest in his purpose to learn, and soon began to show progress.

New things were constantly opening to him as he was brought more directly in contact with the whites, when one day he happened to be in the store of an Indian trader where a post office had been established. He had seen people trading with the merchants, receiving goods over the counter for which they paid money, but he noticed now the merchant seemed to be handing out things for which the people paid nothing. He could not understand it, and his curiosity was so much excited, that he asked the blacksmith, under whom he worked, what it meant. The blacksmith answered that the people were getting messages from their friends; that people could talk on paper to one another although they were a long distance apart. He said no more, but it awakened a hope and set him to thinking, and thus he soliloquized:

"Long years ago, I was stolen from my home. The Apaches stole me. Now, as I think of it, it all comes fresh to my memory. The Indians call me Andele, but my name is Andres. My father, who was he?"

He sat straining his memory, going back, back, over the wild scenes of his Indian life, through the years since he was stolen by the Mescaleros in the little vega where he tended the cows.

"Who was my father?" and occasionally memory would almost catch back the long forgotten name, but then —

"Now I have it!" he exclaimed. "I rememeber now, it is Martinez. Martinez, Martinez; yes, that is it," and he continued to pronounce it, lest it should slip from him again.

It was night, and he went to his bed and lay down, but could not sleep. His mind was full of thoughts of home, mother, the scenes of his childhood. Memories long since dead were revived. He lay there wondering, and the more he thought, the more wide awake and restless he became. Hope began to spring up in his heart, and he arose and made his way at that late hour to the sleeping apartment of the United States physician, Dr. Hugh Tobin. He rapped at the door, when Dr. Tobin bade him come in; for although it was late, he had not yet retired.

"Why, what brings you here at this late hour, Andele? Anybody sick?" asked Dr. Tobin, in the Comanche dialect; for he and Andele both had some knowledge of that language.

"I am come," replied Andele, "to tell you something that disturbs me much, and keeps me from sleeping. I am, as you know, a Mexican captive. I learned to-day that people may communicate with their friends on paper through the post office. I have been thinking it may be possible for me to find out my people from whom I was stolen long years ago when I was a small child. Do you think I could?" and he looked anxiously and intently into Dr. Tobin's face as he asked the question.

"Do you remember the place where your father lived, and do you remember your father's name?" asked Dr. Tobin

"I have been lying awake on my bed, thinking, thinking, oh, so hard, and at last my father's name has come to me. It is Martinez, and the place close to our home was Las Vegas, and my oldest brother was named Dionicio. I remember him well, now."

"Well," said Dr. Tobin, "we will write to your brother, because if your father was an old man at the time of your capture, he is probably dead ere this."

"Will you please write now," asked Andele, as his heart beat in ever increasing interest.

"I will," said Dr. Tobin, and he turned to his desk and penned the following brief note:

KIOWA AND COMANCHE U. S. AGENCY,
ANADARKO, IND. TER., Jan. 6, 1883.
DIONICIO MARTINEZ,
LAS VEGAS, N. M.
DEAR SIR: Did you have a little brother stolen by the Indians many years ago, by name Andres? The Indians call him Andele. If so, write me at once. He is here, and we think can be identified fully. Respectfully,
HUGH TOBIN,
U. S. Physician.

"Now," said Dr. Tobin, "this letter will reach Las Vegas in about ten days, and if your brother is there, he will get it. In thirty days this letter will come back if your brother don't get it. Be patient and we shall hear."

Andele went back to his own bed, but he could not sleep. The vague memories of the long ago came flooding his mind and heart, growing more and more distinct, till they stood before him as but the happenings of yesterday. After a month had elapsed, the letter came back, not having been called for at Las Vegas. It was a sore disappointment, for Andele felt confident that it would reach his brother. Dr. Tobin encouraged him to hope, and he wrote the second letter, but it, too, came back after some delay. But Andele seemed more determined to hear from his people, and he continued to send letters for nearly two years, till one day, Dionicio Martinez, who had years before moved with his family to Trinidad, happened to be on a visit to his mother in Las Vegas, and received Andele's letter.

He did not break the seal of the letter till he reached the house and sat down near his mother. He was so astonished when he read the letter, he could scarcely restrain an outcry; but fearing lest the news should too deeply affect his old white-haired mother, he, with a great effort, tried to conceal his emotions. The quick eye of the mother detected something unusual, and she asked:

"What is it, my son ? Is there some evil news in

your letter? Is some one sick? Tell me at once, for
I see something is wrong.''

''No, mother,'' said Dionicio, ''no evil news, but
good news. I hardly know how to tell you. Will
you please nerve yourself to hear something that will
surprise you much?''

''Well, tell me quick, for you hold me in suspense.''

''Mother, will you be prepared to hear that our
little Andres, whom the Indians stole long years ago,
is still living and here is a letter from —.''

But before he could finish the sentence the white-
haired mother had swooned away, and was falling
from her chair. It was an affecting scene, and here
we draw the curtain.

CHAPTER XXII.

GOES HOME TO NEW MEXICO. — RETURNS AFTER
FOUR YEARS. — CONVERTED AND JOINS THE
METHODIST CHURCH. — GOD'S PROVIDENCE IN
IT ALL.

After correspondence with Dr. Tobin and the
United States Agent, Hon. George Hunt, at Anadarko, and Andele was thoroughly identified, Dionicio
started in a hack across the country to Anadarko to
take Andele home. He was several weeks on the
road, but made a successful trip. When he reached
the agency, and Andele was brought before him, he
looked at him in open-eyed wonder. Andele was
dressed in full Indian paraphernalia, hair long and
plaited, and rolled in beaver skin; face painted, beaded moccasins and fringed buckskin leggings on; but
in spite of all this Indian dress, Dionicio could detect
the family resemblance in the features of Andele, and
after closer examination, his identification was complete.

The Indians called a council, for they were decidedly opposed to giving Andele up unless it was

very certain that his real brother had come for him. But after hearing a full account of his capture by the marauding Mescaleros, and knowing that it was from them they had bought him long years ago, they were satisfied and willing for him to go, but insisting that he must come back after a.visit home.

In a few days he started with his brother for Las Vegas, where he arrived on the 19th day of March, 1885, having been just a month on the road.

It would hardly be proper to intrude upon the privacy of the home and undertake to describe the meeting that took place. The white-haired mother, tottering under the weight of years, under the impulse of a mother's love, knew him as he entered the door, although he still wore some of the Indian paraphernalia. She could hardly endure the excess of joy as she hugged him to her heart, and called him her own little boy.

Twenty long years of sorrowing, in slow succession had dragged their weary length along. Storm-swept and weather-beaten the old earth seemed to have grown gray, but even yet she had been spared to see her little boy. Andres stood before her a mature man, but to her he was still the "Mi Muchochito" (my little boy) of the long years ago, and thus she caressed him with the same fondness and tenderness as in the days of his infancy.

Andres remained with his people till the summer of 1889, and then, after four years, in which he completely recovered the Spanish language, his mother tongue, he returned to the Indians. His wife, "White Sage," had died during his absence, but his interests were all identified with the Kiowas, and he had learned to love them. Besides, God had a purpose in it all, for in the apparent calamity that had come to Andres in his capture, God was overruling it all in preparing him for a life that should glorify him. We shall see as we read on.

God works in mysterious ways, and often His plans are many years in execution.

In the fall of 1887, at the session of the Indian Mission Conference, held in Vinita, Indian Territory, Bishop Galloway presiding, contrary to all expectation and to all apparent wisdom, the author was sent, "Missionary to the Wild Tribes." But satisfied that it was God's direction, and conscious of His presence, he went with a glad heart and began work among them, with headquarters at Anadarko.

Here he had toiled faithfully for two years, having built in the meantime a parsonage with a "church annex,'' when one day out upon his rounds among the tepees, he discovered standing on the banks of the Washita, near the old government commissary building, a Mexican whom he had not before seen. Approaching him, he said: ''You are a stranger here. I have not seen you before.''

''No,'' replied the Mexican, ''I am no stranger here. I belong here, but I have been away for four years over in New Mexico.''

He spoke in such broken English that it was difficult to understand him.

''Well, I am a Methodist preacher, a missionary sent here by the church, and I want to know all the people, and help them where I can. What is your name?''

'' My name,'' he replied, '' is Andres Martinez, but the Indians call me Andele, and everybody calls me by my Indian name.''

''I have a little church right up beyond the post-office, and will be glad to have you come to our services tomorrow.''

''I will come,'' said he.

The next day, Sunday, the little church was well filled with blanket Indians of the numerous tribes that inhabit both sides of the Washita, and a few Mexicans, among whom was Andele. All were attentive listeners, but Andele seemed profoundly interested. He was a constant attendant from that time on.

On Sabbath morning, at the 11 o'clock service, a call was made for all those who felt that they were sinners, and wanted right then to give themselves to the Lord, and be saved, to come to the altar. Andele, sitting in the back part of the house, arose, came forward, and knelt at the altar. Without manifesting any great emotion, he professed saving faith in Christ, and on the next Sabbath asked for church membership.

When he came forward to be received into the church on the next Sabbath, however, it was evident that there was some great conflict going on within. It was not fully understood till sometime after, he told of his childhood home, his capture by the Mescaleros, his transfer to the Kiowas, his training among them, his disappointment in the Indian religion, and after his rescue and return home, his continued disappointment in a mere ritualistic form of worship, and finally, his deep conviction as to the truth of God's word and his own sinfulness and need, as he heard the author, from time to time, read and explain the Bible; and then, amid, but in spite of, much embarrassment, lest he should be ridiculed, he determined to give himself up to God in Christ's name, and in the act realized His power to save.

I have gone over it all in this little volume as he has related it from the beginning. It is no difficult matter to trace the Lord's loving hand in it all. It is the overruling of His providence to bring good out of evil; for brought up by the stubborn and warlike Kiowas, trained in trial, inured to hardships, skilled in their ways, acquainted with their superstitions, a perfect knowledge of their language, and several other Indian dialects as well, and having a fair knowledge both of English and Spanish, there is no one so well qualified under sanctifying grace to lead the Indians to Christ. He is by every token called of the Lord to carry the gospel to the Indians.

A few months after his conversion and reception into the church, he took the place of interpreter and industrial teacher in the Methvin Institute near Anadarko, Oklahoma Territory, in which capacity he labored long and well. Owned of God and respected of men, he goes forward without wavering and without a vestige of superstition clinging to him to the work to which God has, by His providence, called him, and for which He has so well qualified him.

CHAPTER XXIII.

A Civilized Courtship and Christian Marriage.

This chapter must close this little volume. Ti-i-ti, or "White Sage," had now been dead about five years. She had been faithful to Andele, but while he was away in New Mexico she took sick and died.

While Andele had learned the ways of civilized life and had caught the inspiration of a better hope by faith in Christ, he had also, under this new order of things, learned the magic of successful wooing after the approved manner of Christian refinement, and having actually fallen in love, went forth to a conquest difficult but pleasing to his enraptured soul. In marauding expeditions into Texas and elsewhere, he had tried the conflict of war and bloodshed, and it was exciting in the extreme, and dangerous; and now, while in this conflict with love, choking with quickened pulsations and increased heart beats, he woke to a realization of the truth of the poet's song:

"War and love are fierce compeers;
War sheds blood while love sheds tears;
War breaks heads while love breaks hearts;
War has swords while love has darts."

182

But nothing daunted, he pushed his conquest, as we shall see, to a successful ending.

In the spring of 1893, Miss Emma McWhorter, daughter of Rev. P. T. McWhorter, of Indian Mission Conference, took the place of matron in Methvin Institute, an Indian mission school belonging to the Woman's Board of the M. E. Church, South. She was a young lady of substantial Christian character, quiet in manners and reserved, and conscientious and faithful in discharge of duty. She served her place well in the Institute. The Indian children, as well as the old Indians, all seemed to love her, and gave her their confidence.

She being matron and Andele industrial teacher, they were thrown together occasionally, each day, in looking after the children, especially when one was sick, as each had to keep up with the prescriptions and aid in the attendance upon the sick.

One day, stepping unexpectedly into the "sick room," a scene presented itself that afforded both embarrassment and amusement. A little girl, who had been too short a time in the school to understand much English, was lying upon the bed, sick with a fever after a chill, the Matron standing at one side, the Industrial Teacher at the other. Evidently something unintelligible to the Indian girl had been said, but full of absorbing interest to the Matron and Industrial Teacher.

As I stepped in, the Industrial Teacher looked up with a start, and startled was the Matron. The live carnation coursed itself around the cheeks of the one, and the flush of confusion covered the face of the other. The diagnosis of the case before me, not of the sick child, but of the Industrial Teacher and Matron, was easy. It took no skilled physician to read the symptoms. The symptoms of heart yearnings are more difficult to conceal than that of a fever-stricken body.

I stepped on, after inquiry after the sick child, saying to myself, "Evidently Andele is not 'making medicine' now after the fashion of the Indians preparing for war and bloodshed, but

'. . . is working his magic wand
    For wooing a heart and winning a hand.' "

His wooings were not in vain, and his magic did not fail. On the 17th of October, 1893, the writer solemnized the rites of holy wedlock between them, and thus the Matron and Industrial Teacher went into a life-partnership and became one!

And now, in closing, I take pleasure in introducing to the reader, not *Andele, the Kiowa*, but Mr. Andres Martinez and his estimable wife, who will grace the following page as a fit closing to this little volume.

[THE END.]

MR. AND MRS. ANDRES MARTINEZ.

www.ingramcontent.com/pod-product-compliance
Lightning Source LLC
Chambersburg PA
CBHW062149270326
41930CB00009B/1479